# BIGGER THAN HITLER
# BETTER THAN CHRIST

# THE
# RIK
# MAYALL

## BIGGER THAN HITLER
## BETTER THAN CHRIST

HarperCollins*Entertainment*
*An Imprint of* HarperCollins*Publishers*

The Publisher wishes to point out that due to 'contractual obligations', the author has exerted his right to insist that the text of *Bigger Than Hitler Better Than Christ* be reproduced 'exactly like what has come off my typewriter, right?'

In addition, the Publisher has been prohibited from proof-reading or otherwise editing the author's text, and as such all mistakes and infelicities are entirely those of The Rik Mayall.

HarperCollins*Entertainment*
An Imprint of HarperCollins*Publishers*
77–85 Fulham Palace Road,
Hammersmith, London W6 8JB

www.harpercollins.co.uk

Published by HarperCollins*Entertainment* 2006
1

First published in Great Britain by
HarperCollins*Entertainment* 2005

Copyright © Rik Mayall 2005

The Author asserts the moral right to
be identified as the author of this work

ISBN-10   0-00-720728-X
ISBN-13   978-0-00-720728-2

Set in Linotype Sabon

Printed and bound in Great Britain by
Clays Limited, St Ives PLC

## The Rik Mayall Books (est. 2005)

*Give me your hand small ordinary person, and walk with me – for I shall be your guide. You don't have to worry with me for I shall not give you a quick feel-up or anything like that. For I am nice. And a lot nicer than those other cunts who write books and stuff.*

*By the same author:*

Some postcards
A few police statements
Occasional letters page in Razzle
Over 2,500,000 autographs[*]

---

[*] This is true. You can ask anyone. [Maybe delete this? Whose idea was this page anyway? Make sure you don't put it in the book.]

# FOREWORD

Good afternoon. You know how like when you're writing a book, loads of great ideas come to you. Well that's what's happening to me. And you know how you're at the beginning of this book reading this now, well so am I, so it's like we're locked together, you and me, you know what I mean. Not like that, obviously, not dirty front bottom style, although we could be if you wanted, especially if you're a jugged-up kind of bird who's up for it. In fact, thinking about it, only really if you are a jugged-up bird who's up for it*. Anyway, the thing is, here we are together, you and me. Except no, we're not really, are we? Because I'm writing this bit now and it'll be a different time when you'll be reading it, won't it? I mean, you know, think about it, it could be millions of years from now that you're reading it. I mean my now, not your now. Your now would be right now, wouldn't it? See, I was right. About both nows. You might even be someone from another planet. Or someone else from that planet. Or someone from a completely different planet. Or both of them. Or something. Or, oh forget all that. (Unless you are someone from another planet, in which case. Hello. Good afternoon to you too.)

---

* Phone my agent Heimi "M.D." Fingelstein to arrange an audition. Don't call on Thursday afternoons though cos that's when he gets his hair done.

So, basically, no one knows when or where you are reading this. So that's kind of cool isn't it. You know. Mysterious. I mean, this might be written on a cave wall some time after the next apocalyps. I just thought of that. Or somewhere else. Or not even there. But the thing is that none of this really matters so don't worry about it because it's not important because what I'm saying is, loads of people have written loads of books but the thing to remember about this book is that it's better. A lot of books are just a load of old wank so they can fuck off. And if you don't believe me, you can fuck off too. In fact, if you want a fight, I'm there. I'm pretty good at fighting so you'd better watch out. Better-watch-out-he's-pretty-good-at-fighting is my middle name. Always has been. No it hasn't. That's bollocks. This isn't working. Let's start again.

Good afternoon. You know how – oh just forget this fucking page. It's shit.

# INTRODUCTION

In the beginning was the word, and the word was Rik Mayall. Do you see what I did there? That's the kind of guy I am. Unconventionable. And don't say that I'm not because I am. And my career as a showbusiness legend spans decades and all of them (the decades that is) are choc full of successful movies, theatre events in the West End (and other places), cutting edge comedy television formats, number one hit records, funny and challenging chat show non-appearances and, most importantly, a string of highly inventive and genre-bursting (make that exploding and with some serious megatonnage as well) commercial television and radio product endorsements. People do not, and I repeat not, shout "fat unfunny has-been" at me in the streets. That has never happened – read my lips – ever. A lot.

Now, you know me, I'm a nice guy. You can ask anyone. So that's proof. Anyway, I want to tell you what happened to me the other day. Things happen to me all the time. That's what it's like if you're big famous. And I've always been down with my ordinaries*. Did

---

* When I say "ordinaries" I mean the honest normal everyday people who love my work. People like you most probably. And I want you to know right here and now that I love your work too unless you're not working in which case I love the way you sit around all day watching the telly doing fuck all, blowing off and shouting. Actually, that reminds me of a really good story where . . . Oh shit, this is a footnote. There isn't space. Bollocks.

you see that footnote? I wrote that. Anyway, when I say "down" with my ordinaries, I'm not saying, down with them as in "down with Thatcher"*, I mean down as in that expression "down with the kids" meaning happening and cool and groovy not, you know, like, you know, anything else. So, I like to think that I'm down with the kids [maybe change this]. What I'm trying to say is that I like children. Oh fuck, look just erase all this, forget about it. What I'm really trying to say is that I like you a lot and I'm down with you – actually, I need to stop saying "down with". I'm "in with" you – oh God that sounds as though I want to get your stuff all over my fingers. Look, just go to the next paragraph. I didn't mean it and it's all shit.

What I'm really definitely trying to say here and now is that I AM THE RIK MAYALL. Good. That's sorted. Moving on. We're really getting somewhere now.

Picture the scene. Maybe it's a Tuesday afternoon – fuck it, it is – this is my book. This happened, right. It's last Tuesday. I'm in a crowded pub, having the third of three halves – I'm quite a big drinker† – when bang! It hit me straight between the eyes! I say it, it was more of a he – a big hard bloke with tattoos – you know the type. What had happened was that I had accidentally stumbled penis first against the arse cheeks of his girlfriend as I hurried to the Gents toilets to not take drugs. At first, I thought it might be one of those sudden unscheduled violence workshops that my great showbusiness mates‡ often spring on me which look to all

---

* I've had her.
† Although I've never had a drink problem and I've never taken any drugs. Apart from legal ones like painkillers. Although I don't take many of them because I'm quite hard.
‡ Stephen Fry, Hugh Laurie, Adrian Edmondson (very talented), John Sessions, Phil Cornwell, who are all my good friends. And who I respect massively. It's never them. Ever. They don't beat me up.

the world like they're beating the shit out of me but which are, in fact, all part of the acters' craft. Anyway, it wasn't. So forget about that. So, back to last Tuesday, and the next thing I know is I'm carrying out an emergency landing on the pavement outside the pub which is when a small pale man in a red overcoat came up to me.

"You're Rik Mayall, aren't you?" he said to me.

"I am he," said I*.

"Rik Mayall! No, no, I can't believe it! You are The Rik Mayall! You must be some kind of God, The Rik! The son of God or something! You have changed my life! When I saw first saw you in "Boom! Boom! Out Go The Lights" on the television in the early eighties, I laughed so much I coughed up half a lung and had to be taken to hospital. And after I watched you on Top of Pops with Cliff Richard, I was pissing blood for a week. To this day, my girlfriend and I like to tape the Andrex commercials and do sex to the sound of your voice as you bring the Andrex puppy to life with your challenging portrayal. It's the only thing that's kept our relationship together. Are you a God, Rik Mayall? You must be. You are like a shining beacon in the darkness of British light entertainment. And now I see you as just a mass of blood and teeth. You must be having another one of your many Rik Mayall showbusiness accidents."

That. Was the moment. Suddenly there was a thundercrack. I looked up and the clouds parted. I found myself in a blinding shaft of golden light. I'm not joking. This happened. There I was standing in the lesser known alleyways of London's Soho as if chosen, locked in a vast sunbeam of divine glory. It suddenly became clear to me. I was in the middle of having an epiphany. It was a sign from above. It was my divine destiny calling to me. It was everyone's divine destiny. For I realised that what the people of this

---

* I'm known for my good dialog.

great land needed – this good ship Albion as I like to call it (although it's not strictly a ship, it's more of an island really) was a book. By me. It would provide a sauce of happiness and solace to my ordinaries (who I love) as they have to face up to living with all the shit they put on the television nowadays. (Have you seen it? It's complete bollocks isn't it.*) It would be like a gift to all my fans. Well not strictly a gift as they'd have to pay for it but you get the general idea. What's a few quid when there's people starving in the world? You haven't got an answer for that, have you?

"I'm going to write a book," I said out loud.

"Wha-wha-wha-wha-what?" (He was stammering, that's not a typo. It's actually rather good writing. I don't know why he was stammering. Perhaps he was masturbating while looking at me. It happens.) Wha-wha-wha-wha-what?" He repeated. "The Good Book?"

"No, The Great Book."

On hearing my plan, the man in the red overcoat – you know, the one I was talking to a minute ago outside the pub – his bowels spontaneously evacuated and he dropped to his knees, trembling.

"Oh God in heaven help me," he intoned [or something that means speak only kind of grander].

"Yes, you heard right Roger [check name]. Pretty soon there are going to be only two types of people in this world: those who have read my book and those who haven't. The line is drawn in the sand and you've got to decide which side you're on."

"Crikey Rik Mayall, you're so right there like you always are and I respect you for it."

"I know, thanks."

So, as you stand there with this book in your hands (maybe you're

---

* Have you ever tried to count all the programmes there are without me in them? It's a lot.

at home in your "front room" or whatever ordinary people call their living areas – or maybe you're in that Godawful shit hole for the friendless, with the coffee and the easy chairs – what's it called? – Waterstones, that's it) you can think to yourself that you are part of this call to destiny and you can see that this is a whole new front that I've opened up here on my war on showbusiness. And I bet you anything you like that this will be every bit as successful as all the other great stuff that I've done over the years. And if you don't believe me then I've got just one word to say to you: fuck off. (I did it again then, did you get that? What you've got to realise here is that you're stuck slap bang in the middle of a firestorm of red hot literary cluster missiles of explosive word play and punctuation.

Hold on . . . ) There you go.

As my old Gran used to say – actually I don't want to get into that now, it's too sordid. Just forget it.

Anyway, what I want you to know is that whatever else happens in the next few hours or days or weeks or however long it's going to take you to read this book, I'm going to be honest and true to you my viewers. Notice I said viewers there and not viewer because I know what's going to happen. This is going to be massive. We're talking daytime television here. I'm going to rip apart the very fabric of popular culture and put it back together again in my own image. This is a whole new world order and this one is screaming in your face to get your kit off, and go for it. I worship at the church of excess (and I don't mean like those Australians, In Excess – I don't remember them biting the head off a whippet). So you'd better watch it. I'm a swear-word-using hell-raising bare-bottomed anarchist at the gates of dawn and I can say what the fucking hell I like and if you want some failed celebrity's wank book, you can stick it up your arse* because this eagle has

---

* Be careful, this can be dangerous. I know.

landed. When I come for you, you'd better be ready, you'd better grab hold of something, put your head between your knees and jam a cork up your arse because when you read what I've got to say, you're going to shit your kidneys. And if you don't like it then get out of the way. This is the new bible, motherfucker*, and it's me at the controls and I'm coming straight at you – in your face, down your throat and out your trousers. I live on the edge. I'm out there in Edge City – right on the very edge of Edge City, teetering over a byss.

Now this baby's written, just remember that it's always out there. Everything is always out there. You must never forget that. Everything is out there doing everything to everyone. Sometimes for everyone, sometimes not. Who's to know? I'm not everyone. Nor everything. No thing is everything and no one is everyone. But I'm more than most. A lot more than most. No, a lot more than everybody. I have a theory. But that's a secret. Oh sod this, it's late now I'm going to bed.

---

* No offence.

Harper Collins, Esq.
77-85 Fulham Palace Road
London W6


August 5, 2004

Dear Harper (if I may call you Harper - I mean apart
from last night I've never met you before but I think we
have a deeper understanding now – and if I can't call
you Harper then you'd better stop reading now because
believe me, I'm going to call you Harper for the rest of
the letter and if each time you look at Harper and see
that I haven't put Mr Collins and then get offended, well
you're just going to have to pack it in Harper and stop
being so pathetic).

All I'm trying to get the chance to say is, thank you very
much for last night. The food was absolutely delicious
and please accept my apologies for the wallet incident.
You must admit that the leather trim on yours is very
similar to the one on mine even though it is a different
colour. Apologies also for calling you a spod-faced fuck-
hole, I think maybe one of the waiters might have spiked
my drink. It happens sometimes – there are people
everywhere trying to mess with my head. Anyway, it's all
in the past now and we're both man enough I'm sure to
rise above it and move on. But don't get me wrong, I'm
not coming onto you or anything Harper, I'm not that
kind of guy as I'm sure you're not - or indeed Mrs Collins

for Christ's sake. I mean look at her. I have. I mean, I would. That's a compliment. Oh fuck, don't read that last bit you've just read. Oh, you know what I mean. Christ, writing letters is a bitch isn't it? I'm just saying that I'm not calling you a whoopsie, all right? Not that I would have a problem if you did drop from the other bomb bay, so to speak – I'm an all-inclusive kind of guy and I'm everybody's friend. In life, I don't really have any enemies. None at all. Well, apart from some other professional live "performers". Well, quite a lot really. But let's not think about them. Cunts. I just ignore them. Apart from them, I have no enemies – least of all anyone in the minorities. That's something that I think Tony B has taught us all. Tony and I are such good friends – I don't think I need to say anymore – walls have eyes or whatever it is they have. Wallpaper or something, I don't know. How should I know? Ask a fucking builder.

Anyway, I digress. What I really want to say to you, Harper, is that I'm well fucking happy that you have agreed to publish my book. I knew that once you'd met my agent Heimi you would know in your soul what the best decision would be. I know he has a peculiar manner, especially when he mentions your family and the leaking gas main, but that's just his way. And don't worry, the "Mad Dog" in Heimi Mad Dog Fingelstein isn't a nickname or anything. Heimi Mad Dog Fingelstein is his actual name. And having said that, it is true about his close relationship with the current Chief Inspector, so he would walk away if anything came to court. It's all food for thought.

The thing is, things only happen when they're happening, so let's happen them Harpo, and seeing as things ended on a sour note last night, I thought I'd set our balls rolling (that's a media expression) on some hot ideas for my book. First off, I'll need a researcher. This is important. I've had a massive career – even though I'm only in my late thirties (and firing on all cylinders in the trouser department before you start) – and there are so many pinnacles in light entertainment that I have conquered, that when I try to remember them all, I see a vast mountain range. Like the Alps. Or maybe the Himalayers. Whichever are bigger. Something like that. You know what I mean. I am an equal opportunities employer as well, so be cool, but she will need to be quite young and fit and I will need to conduct auditions. I'm sure you must have sorted yourself a bit of top bird to work in your office – well if she's got any mates or sisters then perhaps they could apply for the job. It's also important that applicants don't scare easily as I can form violent sexual friendships when I'm deep in the cut and thrust of creative thought. I must say, I'm really looking forward to blouse-storming (just another media expression Harper, drop the valium and keep up) with my researchers so it might be a good idea to hire a hotel room for us to work in, preferably without windows or curtains that function. I will supply a rider (this is a show business term for a list of stuff like drugs and gin/sherry which stars have to have in their dressing rooms) (not that I ever take illegal drugs) with all my requirements on it like lubricants (creative ones) and juice (this means alcohol) and drugs (legality is irrelevant because I don't ever take any, so get loads). Although actually you'd better definitely slip in some illegal ones, you never know what chicks are going to pop. Or where. Or sometimes how. The fuck. Did. She. Do. That? Eh? Sort of thing. You see, Herpe, it's important to have everything you need when you're bouncing ideas around (another media biggie Herpes – this letter is shaping up into being a bit of a Krakatoa of happening media and marketing buzz expressions isn't it, me old arse-wrench?). In case you're wondering, buzz expression is a buzz expression in its own right.

Oh yeah, listen up Herpar this is important – you know how last night you mentioned something about someone or other editing my book? Well, I want to say right now and I'm doing it right now and what I'm saying is this – no I'm not, I'm commanding it (in a close up), NO ONE FUCKS WITH MY WORDS. Read it again, you lefty twat, NO ONE FUCKS WITH MY WORDS. Because if I read through my book and find that someone's been messing about with my oeuvre, I'll be straight round to your little office with some of my associates to rip your head off and shit in the hole. And I won't wipe my bottom. Is that clear? You've been warned. I'm pretty sure it was the great Graeme Green himself who said, "don't fuck with my words, man," and I'm down with that. (Down means down which means – oh just look it up). And another thing, Harps, and this is a biggie. A really important big biggie, so take all your clothes off and kneel down in front of me, sweating and paying attention. Right? I have got in my possession a fabulous mesmerising archive of correspondence that has been gathering and breeding and swarming around me like napalm throughout my raging blood-drenched Hiroshima of a professional north AND south career. See that! Did you see that? That's creative writing that is. And that's what I'm going to put in my book. Everything I've ever written and ever done in my life is creative and it's all going in, man. Notes, poems, journals, letters, great letters too. That's what they are. Great ones. And if you don't think they are then you're a cunt. Point proved. Anyway, I just want you to know that I'm very very very very committed to righting enough words. Who knows, I might even put this letter in. No one likes a little one.

As far as publicity for the book is concerned, this is really where I'll come into my own (that's not a media expression although I did once see someone do this in Bangkok – not that I've ever been there). I am very well known by all the global media networks – they follow my every move – I only have to crack one off and it's in the papers. I'm talking metaphorically, I have never – repeat never – been caught masturbating.

So, I think that just about raps things up. I'm sure Heimi will be in touch soon to tie up all the loose ends contract-wise.

Big up Harpo, respec (that's "street" slang),

Rik Mayall, The.

P.S. Don't fuck any of this up Harper – you're dealing with frightening people here.

P.P.S. Love to the wife.

P.P.P.S. Did it heal up for her?

## DIARY EXERT

March 7th 1966

A prare to God.

Dear R. Father, what are in heaven, hello
be they name. How are you today? My name
is Richard Mayall. And that's not a lie.
Firstly, many thanks for choosing me
above all other people. I want to make
sure that thine choice is the right one
oh Lord. And it is so thou knowest that
already. I want thou to know that I have
never doubted you, ever ever. I wanted to
ask you a question which I thought I would
write in my diary so thou could read it
as well. We could read it together – thou
and me – as I write it. I am going to
start a new paragraph now Lord because
I want this question to be important.
  There. You see, Lord, what it is is
that often in the middle of the night
I find myself thinking about the angels
and the heavenly host – and hostess –
and I was wondering, Lord, if thou could
clear something up for I. You know how
like in the pictures of angels that you

see in books, all the lady angels always
wear sort of short white shirt kind of
things, well if I were to be surrounded
by angels, both man and lady angels, and
they are all flying around above me up in
the air over my head, and if I looked up
in the air and saw these angels flying
above me and thought to myself "Oh look,
there are some selestial bodies. I'm so
glad that God has chosen me to be his
special one." Well, what would happen if
at that very moment I looked up and there
was a lady angel just above me and I
accidentally saw her girl's pants? Would
I go to hell? And if I did, would I have
to fall all the way down from the sky to
the middle of the earth and hurt myself?
And will there be hospitals in hell for
me? I've been worrying about this a lot,
dear Thou. If you could clear this up for
me as soon as possible, I would be
eternally greatful.

I hope thou ist keeping well.

Best wishes,

Richard Mayall.

Mr Clutterbuck
Masters Common Room
King's School
Worcester


August 20 1969


Dear Sir,


I know you said I should not write to you again because
you might have to tell the Headmaster but I felt I should
tell you that I now know who let off the fire alarm during
break last Thursday. It was not me, it was Lancaster, which
proves that he is not handicapped because he would
have had to stand up out of his wheelchair to do it. I also
saw him doing the hundred yards sprinting practice last
week as well so he is a bloody liar. Sorry to swear Sir,
but it makes me so cross when other pupils break
school rules. If you like, I can help you lift him out of
his wheelchair so that you can beat him. One day he
will thank us all for this.

You are very good at beating, Mr Clutterbuck. You have a
very good slipper action and it certainly hurts a lot. You
are much better than Mr Cunley, who said he was going
to beat me the week before last for cribbing and then he
put his hand down the back of my trousers. I am sure this

is against the law but I do not like to tell tails. He smells
of LSD and he doesn't cut his hair very much so I think
he must be a hippy. I will say no more.

I hope you have a very nice holiday in Benidorm with
Mrs Clutterbuck.

Best wishes,

Richard Mayall.

# MY GREAT LIFE

"Fucking hell, look at the size of his cock!" said the mid-wife who delivered me. "It looks like he's got three legs. Perhaps he should be called The Tripod." This is true. She really said this. But I was called Richard instead and the rest is history.

I went to school at the local primary school, right? That's where I went to school. I didn't have to pay anyone, I just got in. No questions, no bodies. I was in. The infants. I don't want to talk too much about it because it was like sucking shit through a shoot. But I tell you what. And I'll tell it you now. It was a Tuesday night, 17th December 1968. Choir concert. Got that? Me too. All the infants were there. All the parents were there. This is true, this. My fucking class teacher, Mrs "please kick me in the face violently" Andrews lined up all the tables against the wall and told us all to stand on them facing the audience.

"Call that a stage?" I thought, "I'd rather slam my bollocks in the fridge door." But I got on the stage and I was right, it was a shit stage. And that bitch Andrews stuck me right up at the left hand side of it, right at the edge and at the back. I was practically off stage (which means not on stage). And I'm never off stage. I'm always on. I'm on now, look. And guess what. No but really, guess what. No don't actually, I'll tell you. I'm doing it right now or I will after I've done this sentence. And I'm getting there now. Right here we are, I'm there. Told you I would be. So shit off if you don't believe me. Right what was I going to say? Bollocks. Oh I know, shut up and listen. New paragraph – this is good.

Mrs Andrews said to me – and get this because this is true – "Now Richard, pay attention and stop doing that to Penelope. I have something important to say to you. The success of the whole of this evening's concert depends on it. So pay attention, it's very very important. Now Richard, I don't want you to sing this evening. Not at all. Not one note. I want all of the other children to sing but not you. Because you've got a horrible voice. So what I want you to do is just move your mouth as if you're singing but not actually sing. If you sing, you'll spoil the whole evening's entertainment. Have you got that?" she said rather too emphatically an inch from my face. What do you think of that? Me too. I wasn't going to take that. Me neither. Or me. She was dealing with Rik Mayall (i.e.* me). That's what she didn't know. She used to call me Richard. Bitch. I wasn't going to take that lying down. "Right, Richard," I said to myself. "What are we going to do? I'll tell you what we're going to do. We're going to steal the show. Let's do it. (Like a firestorm, obviously.)" So, what I did was just that. Fantastically too. I pulled faces at the audience while I was mouthing the wrong words to Away in a Manger, made extremely vulgar gesticulations and upstaged the entire cast (there were about thirty opponents up there, don't forget. This was thirty to one.) I transformed the whole evening into a breakthruough comedy entertainment format. You should have heard them laugh when Annette Jennings' knickers and tights suddenly came shooting down her legs, tangling up her shoes and she fell into the front

---

* This is Latin.

row. It was all going on. Hilarity prevailed. Quite a few people had a good time until suddenly, the Headmaster grabbed me by the ear, pulled me off the stage onto the floor of the auditorium (form 3B) and marched me to the corner of the room and made me stand face to the wall in FULL FUCKING VIEW OF MY AUDIENCE thinking it would humiliate me. Like fuck. That's when it all kicked off big style. So the Headmaster ordered me out of the hall. And that's when I threw my first really good tantrum. I bit Mrs Andrews in the face, ran a mock with my matches in the cloakroom causing over eight thousands pounds worth of damage, flooded the girls' toilets, and shat in the gym master's holdall*. As a seven year old, you can only take so much.

The thing is, I was very misunderstood at school. Quite often, when the other children were playing kiss chase in the playground, I was tied up in the toilets with my pants stuffed into my mouth. Even the teachers used to spit on me as they passed me in the play ground.

I'm putting all this in the book, viewer, because I want to show you what a hard life I've had and how I rose above it. It's really very Jesusy when you think about it. I remember as though it was yesterday when the Headmaster was beating me in his study one day and I looked up at him and said, "Judge not lest ye be judged you fat motherfucker." He just went on beating me. His house burnt down shortly afterwards. I had nothing to do with this.

Picture the scene: Spring 1967. Got it? Everyone else was on the Isle of White watching Jimmy Hendrix burning his guitar but I was at school. They had decided to change the state school system so that no one would be equal anymore. The rich would go to one sort of school and the poor would be put in holding pens before they were taken off to factories. It was different in those days. We had factories and people went there and made things. They were

---

* There's more to this but this isn't the director's cut.

called jobs. You don't have them now. There was still a Labour
Party in those days. Nowadays there are just slaves on the other
side of the world that make stuff for us. Unless we bring them
over here to do it. Then we call them immigrants and pay them
fuck all and make them live in the old holding pens that the white
working class used to have. Until they're fucked up and knackered
and useless and then we send them home again. Or to somewhere
in Croatia where they're made into dog food.

Now, it's worth knowing, viewer, that the old education system
was governed by an exam called the Eleven Plus. This was an exam
which separated the creepy frightened kids that behaved themselves at school and managed to learn something from the stupid
kids who didn't give a shit and were happy. You took it when you
were eleven and, rich or poor, you were divided into two groups
and "educated" in one of two separate schools depending on your
ability. But the rich who were in control of the state at the time
decided that they were going to destroy this system and replace it
with two different kinds of schools – good well-equipped schools
for the children of the wealthy, and sad empty blank voids for the
children of the poor. So, I was in the shit. Big time. Lots and lots
of shit. You had to be eleven to take the Eleven Plus, you see. It was
the last year they were doing it before they scrapped it forever and
I was only nine! Plus my mum and dad weren't rich so I had no
chance of an education. Fucky-fuck-fuck, shitty pants and deary
me, I'm bollocksed, I thought. EXCEPT, my mum and dad just
happened to be teachers*, so they prepped me up for the Eleven
Plus exam and I got into an expensive school full of posh kids
called the King's School Worcester – when I was nine! How's about
that for cool? And that's where I taught people how to drink and

---

* Teachers are all you've got left, kids. Don't listen to anyone else. Especially
  the BBC.

lose their virginity and be happy because I was a nice bloke and they were all wankers. I've always been like that, I've always offered a helping hand to others on life's, you know, whatever. I was the youngest in the school but almost straight away I fell in with the hard guys like Simon Rex and that other one with the ginger hair, you know, that psycho who liked to do that thing with cats and a screwdriver. He's dead now, thank fuck.

So nobody knew anything about anything. No one found the bodies. There were no traces and I passed the Eleven Plus! I did it. All on my own. Yes I did. Prove it if you can then. Get this, I was the youngest kid in England to ever pass the Eleven Plus. And I still am. Didn't put that in the credits for Filthy, Rich and Catflap did they? BBC fuckholes. I'd got into a big posh school. But it was the very last year they were allowing kids like me to sit the Eleven Plus. After this, ordinary kids weren't allowed to have well-equipped schools and teachers that could teach. But then. Now wait for this. You'll like this, this is nasty. Just when everything was great, suddenly there's this other kid at King's called Gretisson who grassed (this is cool prison slang for told on) on me to Mr Cunley. The little shit (ugly too. And probably still is. I hope so.) gave him a list of all the boys who he thought were smoking and Cunley went through our desks at lunchtime and found our cigarettes. It was either six of the best or a one pound fine.

"How about this?" I said to him, "what about a ten shilling fine and three of the best? Do you play that kind of game?"

"Hold on a minute, Mayall. Did you say what I thought you just said?"

"Believe it if you need to, Mr Teacher Man," I intoned moodily. Or was it huskily? It was a long time ago. I can't remember[*]. "How do you want this baby to come down?"

---

[*] Don't tell the publisher.

His face fell. He held both of his hands up defensively, backing away. "Whoah . . . Hold on there Mayall," he croaked (no he didn't really, he died a long time later. I had nothing to do with that either.) "Listen, I'm way out of my league here or whatever it is that they say in films. I'm not used to dealing with guys like you. I'm scared, man."

I leant forward, took my ten Number Six back out of his top pocket along with the five pounds that he had fined the other guys in my posse.

"Shall we just say this never happened?"

"Thanks."

"Not a problem, friend," I said and patted him encouragingly on his shoulder. Then I turned on my heel.

"Ow fuck," I said, "why do I keep doing that to my heel?" And I breezed, well, hobbled, looking cool, out of the room. Closing the door. After I'd left, obviously. Never works the other way round. I've been in that situation before. Told you it was nasty.

I swore a lifelong debt of hatred to Gretisson for that. And as for Cunley, I still have sharp stabbing memories of him when I run up the stairs quickly. Enough said.

I fucked up my "O" Levels not because I was stupid and naughty but because I was a wide-eyed anarchist at the gates of dawn even then and the world was against me, especially the teachers and the examination board because they had heard of me and they were jealous. I was like the Outsider and I don't mean like the one in that shit book by Albert what's-his-face. The only "O" Level that I did get was in English – it was a breakthruogh cutting edge grade six. And that was a pass, not like they say. That's right, a pass. And that's a fact, viewer. Rik Mayall got an "O" Level. In English. Go back and read that last sentence again – and read it out loud. Go on. Although what you do is your own business. That's the thing about life. People. They're all over the place. It's exciting – and dull. And you don't even have to do what I say if you don't want to because I'm Rik Mayall, so don't worry about it or even think about it. It's as though you haven't read the last paragraph which if you haven't, well then, that's fine. See if I care. Which I do and I don't. See? That's the beauty of my enigmas.

Headmaster's Wife
Headmaster's Office
King's School
Worcester


April 14 1972

Dear Headmaster's Wife,

I think I might be in love with you. I have seen you
looking at me and I think you would probably like to
do some fucking with me. Please do not tell your
husband because he is a real old bloody bastard and I
bet he cannot get erections like I can. I bet he needs that
stallion cream like they sell in nude magazines. We could
make love to each other on his bed. I want to do this to
you because I am Gretisson, the nasty one with the curly
hair. Please do not tell your husband because I will be
expelled. My parents vote Labour as well. Please come
round to my study and masturbate me whilst I read my
magazines with naked women in them. You can even see
my balls if you like and smoke some of my drugs which
will make you high like a hippy at Woodstock and you
can take all your clothes off and wear flared trousers
and show off your midriff and not wear a bra. And you
can call me Man and we can masturbate together to
the Beatles (but not their disappointing phase) and wear
those ridiculous blue glasses like John Lenin wears and
sit around and talk about the sky and the trees. We could

go and watch Bob Dillon singing out of tune and complain about the Vietman war together and read Oz Magazine and fight the power. I am Gretisson and I want to do it with you all night long.

Best wishes,

Gretisson.

Mr Priddy
Masters' Common Room
King's School
Worcester


April 15th 1972

Dear Mr Priddy,

You are a complete spasmo. That's what I think. And if
you give me yet another straight "A" in class for one of
my appalling essays which I crib anyway, I will creep
into your bedroom in the middle of the night with a
knife between my teeth like in that film that was on the
TV a couple of weeks ago and I will kill you in your
sleep. Yes I will. This is not a joke. This is for real. I know
where you live. Just off the parade – the one with the shit
orange curtains. So just watch out. Please don't tell the
headmaster that I have sent you this death threat because
I will be expelled.

Best wishes,

Spencer (the one with the speech impediment and the
girl's haircut who's always blaming Mayall when he gets
pushed down the stairs).

## DAIRY EXERPT

January 14th 1970

I think I did a bit of a fib today Lord
because I felt obliged to tell Mr Townsend
that Gretisson had some what are called
"gentleman's publications" if I can use
such disgusting words in front of you dear
Lord. Sure enough, when Mr Townsend went
to Gretisson's locker he found some. And
thankfully, Gretisson has been suspended
for this outrage. Of course this action
means that I will now have a much better
chance of getting the part of Othello in
the school play. So if I might ask for
forgiveness from you dear Lord for any
advantage I may have got by telling Mr
Townsend this but, in its own way, it was
a selfless act Lord meaning that the part
of Othello will be performed so much
better by me and bring more joy to the
audience which is my motorvation. All I
care for is my fellow humans on yours
and my planet. That is why I stitched
Gretisson up and used my superior
intelligence to take care of matters.
He will thank me in later life. Thou and I
both know that oh Lord. It is good that I

know how equal everybody is aren't I. If
only the people in the government were not
more like me. I have got nothing against
Harold Wilson, I mean I know he doesn't
comb his hair very well and his pipe
smoking is a bit common but he does his
best. Maybe one day I could be Prime
Minister. It is up to you dear Lord.

Thank you for making me milk monitor
this term. As you probably already know,
this is a very important position which I
am going to take very seriously and I told
everyone in the class that we should not
drink all the milk and save it up and send
it to the people who are starving in poor
countries. But Redfern got some other boys
together and they punched and kicked me
after double maths. I knew that this was
a test oh Lord and I took the test and I
didn't cry and I remembered all of their
names when I reported them to the
Headmaster. I had almost all of them
beaten and three of them were put in
detention. A job well done. I have got
three boys expelled and two boys,
including Gretisson, suspended since the
start of term. I trust I am doing what
is required of I.

I hope you are keeping well.

Fondest wishes,

Richard Mayall.

# SHOWBUSINESS GOLD*

Literally anything can happen twenty four hours a day in show-business. That's just what it's like. There are secrets to be told and lives can be ruined. It's all true, every syllable of it. But what I do NOT do is drop litter on the showbusiness super-highway. I'm a careful driver I am and I always use litter bins although they can be difficult to find when you're doing 127mph in the outside lane. But if you're really cool, you should always drive with the lights off at night – that way, you're just part of the darkness. There are autograph hunters everywhere. I'm often thinking to myself, is that a road pile up ahead? Or is it another autograph roadblock? Not that I've got anything against autographs. I live for them. Fans are always hurling themselves into the road – metaphorically speaking obviously – to stop me driving past without giving them an autograph.

Anyway, what was I talking about? That's it – acting. Rules for good edge cutting acting: first off, try not to allow any other acters on stage when you are on it. They will deflect attention away from you. If they do manage to get on, make sure that you stand in front of them. But before any of that, before you even get on stage

---

* Maybe this should be platinum? Check which costs more.

or even turn up for rehearsals, make sure you've got the biggest part (see fourth sentence of last paragraph). Sometimes it's worth taking money to the auditions. And if you are a love interest in the play then make sure that you beef up your love equipment. Two tennis balls is good but three tennis balls and a cucumber should really hit the nail on the head. But worth remembering that you should try to make sure that your part does not involve running around because the tennis balls will fall out. If you think this might happen then make sure that you superglue them to your genitals. It might hurt a bit, but it's worth it, you really don't want tennis balls falling out of your Elizabethan trousers during a Hamlet monolog. It will take away the audience's focus (that's a theatrical expression for people in the audience saying, "Oh for fuck's sake, this is shit!" too loudly) from your face.

So, you're on stage now with the biggest part and lots of tackle enhancers (that's another theatrical expression) down your pants. Now is your time and it's vital to remember that when you are acting you must shout and point at yourself and stand at the front of the stage. Shouting at the audience is called projecting, like they do in cinemas. This is what they teach you at acting school although I didn't go to acting school myself. I don't believe in acting schools. Acting schools are shit. You've either got it in your blood or you haven't. You can always tell someone who's been to acting school because they can't act. And they're on the television all the time and get all the parts in all those shit television dramas like that police thing with all those balding overweight arseheads. Bob or somebody.

It is very important that you make sure to learn all the words in the right order before you shout them at the audience. It often helps to have a young woman to help you with your words. This is known in the industry as your word bird. Now, you know that hole at the front of the stage in between the stage and the audience?

That is what is known as the orchestra pit and that's where you will need to put your word bird who can tell you what the words are if you forget them. She must be able to read as well and speak and she must have the book or the script (which is a technical term) with all the words written in it. And for God's sake don't have any mouth action with your word bird before you go on stage because if all her teeth are stuck together it's a "no no" for tricky speeches (which means no good).

When you are at the zenith of your career like I have been for the last thirty years (even though I am only thirty-seven*) you, erm, something or other. Got it? New paragraph.

Hey, we're moving on this one. We're moving down the page. Hang on a minute.

That's better. I needed that.

Right, here we go, you know this bit anyway but I'm going to have to put it in here all the same because you never know what kind of stupid twat is reading your book, do you? Right, so the audience are the people who sit in the theatre. But they don't sit on the stage. That's where the acters stand, or sit and that's where they stand or sit† and shout at the audience. The audience are in the dark with their sweets, rustling things and coughing occasionally. They're arseholes, don't forget, but they're also your friends. You love them. Sometimes you can tell them the number of your room at the Travelodge (always get a double smoker‡) and they

---

* I want to get this sorted here and now. I do not lie about my age and anyone who says that I do is a cunt. Lines in the sand – I will say no more.
† Or maybe lie down. Or squat. Or, you know – whatever. Look, they can do what they like, okay? So get off my back about it. Who do you think I am, Albert Speer? Get a life. Who cares? I don't. Bollocks to the lot of you. No, not bollocks, oh look just go back up there and read the rest of the book will you.
‡ This is a hotelier's expression which means a room with one big bed and you can smoke cigarettes in it.

can visit you later. It also helps if you tell the audience that you are having trouble with your marriage and you might be available for some tragic lonely adultery but without anybody finding out, of course.

Waiting for Godot is a play by that great playrighter Samuel Beckett. We did it at school (and I did it a few years later in the West End with Adrian Edmondson who was much better than me in it and is much more talented than me in everything he ever does). There is a lot of waiting around in it and I found out that if I sat at the front of the stage, the audience would look at me rather than Pozzo (he's a bloke in the play). I found out that if I coughed a lot during his speech, I could deflect attention away from him onto me. I even put some grease on the stage one night and he slipped on it. Unfortunately, he didn't hurt himself badly and it didn't work out very well at all really because everyone in the audience looked at Pozzo falling off the stage and not at me. But I was learning my trade.

I was like a kind of impresario at school. I managed to get loads of games of sports cancelled in the new school gym so that I could stage decent rehearsals (rehearsals are what you do when you are rehearsing for a play) (rehearsing means practising). I managed to bribe other boys to bully smaller children whose parents had not bought tickets to my productions. When we did Rosencrantz and Gildernstern Are Dead (top play), three of them were thrown in the River Seven along with their geography projects, for example. And it worked, we had packed houses for a week and some wonderful reviews in the school magazine. Fair enough, I was the theatre critic on the school magazine at the time and wrote the review myself. But when I wrote how great I was, I was only being honest. Because I was great. If I'd written anything else, I would have been lying. And I don't lie. If you were to cut me in half, I would have "truth" written right through me just like those sticks of rock they sell at the seaside that have the name of the seaside town written in them all the way through them like Blackpool or Brighton or Skegness or whichever town you happen to be in at the time. See how much stuff I know? You didn't waste your money on this book did you, Shylock?

So, after the raging success of Rozencrantz and Gildernstern Are Dead with my packed houses and fabulous reviews, I knew where my future lay. I could see all those future edge cutting performances stretching away in front of me, performances that would be so much better than everyone else's. I won't mention them now because I don't want to demean the work of other fellow professionals. It's not that I can't remember who these people are and it's even more not because I think they're a bunch of tossers. I don't say things like that. I'll just let you make your own mind up. It's a free country. It's just that some people are bad people and I'm striking a blow for you my viewer and friend. You are freedom and freedom is my missile. We are rolling around together in the freedom bed, deep in the bunker of war. There are bullets, there is blood, there are chicks and there is fame. Feature films as well. Major worldwide tours and groundbreaking radio voice overs obviously. Some are for grocery products and some not. I know about marketing and the global media worl. I know that media is the plural of medium, a medium being something like BBC1 or ITV or the Sunday Times – and Readers Wives obviously. And Doris Stokes. That's not a joke. Although it could be if you wanted it to be. I can do anything. You must never forget that you are riding on board an out of control pantechnican roaring down a steep hill with the brake cables cut and a pelican crossing of school children and a lollipop woman up ahead. But fear not, viewer, for I am at the wheel and I can tame this mother.

Mr Wallace
Masters Common Room
King's School
Worcester


April 28 1972

Dear Mr. Wallace,

As you can see, I did not call you Fatty Wallace – I strongly
disapprove of the hundreds of boys who call you that.
I have told them too, although they do not pay any attention
to me. I do not think you look fat, I just think you are well
built. In fact, I think you look really handsome today sir.
I like that jacket and your tie really suits you. Also, I was
waiting to be beaten last week outside the Masters Common
Room and I could not help but notice how much more
stylish your cubby hole is than the other Masters. I have left
a Penguin biscuit in it for you today, sir. I know how you
prefer Club – I have seen you eating them at breaktime –
but they sold out of them at the tuck shop I am afraid.

I also think your flared trousers are very with it and the
height of fashion and I do not find it funny when your
shirt becomes undone when you bend down and we can
all see the top of your buttocks. I have never tried to flick
pieces of paper into your crack – sorry, cavity – and
deplore those boys that do. I hope I have hair on the
top of my bottom soon too.

I want you to know that I am really enjoying the Othello
rehearsals. I have been watching you in rehearsal and
remarking to myself how remarkable your directing is,
although dare I say it, you have made one fundamental
mistake in your theatrical stratergy. Dewsbury is mis-cast.
Othello requires an acter with intelligence, with looks
and sympathy and what is more, he cannot even do the
right axent. He sounds as though he comes from southern
England. He has obviously never even seen the Black and
White Minstrels. I, on the other hand, am from the West
Midlands and the place is teeming with darkies. So I have
been practising my accent. I spent some time in Newport
Street Bus Station in Worcester as research for the part.
Luckily I am a day boy and not a border and because of
that, I encounter the working classes and the immigrants
much more. So what I am saying is that I am ready now
to play Othello. I am sure your mistake was only made
out of kindness for Dewsbury. Which is why I feel it is
only fair to tell you that it was Dewsbury who actually
thought up the name Fatty Wallace for you and he flicks
ink on your bald head when you turn around to write on
the black board.

I also wanted to tell you that you spent the whole of the
double lesson last Thursday with a sign on your back with
"homo" written on it. Gretisson put it there – he forged
my handwriting.

I hope you do not mind me saying this but last week
I saw you in the Common Room and none of the other
Masters were talking to you. It must be hard being so
unpopular but I want you to know that you can count

on me as a friend. And what is more, I can be your eyes and ears in the school and tell you when I hear boys and other Masters saying nasty things about you. Any time you feel lonely or any time you want a shoulder to cry on then please feel that you can talk to me because I am a Christian, unlike the other boys.

Something that you might like to know is that I think Mr Tooley is an alcoholic. I have seen him drinking whisky in his car. He keeps the bottle under the seat. If you were to mention this to the Headmaster or maybe if he were to "accidentally" find out then it might improve your chances of becoming Head of the English Department. It is worth thinking about. There is nothing wrong with ambition.

With best wishes,

Your secret friend, Richard Mayall.

P.S. I think Harold Pinter is a really great playwriter too.

Mr. Powell
Headmaster
Headmaster's Office
King's School
Worcester


April 30 1972

Dear Mr Powell,

Hello. You might have already turned over the page to
see who has written this letter but if you have not done
so then I will save you the bother because this letter is
anonimous. So, I can say what the fuck I like and swear
and call you a wank bag if I want to and you cannot do
anything about it. And if you try and pull one of those
"everyone will have detention until the culprit owns up"
stunts, I want you to know that I will not crack. I am
quite hard and will survive much longer than some like
Renshaw and Burwood who will blub at the first sign of
pain and admit to writing this letter even if they did not.
So have a think about that.

Now, down to bizness. Mr Wallace has miscast the entire
school play. The man is an imbaseal. I presume you are
responsible for recruitment of staff and I want you to
know that the day that you employed this man was a
dark day for King's School. He has cast Dewsbury as
Othello and any fool can see that Dewsbury cannot act.

Also, I saw Fatty (that is what everyone calls Mr Wallace
– I invented it) helping Dewsbury on with his costume in
a dress rehearsal and Fatty was doing it a bit strangely if
you ask me and Dewsbury looked like he was enjoying
it. I thought you ought to know. I think they might be
doing some having it off. I should imagine that a sacking
and an expulsion are what is needed right now and the
part of Othello should be given to a much more talented
boy. I shall say no more. There are moles everywhere.
Moles is prisoner of war slang for people who dig lots
of tunnels and it also means people who tell on other
people.

Best wishes,

Anon (that means anonimous).

P.S. I saw your wife smiling at Mr Greenfield last week.
I think they might be doing some having it off as well.

Julie Newport
Alice Ottway School
Upper Tything
Worcester

November 30th 1973

Dear Julie Newport,

I know who you are and I know you know who I am.
That's right, I am the one with the sideboards who looks
a bit like Jason King. Do you like sports cars? I know girls
do. I am going to get a super-charged Ford Capri RS3100
with run faster stripes when I pass my test. I also smoke
cigarettes. A lot. And I have a French cigarette lighter.
And it works. My favourite fags (which is what I call
cigarettes) are Sobrani Black Russians. I've got five
different LPs at home. I think you are a really smashing
portion of skirt crumpet. Maybe catch up with you some
time. That is American street slang for meet you in a
coffee shop one afternoon after school.

So long (that means best wishes),

Richard Mayall.

# MANCHESTER

This is a charming story. You'll love this viewer, I was recording something or other in Manchester (a place somewhere in the north of England – quite unpleasant) with some great showbusiness friends of mine whose names momentarily escape me. I knew I was working that particular day because I woke up with the make up girl. I knew she was the make up girl because she had my wake up call (this is what acters use to wake up in the morning) written in biro* on her back. And here's a word of advice for you if you're going to write your wake up call on the make up girl's back, always make sure you put her name there as well so as to avoid confusion, impoliteness and fights. And put Wendy I love you or Christine or whatever her name is so that when she sees it and reads it backwards in the mirror in the bathroom later she'll feint with affection so you can always tap up her up for a loan or lay her aside for a shag later. The only bitch is when you bump into her in the street a few months afterwards and you don't know who the fucking hell she is. Or worse, she might be carrying your child. Fans are bad enough when they are carrying your children.

---

* Rik Tip (and I'm not talking about my penis): If you're going to do this, don't write it in lipstick because it'll get everywhere and might look like she's bleeding.

The very great Bobby Ball himself once gave me this: "Rik, never ever ever fuck the fans." So all I ever say to fans in bed is, "remember, this never happened, bird. I've got relatives in the police." He's a great man, Bobby Ball, and always will be. And Tommy of course. I have never had sex with either of them.

So, anyway, when a pregnant make up lady confronts me in the street, my heart turns black and my wallet does a triple back somersault. Before this wretched fame thing took over I could always protect myself with a different name. I was Kevin Carruso for six years. The child support agency is after him big style. It's important if you want to be a top international acter that you learn the ropes.

Anyway, back to the make up girl in the hotel room in Manchester. (And yes in case you're wondering, repeatedly and rather well and about half a pint but don't tell Miriam for fuck's sake.) I was chatting warmly and entertainingly to her about how I had gone to university in Manchester and she was thrilled to bits – tiny but nicely formed bits with breasts – and said what a fun guy I was and how nice I was and good in bed/big cock etc.

"But you look so much better in the flesh than you do on the telly," she said to me.

"It's just a make up thing," I breathed. "I studied in Manchester. I got a double first in Philosophy and Ancient Chinese Literature and the house that I lived in here, in this very town, was the inspiration for the house in The Young Ones."

"The Young Ones," she ejaculated, "that legendary situation comedy that exploded in the cultural wasteland of the early eighties like a five megaton nuclear warhead thereby forever changing the face of British broadcasting and leaving a big fuck off crater in the middle of it?"

"The very same."

And the make up girl – we'll call her Wendy for safety (her real name was Carol) – asked if we could go and take a look at the house later that day after I had finished doing my edge cutting acting in whatever it was I was there to act in [get someone to look this up, publisher]. So we did. We got a taxi and I paid for all of it – I didn't split it 50:50 or anything. When we got there, we got out of the car. It was as if the rain was falling. No, the rain was falling. We got out of the car. Sorry, done that bit*. Look, we got out of the car and it was raining, okay?

"This is what saved BBC2 from being cancelled," I told her. But when I looked round, she was crying.

"What's the matter?" I asked careingly. And she pointed with her hand. Like that. And I looked up and saw what she had just seen. They had knocked down my Young Ones house! She fell to her knees. What could I do? What do you think? It seemed to help a bit. Then I walked off into the sunset (although it was still raining) and I never saw her again. Good job too. You should have seen her teeth. Disgusting.

Manchester University drama department didn't know what had hit it when I arrived. (This is years before. Not with the make up bird. That story's over now. File closed. Move on. You'll thank me for being brutal with you viewer, when you hit some really serious wordage later on when I spill the beans (this means sing like a canary†) on where the corpses are really buried. It's a blood drenched, charnel house of bodies and still-quivering organs when we really get up to our elbows in the viscera and gristle of British light entertainment. In the meantime I'm going to tell you about the young Rik Mayall in Manchester when he meets Adrian Edmondson (a towering inferno of genius – even more towering and inferning then me – and I don't say things like that lightly.

---

\* You have to watch out with me, don't you. Funny jokes can pop up with me any-old-where. I'm crazy. But that's enough. Back to the book. Now.

† Check what this means.

You're hanging with the big boys now. I remember once when we were writing a Bottom series together (an earth-shattering genre-busting situation comedy that has been butchered, raped and copied by every successful comedy series since), I say we, really it was all just Adrian, but he kindly let me put my name on it as well so that I could earn some more money in order to meet my payment schedule to him*. Anyway, we were sitting in a pub in Soho. Adrian had the pad and the biro and it was my job to buy all the drinks and the food and fetch it all from the bar and clear it away and fetch coffee and cigarettes and pay for Adrian's executive massage around the corner afterwards. It was so funny. Honestly, we were roaring. And other people in the strip club, [delete this], pub looked around and saw the two of us and commented, "Look, there are the two giants of British comedy, laughing together – what great mates they must be and what great lives they must live as they ride the out of control rollercoaster of hilarious crazy good times together." And they were right, of course. And the reason we were laughing so much was – honestly you're going to love this, we [fill in amusing and heart-warming anecdote here].)

I was terribly excited on my first day at Manchester University. I put on my student's uniform, got there early and bagged the best place so that the lecturer would see that I was the keenest. At King's School, we were all very well brought up and when Sir came into the class, we all stood up. So when Professor John Prudhoe, the man who invented the Manchester University drama department, came into the lecture theatre, I, of course, stood up. But I was the only one. No one else moved. They just sat there

---

* I want to make it perfectly clear here that Adrian has never blackmailed me for large amounts of money and taken members of my family whenever I default on the payments. He would never do this. He is kind. And very talented. More than me.

looking at me. Then one of them laughed. He didn't even have a proper student hair cut. He had long wispy nasty hair and had his feet on the desk and he was smoking a cigarette. Smoking a cigarette in lesson! In LESSON!!! Was he suicidal? He would get at least six for that. But he didn't seem to care, and Sir didn't seem to bother about him either. This fellow student was the Adrian I hadn't yet met and he just stared and pointed at me and he said, "look, look!" and everyone started laughing at me. I mean, I know I'm a comedy genius but I didn't really know what the gag was. Had my fountain pen leaked ink or something? And then I saw that the Professor was laughing at me as well. Ice ran down my spine. So this was university was it? I thought to myself. Anarchy, no laws . . . no future? Punk type pop music? What sort of world had I got myself into? I quickly unbuttoned the top button of my shirt and tried out some swear words. I was evolving. This pack of freedom-fighting wolves had a new brother with them. It was Rik. Okay, I couldn't pronounce my Rs very well, but I knew that as soon as I reached the onset of puberty, I wasn't going to shave. I was only seventeen. Who was this innocent young seventeen year old I could see them thinking. We'll have him for breakfast. Sweet seventeen and never been kissed? I don't think so. You've got a Rik Mayall on your hands I said to them. Well, I didn't actually. Not out loud. But I wrote it in my notebook. My special secret one for "certain" occasions.

The wild terrifying unconventional non-sexist hell-for-leather student accommodation that I collectively occupied in Manchester with my three undergraduate amigos, Lloyd*, Ivor and Max, was like living in Golgotha. No, Sodem. No fuck 'em. No fuck it. No fuck it all. Bollocks. Oh Christ, look, we were just dangerous guys

---

* I'm not going to write anything here about shagging Lloyd's girlfriend and if you see him reading this book then please take it from him and tell him he never saw it and you don't know what he's talking about.

who lived life to the max right, and pushed everything to the hilt despite the endless homework and cleaning and squabbles about the washing up rota. I'd like to see Charles Bronson survive in that frightful little house in East Allington that only had one name, Limes Cottage. Anything could happen and often did. Sometimes we wouldn't even do the hoovering for a fortnight and sometimes we'd come home from the chip shop and instead of putting the fish and chips on plates, we'd eat them out of newspaper on the floor just like we were really working class. It was extraordinary. Regularly, I quite simply wouldn't do my homework when I was supposed to. We were the hard guys, the four horsemen of the apocalypse. There was strong drink, sex, and drugs all over the place (that none of us ever took). We even got dirty videos out from the video store. And Max's mate rode his motobike* up the stairs, turned left and went straight into my bedroom and parked it on my bed. He did. He bloody did. I'm not lying. This was serious. No way could I accept that. There was going to be a fight. And there was and I was so badly beaten up that I nearly had to go to hospital. I'm not going to put his name down here. Not because I'm scared or I can't remember. Just because I'm hard.

Every Monday night at Manchester University, the drama department hosted what was called Studio Night which was where all the students who went to lectures and knew how to write used to put on their very own productions. Anyone could get up and do their thing† – like a sex machine man – sorry, wrong format. Someone might think of a monologue or a play or a love affair with a chair. That was where me and Ade started. Or rather, where Ade let me start with him. No, that sounds a bit rude. It was where Ade and I started to do our thing together. Not that we

---

\* This is a fashionable term for a motorcycle.
† This is a happening way of saying they did something.

had a thing or anything. We've never done it to each other. Not like that. Well, not in any way at all, really. Adrian is far too great a talent in the world of international showbusiness for me to ever dare assume that I might try to cop a feel. So, just leave it now and move onto the next paragraph. Pretend you didn't read any of that last bit. It's just a blanket denial, okay?

So, me and Ade started doing our stuff together on a Monday night at the studio until we thought bollocks to the Marxists (some of the students were terrifically well educated) and went into Manchester and started doing our thing in pubs where we got paid and got to drink more. We were known as things like Twentieth Century Coyote and Deathsquad Theatre Company. We learnt how to be funny (although Adrian was always funnier than me) and how to live life without rules.

If it wasn't for Adrian I would never have met Little Ben-Elton. Me and Ade were in the third year and one day I masculined my way into the drama department and heard this disgusting squealing animal noise. Jesus, it's a fan I suddenly didn't think because I wasn't huge famous yet although I was deeply popular in Manchester. Doctor Nightclub they used to call me. Anyway, one of the things that I love about Ade in a butch matey kind of hard sort of way is the way that he likes to beat people up, and sure enough there was a churning maelstrom of blood and flesh and good looking fists and savage well placed kicks to the face of a weeping screaming little schoolboy.

"Cool thing to do, Adrian Edmondson," I said.

"Get me a drink, this is thirsty work," he said. So I did, even though it was only nine o'clock in the morning and he had already had four pints (but he has never had a drink problem*).

"Here you are, great mate Adrian," I said giving him his beer.

---

* Ever.

39

"Fuck off," he said amusingly.

"What are you doing?"

The violence stopped and the quivering little mass whimpered and recoiled and tried to make itself even smaller in the corner of the corridor. Adrian swung around and locked me in an El Alamein of a glance.

"Look," he slathered, "the new first years have arrived and look at this one. It's a fuck pig."

"Ha ha ha, great joke, Adrian Edmondson," I said, "let me help you to stamp on him."

But at that moment the little mite looked up at me and said, "Help me, good looking third year, I'm Little Ben-Elton. I just want to study drama for three years and behave decently and become one of Britain's foremost dramatists. I've got an enormous output of avant guard work which means that I like to write a lot."

"Hey, Adrian Edmondson," I said with compassion for the little tot, "why don't you eat my thesis and take my wallet and cigarette lighter so you can go to the pub and do some more of your drinking which you do so well although you're definitely not an alcoholic."

"All rightey dokey," quipped Ade and it was as though a whole new seam of comedy had been mined in a flash. I'm looking at Eddie Hitler I thought. And with one more good-natured snap of Ben's thigh, Ade (although even then I felt like calling him Eddie which was a tremendous creation as was all of Bottom which he wrote all the best parts of) made his way to the pub.

And that was how I befriended Little Ben-Elton. We swapped comedy ideas while I was taking him to Casualty past a burning pub – The George and Whippet which burnt (look it up in any local newspaper of the time) down on December 3rd 1977 and Adrian had nothing to do with it.

I actually went back to Manchester a few years later and performed in a play called Man Equals Man by Berthold Brecht who is probably the worst playwriter who has ever been allowed near a type-righter. No one even knew he was a German until I "let it out of the bag", and the play has never been performed since. I managed to expose how bad his play was. I realised it for the audience. It was a definitive performance. Up until then, everyone had enjoyed his plays, but during that run, I managed to alienate the audience so much that by the end of some of the performances there was no one left in the theatre. Even some of the cast had left by the time I had delivered all of my five lines. Beat that Paul Bradley.

The Man Booker Foundation
Equity House
Irthlingborough Road
Wellingborough NN8 1LT


February 15th 2005


Dear The Man,

Re (means regarding) your Booker Prize thing

The Rik Mayall here – yes that's right – Rik Fucking
Mayall in your letter, in your hands. Read it and weep.
Well, not weep really, more like, rush around the office
with tears of joy streaming down your face shouting
about me. All right, that's enough, let's be sensible.

Now the thing is, I'm writing a book. Yes, go back and
read that line again. You don't need to bother with the
"now the thing is," bit. That's not important. Just the bit
about writing the book. That's the meat of it. Which
means that that is the important bit. The bit about writing
the book. Anyway, just concentrate and we'll move on.

I am writing a book. I'm just taking a brake from it to
write you a letter to tell you about it because it's kind of
important that people like you are aware of what is going
on in the white hot raging furnace of bang-up-to-date Eng

Lit. Now some bloke that I met the other day at the
market on the end of our road told me that your prize is
the really top prize to win if you've written a book. So,
already you're probably beginning to get a sense of what
kind of shit I'm going to throw down for you. This is
media speak for what ideas I'm going to tell you about.
It has nothing to do with fouling the carpet.

I'd only gone down for a few vegetables. I could have
said I'd gone for a leak but that's just a really unfunny
play on words that one of those oldtime comedians might
have come out with in a northern working class working
men's club in the mid-seventies and been thanked for it.
(Although I'm down with the working classes – which
means I like them and empathighs with them – I've
always been a socialist.) Besides, they might not have
had any. Anyway, this guy came up to me and we got
to talking, you know, like "Hello, are you Rik Mayall?"
"Yes." "Oh Crikey, I'm a really big fan, I think you're
probably the best acter working in Britain or indeed any
English speaking country etc." And I told him about my
edge cutting new book. And that's when he said that I
should try and win your prize because it helps to sell
lots more copies.

So, here I am. And let me tell you that the book I'm
writing is shaping up to be a total cock-ripper (which
means it will be very amusing and interesting in every
respec). So what I want to suggest is that if we agree that
I can have the prize here and now then I'll split the prize
money with you. I know it's only fifty grand and I get that
for taking a piss in a commercial voice-over studio toilets

as a rule but it's the kudos that I'm looking for as much as anything else. And it will be a win win situation for you because once you've decided to give the prize to me, you won't have to read all the other pretentious nob-dribble that gets sent to you. Everyone's happy – we're all floating around on big inflatable lilo things in sun-drenched swimming pools with fabulous topless birds fighting over which one of them is going to blow us off first. I'm speaking hypo-allegorically of course.

So, please let me know when the ceremony is and I'll make sure that my agent, Heimi Fingelstein (you never read that), can get it in my diary and I can think about my acceptance speech. Let me know if you would like a mench (this is showbusiness for mention) and if I should give a mench (see last set of brackets) to any other products you might want me to plug. I can also do this on any daytime chat show you like – or onstage at the Olivier. I see that your company is something to do with food so perhaps I could let people know if you've got any special offers on at the moment – frozen peas half price – that sort of thing.

So there we go. Letter written. Job done. Please get back to me soon.

Regards,

Rik. The.

# CONQERING AMERICA

I woke up this morning and I thought "New Chapter" so I wrote it but I'm not going to put it in the book for personal reasons. I'll keep it here though, so if you want to see it please forward some cash and I'll send it to you although it'll only be a copy because I'm keeping these "lost" chapters for a book of outtakes from this book. It'll be like a book version of one of those Denis Norden bloopers shows, only thrusting and vital and like viral media anthrax, of course. Interested publishers, please get in touch. I feel another fat advance coming on and I'm not talking about an over-weight predatory homersexual. Which reminds me of a story.

It was the 11th of October 1992 and the first Tuesday in the month. And as I always do on the first Tuesday of every month, I decided to do something special. So I thought I'd telephone Christopher Biggins and invite him around for elevenses. Now, the telephone is next to the fruit bowl in my house – you probably have different arrangements in your house – so I approached the fruit bowl with my hand extended and although I was reaching for the telephone receiver, I actually grabbed hold of a banana. Now, the banana is the quintessence

It was the first Tuesday in the month and I decided to do some-thing special. Christopher Biggins I thought for elevenses. Cups of coffee and rich T biscuits. Showbusiness gossip. So, I reached for the fruit bowl. Now, as everyone knows, the banana is the quintessence

It was October 1992. It was a Tuesday. It was the first Tuesday in the month. So what did I do? I thought Christopher Biggins for elevenses. Sponge fancies, chocolate fingers and a big fat pot of tea. I approached the telephone. I don't know about you but in my house that's where I keep the bananas. Now, the banana. Is the quintessence

The first Tuesday in the month. Sponge fancies, pots of tea and approaching telephones. I don't know about you but I thought "Christopher Biggins". Elevenses in a fruit bowl in my house. Chocolate fingers and something special. Now, the banana is the quintessence

Oh sod this, abandon anecdote.

[Note to editor: I'll right some stuff that can go here about when I went to America after I'd left college and toured around in a big bus on the wrong side of the road with loads of other acters. I can mention about all the burning theatres, police car chases, drugs (that I never took), helicopter incidents, speedboat getaways, shoot outs with real guns, explosives, breaking Jon Plowman's arm etc. Don't worry, it'll be great.]

# CRACKING THE SMOKE*

Imagine the scene, and if you can't then bollocks, I'm just going to keep my legs together on this one and go for it. 1980. That was the big year last century. Because that's when me and Adrian Edmondson came down and hit London. Only it wasn't 1980, it was 1979 but that's not important. What's important is what year it was. And it was that year. No question. BLAM! No, sorry, hold on a moment.

BLAM! That's better. We had just done a fantastic show in Edinburgh called Death on the Toilet. It had got everything in it: violence, and lavatory jokes. It was a massive hit. We made such a profit, actually, no, we didn't. If you're a tax inspector, you never read that, and if you did, it was a joke. And with the profit – not that we made any – we came down to London to stage a spectacular theatrical touring show. Which we did, and it was called King Ron And His Nubile Daughter. It had sex in it. Well, nubile sounds quite sexy. And we thought that Ron was quite a funny

---

* Note to printer: careful with this. I've never done crack in my life. Well, not that sort of crack anyway. Not the sort that you need a pipe for. Although there was that time with Beverly Marwood but that doesn't count because half the pipe broke off in there and it took us two hours to get it out. Anyway, just be careful and print it as it's written.

47

word. The whole thing was a disaster. We played twelve different venues, put up the poster ourselves, several times (and it was quite well drawn) and all in all we attracted an audience of eight people. That's true that. An audience of eight spread over a tour of twelve venues. Not bad. Actually, it was worse than that. It was a total and complete abortion. But God was looking down on me and thinking, "That guy's good. I want him on the telly, and I want him on the stage, and on the cinema. I want him to be a name. He's really got what it takes. And I should know because I'm God. I made him myself. That's Rik Mayall and I'll keep my eye on him."

So, because he liked the look of me and had big plans for me, God sent a reviewer from the Times to see us one day at the Tramshed, a kind of little theatre bar thing in Woolwich, South London. There were only three people in the audience, well two and a half actually, because one of them was a baby in a pram with its mother who was only there because it was raining outside. But at the back of the auditorium there was this weird dark presence. I came on stage and soon, everyone was howling. And the next thing is that I'm being called a "very talented young maniac" in the Times. The newspaper! Me, in the paper! Fucking hell! That's it, I thought, I've arrived. Look out everybody. Lock up your daughters and hide your drugs (not that I would be looking for them because I never touch them).

"Seen that, Ade?" I said and showed him my review.

I think it was about a week before the bruising went down on my face.

Luckily, a lot of English students had come to London to try and get into publishing – like twats do – and a lot of English students are girls. So I had a lot of places to stay. I might have been homeless but I wasn't twadgeless. I ended up in Clapham with some girl whose name I can't remember. But I remember her boyfriend was called Richard. He was a nice guy. Used to work all day in an office which was fantastic for me and his girlfriend. One Friday night he came home from work, completely pissed as is obligatory if you work in the city, and he told me he had heard of a great new place that had opened in London and it was called The Comedy Store. That was the original one, viewer. It was good too. It wasn't like one of those shitholes they have now that are full of non-entities trying to copy me.

So, I went down there to this new Comedy Store place which was just a tiny doorway in the middle of nowhere. I stepped in and there was nothing apart from a sort of tiny cupboard with a lift in it. So I got in the little lift, went up, got out (like you do) – and get a load of this – it was a strip club. Fantastic I thought. And the bar was all made out of gold and all the birds were topless which means they were wandering around with their breasts all over the place*. The drinks were terrifyingly expensive, about forty quid for half a can of warm lager, and I was the tallest guy in the place because all the other men were Japanese. But at 10 o'clock the strip club turned into The Comedy Store. All the Japanese businessmen suddenly disappeared and all the punky threatening dangerous young maverick outlaw comedians started coming in. I'd never seen anything like it: Keith Allen, Tony Allen, Pauline Melville, Maggie Steed, Jim Barclay, Alexei Sayle, Andy de la Tour, Arnold Brown (deep pulsating respect) and maybe ten or so others (sorry guys, blame my memory on the quadbike) – and let me also take this opportunity to pay my respects to Peter Rosengard – there's nothing wrong with being Jewish – that's what I always say. And to the great Don Ward. Men I owe a lot to. But not money.

---

* Very big thing in those days, viewer. The 70s was the Breast Decade. They were very important for our generation – they still are really.

The rule was that if you were shit you were gonged off. I'm the only person who was never gonged off. That's true. As well as being a cool thing to say. Everybody was raving about me because I was the best. The others were quite good but let's face it, at the end of the day, they weren't Rik Mayall. I can't put it more kindly than that really.

Then suddenly, from nowhere, in strode a canny independent-eyed West Country rebel called Pete "Peter" Richardson with his comedy partner Nigel "excuse me, where am I?" Planer. They were known as The Outer Limits. Now at the Comedy Store, if you didn't get gonged, you'd earn a tenner for doing about fifteen minutes, but if you were a double act, you only earned fifteen pounds between you which meant that you got seven pounds fifty each. Well that's what the other double acts got. Ade handled our cash and I got a quid. Nice of him. Clever guy. So, anyway, Pete decided we should work six nights a week instead of one so we could earn lots more money. So he went over the road to Paul Raymond's Revue Bar and he put on a comedy club there which was called The Comic Strip. Because it was in a strip club. And we were comedians – allegedly. And he took Alexei Sayle, Nigel Planer, me and Ade, and the great Arnold Brown with him. And that was when a double act came to audition for us. They were called French and Saunders. They were so repulsive and unfunny that we gave them the job straight away and Dawn and Jennifer made me and Ade look stupendously funny. And that's how it all happened. I was on a roll. From one night a week at the Comedy Store to six nights a week at the Comic Strip. The place was frocking. Flocking. Something. Well, whatever it was, it was doing it. Big style.

Someone had asked me to audition (not that I do auditions) and when I went to it I found out it was for a sketch show called A Kick Up The Eighties with Miriam Margolyes, Tracey Ullman,

Roger Sloman, Robbie Coltrane and Ron Bain. But when I went to see this guy called Colin Gilbert who was the producer, I didn't realise that you were supposed to have prepared something to perform for them so they could see if you were any good. I thought, fuck! I'm in the shit! And I'm on in five minutes! What shall I do? Panic? No. Come on Rikki – you've got no dialogue – DO SOMETHING – so I did. God blew me a kiss and on the spot I invented a character who came from Redditch in the West Midlands, which is not far from where I come from, and could talk about anything at all – from a paper clip to another paper clip – and never stop – ever. (He's still talking now.) His name was – yes, that's right – Kevin Turvey and he became an overnight sensation. I was born. I took my name off the show's credits as well which was a stroke of genius because everyone thought that Kevin actually existed. I'm so addicted to modesty it's a curse sometimes. And that's where I saw this stonking make-up bird called Barbara – fuck me what a lay – the best in Europe without a doubt. Anyway, don't tell the wife.

So you see my dear viewer, what me and my magnificent cohorts were doing was taking the comedy rulebook and tearing it up into little pieces, eating it, letting it pass through our bodies, picking it out of our brown stuff and burning it and dancing naked on the ashes. Smell the legend viewer, smell the legend. Sorry about that. You only get one life to wank yourself off in an autobiography.

Suddenly, we were wanted on the telly and not just the telly, no, the big screen* was beckoning. I offered Donald Sutherland a sandwich in Eye of the Needle, played draughts with Brian Glover† in American Werewolf in London and performed in the

---

* This means the cinema. It makes sense.
† The very great Brian.

breakthuogh Rocky Horror Picture Show sequel Shock Treatment with my great mate Barry Humphries and his great big swinging comedy equipment. [Fill in anecdote here and make it a good one because he knows where I live.]

Julien Temple made a movie about us all which was called The Comic Strip and Julien Temple is cool. If you haven't heard of him, you're not cool. Not only am I cool but I took him some tea once. We did tea together. And it was in Soho. Life was changing, things were happening. I was making tea and movies and great cutting edge television like Boom Boom Out Go the Lights and Whoops Apocalypse. But something even bigger was stirring in my trousers. Something that would take the burning meteorite of comedy and acting talent which is what I was and am and shall be throughout all time and space and make it go supanova (which means that the meteorite would go even faster and further and brighter across the sky – at night preferably because you can see things like that better when it's dark. Not too dark obviously because you won't be able to see anything. Anyway, wrap up warm.)

Er, that's the end of this chapter. So fuck off. These words need to sleep.

# WHY I WAS NEVER IMPRISONED FOR
# BEATING ESTHER RANTZEN TO DEATH

My first question to any producer who wants me in his play is, "Does the character smoke?" This is important because I do very powerful acting-smoking. Motivation and character arks (these are technical playrighting terms which mean stuff about the character who is the person that you are pretending to be) are important to me but more important is that I have a packet of fags and that my character has a good bird (NB*: no clap or syph – and she must bring her own condoms. I can't be seen wandering around buying condoms. I'm Rik Mayall. It's also quite handy to find out where she keeps her purse.) I know you think I'm taking the piss but I am the piss and I've not been taken anywhere. I go where I want. I am the freedom piss in the toilet of oblivion flushing myself away into the sewer pipe of broken dreams. That's not bad actually – seems a shame to just read it once. Go on, I'll wait for you here. Done it? Good. Anyway, what I'm saying is, you tell me one play that I've been in when I haven't smoked and I won't listen. Probably because I won't be in the same room as you.

---

* This means you've got to check.

Being in a play is great for having it off in the afternoons so it pays to have a bed in the dressing room. But don't install any webcams. Look at what happened to Dirty Dan.

It's also very important when you are starting out as a leading acter and comedy giant to get yourself a business partner. This is what is called an agent. This is not a secret agent (although they can be secretive) and they don't as a rule have guns in their pockets. Although mine does. An agent is a person who finds work for you and makes sure that you're happy with all the arrangements for things and sometimes even gets you money for what you are doing. They take the lion's share obviously, which is only fair after all the life-threatening negotiations they have to do.

I remember it so well, it's like it was yesterday. I was at a Celebrity Squares aftershow party. All the greats were there: Crowther, Biggins, Cheggers, Hull, De Courcey, Rogers, Lynch, Russell Grant (obviously) and there we were all howling and gibbering and convulsing and spasming and evacuating our bowels with hilarity as Lynchy and I did some of our verbal swordsmanship when Roger Moore took me to one side and said, "Hi Rik, love your work, I hear you're looking for an agent. I know a guy called Heimi Fingelstein." The dye was cast (which means that something big was going to happen). My personal favourite 007 gave me the address of a post office box which I wrote to. The following spring I had a phone call from Heimi's assistant, Big Joan, who arranged for me to come in for a meeting.

Roger told me something amazing that he had learnt in the secret service but it's confidential and I can't tell you what it is. What he did tell me that I can tell you about is that for important meetings it's always good to wear a wire which means you can record your conversation on a tape recorder which is sellotaped to your chest. Unfortunately, this being the late seventies, the tape machine was quite large and cumbersome and took a lot of sellotape to hold it in place and a lot of baggy jumpers to conceal it satisfactorily. What follows is a transcript of my first meeting with my agent, Heimi Mad Dog Fingelstein*.

*Tape starts. Sounds of rustling sticky tape and various doors opening. Footsteps on stairs. Sounds of lots of sewing machines in the background and the occasional female scream.*

```
RIK:      Hello, I am The Rik Mayall: acter,
          comedian, wit, satirist -

BIG JOAN: I don't need to know any of that,
          mate. I just answer the phone and
          take messages. What you do is your own
          business. Now, just go through into his
          office and once you're in there, look
          straight ahead and don't turn your back
          on him.

RIK:      Thank you.

BIG JOAN: Don't thank me, in fact, don't look at
          my face. Oh and just one last thing, what
          blood group are you?

RIK:      Rhesus Negative.

BIG JOAN: Oh well, never mind. In you go.

          Sound of door opening

RIK:      Hello. You must be Heimi.

HEIMI:    No, he passed away tragically. I was
          there. Who are you?
```

---

\* Note to Editor: as I mentioned in my postcard to you last week, I'm not sure about putting this section in the book because Heimi might not be very happy. It's not good to antagonise him. I'll put it in the first draft but we both need to think seriously about what might happen to us if we upset him. Look at Michael Barrymore.

RIK:   I'm The Rik Mayall: acter, comedian, wit, satirist –

HEIMI:   *Into intercom*
Joan, send in Neville with the acid bath, it's another one of those Panorama reporters. You're sure? Oh him, right. Rhesus negative? Maybe the organs then? All right, well, if you could pick up my dry cleaning and while you're out, I'll have a sandwich. Extra mustard, that's right.
*Switches off intercom*
Rik, my boy! I've always loved you, how are you my darling?

RIK:   Heimi?

HEIMI:   Possibly. Now, sit down and let's talk fame and cash.
*Intercom buzzes*
Excuse me.
*Into intercom*
Who is it? Okay, I'll take it.
*Picks up phone*
Ah, Chief Inspector! Very well, very well. How is Svetlana settling in? Sauce? Oh sores, well that's because of the lorry journey – it's a long way from Hungary and they are packed in tight. They'll heal up soon I'm sure. Besides, if you're not one hundred per cent happy, I'll send you another one, although I'll have Svetlana back if that's okay as she's a rare blood group and still has a kidney left. Your wife? Oh yes, I remember. That house she's set her heart on and the occupants won't sell. Nasty business. You just leave it with me Chief Inspector. There will be a tragic

DIY accident this weekend so the house
will be on the market soon. I'll have
my assistant get the address from you.
Don't mention it. We aim to please. Yes,
business is good. I've just added a dog
food factory to my portfolio. Yeah,
that's right Inspector, dogs'll eat any
thing won't they? Who's to know? An
Alsatian's not going to take the oath is
he? There's always a smile on someone's
face. Okay, well, be lucky. Speak soon.
Good luck with the riot. Bye for now.
*To Rik*
You never heard any of that okay?

RIK:      Oh okay, ha ha ha…

HEIMI:    Squeal and your dead.

RIK:      Right.

HEIMI:    Now, first things first, how big's your
          schlong?

RIK:      I beg your pardon?

HEIMI:    If you want to make it in the adult film
          business, you've got to have a big one. I
          don't make the rules.

RIK:      No, I think you must have mistaken me for
          someone else. I'm the highly original new
          radical socialist acter and comedian.
          Although I do have a very large penis.

HEIMI:    I was misinformed. But don't worry my
          boy – anything can work to someone's
          advantage. In fact, thinking about it,
          I've got a lovely bit of work for you
          Rikky my favourite client. It'll play to
          your strengths in every department, and
          there'll be some serious cash as well.

RIK:      Great, now you're really talking.

HEIMI:    Can you run fast?

RIK:      Like an Olympiad.

HEIMI:    Good. Like dogs?

RIK:      Like dogs is my middle name.

HEIMI:    Looks like we're in business then. I'm
          smelling money already.

RIK:      What is it?

HEIMI:    Police.

RIK:      Are they bringing Z Cars back!?

HEIMI:    No, pretty Rik, grab a hold of something
          solid, it's even bigger than that. Hold
          your breath.
          *Intercom buzzes*
          Oh fuck, hold on Rik.
          *Into intercom*
          What is it? Oh right, put him straight
          through.
          *Picks up phone and becomes nice*
          Hello Director General. I take it you got
          my message... That's right. She's fourteen
          and she's prepared to testify. Add to
          that the photographs that would be
          found in your house should there be an
          anonymous tip-off leading to a police
          search, and I think you're looking at
          about fifteen years. Of course I'll hold
          for a moment.
          *To Rik*
          It is police and it is television but
          it's not exactly a police television
          programme if you get my meaning.
          *Into phone*
          Ah that's quite all right Director

General. I'm glad that you have reached
the right decision. It's not a good
programme that Panorama. I should drop it
if I was you… Beg pardon? The reporters?
The ones that came here to question me?
No, I have no recollection of any
reporters making contact with me and
neither does my assistant. All my very
best wishes to you and your wife, Director
General. We never had this conversation.
You don't know me. Bye for now.
*To Rik*
Oh dear, sorry about that, I should have
mentioned you whilst I had him on the
line. Anyway, where were we?

RIK:       The television work you're lining me up
           for.

HEIMI:     Ah yes, the police dog training video.

RIK:       The what?

HEIMI:     The police dog training video – they're
           looking for someone to play a hooligan.

RIK:       Oh I see, it's a joke, very good Heimi,
           ha ha ha!

HEIMI:     Do you see a smile on my face?

RIK:       No, sorry.

HEIMI:     Good, now let me see.
           *Consults diary*
           You're not going to be anywhere near
           Watford on Friday morning at about 10
           o'clock are you?

RIK:       No.

HEIMI:     Just as well. There's going to be a nasty
           gas explosion. It'll be very tragic. But

business is business. Ah, now, let me
see. You need to be at Hendon Police
Training Centre next Wednesday at 8.30am.

RIK: Will they send a car for me?

HEIMI: Oh good heavens no.

RIK: And what sort of deal are they offering?

HEIMI: Deal?

RIK: Money.

HEIMI: Oh good Lord, he comes in here and he
wants to talk to me about money. Trust me
Rikky-boy there will be money. There is
always money somewhere along the line.
*Sound of Heimi standing up and Rik
getting suddenly very nervous, and very
carefully not turning his back on Heimi.*
Lovely to see you again Rikky, make sure
your health insurance is up to date and
don't mention anything to anyone.

RIK: Thanks Heimi. Thank you very much. I love
your work Mr. Fingelstein.

HEIMI: I can neither confirm nor deny my identity
at this juncture but I would like to take
this opportunity to wish you all the best
for the future. Now, make sure you leave
all your details with Big Joan and I'll
be seeing you soon.

RIK: All right, well, bye then Heimi.

HEIMI: Be good. This conversation never
happened.

*Sound of the door opening followed by the sound
of sticky tape tearing away from skin and a large
cassette recorder crashing to the floor.*

And that, viewer, is how I came to be represented by Heimi Mad Dog Fingelstein. It's just like that dear dear friend of mine, lovely Peter whats-his-name used to say – no, sorry, it's gone.

# CHAPTER SEVEN

## THE YOUNG ONES

Bang, bang, bang, bang, went her head against the toilet door. I'm always doing it with starlets in toilets at film premieres but this film was one of the best I'd seen. I wasn't in it but it was great all the same, although I did have three lines in that one with what's-his-name in it – the bloke with the leg – but it wasn't much to shout about. The main thing is that I'm hard and cool. Like a Kidderminster Bruce Willis.

"Oh Rik, you're the best." She could barely speak. Back bottom stuff is always best with American girls.

Bang, bang, bang – her nose went next. I've always been such a passionate lover but I thought crikey, I'd better get out of here. There's blood and teeth everywhere and there's papperatsi* all over the place outside.

"Check you later, babe, which is American for cheerio, thank you for a charming afternoon in the toilet. I have to go now."

"Oh Rik, you're the best lover ever, I can't wait to not tell anyone about this and keep our secret safe," she said. "Thank God British television is so shit nowadays. Everyone will go and see my movie now."

---

* Papperatsi means Italian photographers.

That's when my blood ran cold. That's right, my blood ran ice cold at that very moment. She's right, I thought. The condition of British television is beyond repair. The art form is dead. A year from today there will be just a vast pyre of useless TV sets as the British public go streaming to the cinema instead. This is a situ-fucking-ation. I left the toilet cubicle like a car bomb and went outside.

"Hey Rik Mayall, give us a smile," said a papperatsi. Whap! Half his camera went back into his eye socket.

"Leave the fuck me alone, I'm incognito," I howled enigmally and was gone.

The rain was lashing down and I was looking a lot like Clint. In fact, a lot of people walking past me said, "Hey bloke, you look a lot like Clint, only better."

"Thanks complete strangers," I said, and carried on my way muscularily.

"Excuse me sir," said another one.

"Yes non-entity."

"Are you going to be Rik Mayall, international light entertainment leviathan?"

"No," I said.

"Get away."

"Don't talk to me like that."

"No I meant 'get away' as in you <u>are</u> going to be Rik Mayall."

"No, I'm not. I'm going to be The Rik Mayall and much more besides."

"Blimey bloody crikey, can I have your autograph?"

"Not yet – I am only a partially formed foetus of a comedy legend. Give me a chance."

"Thanks anyway."

And that was his fifteen minutes gone. Like that ridiculous blond painter Andrew War Hole used to say. Even though they only lasted about a minute and a quarter.

On I mooded into the nearest pub. I won't tell you the name of it because it's important to protect the privacy of pubs. Pubs have far too much unwanted intrusion these days. Anyway, the thing is, huge genre-shifting ideas like The Young Ones don't just come along like that. But this one did. There I was at the bar ordering a drink:

"I'll have a pint of hang on a fucking minute – I've got an idea. I'll write a situation comedy."

Close up on the Rik doing that eye thing. Chicks gasp. Guys slit their wrists. End of shot. I'm young, I thought to myself, there's one of me, so I'll call the show The Young One. But no, I won't be selfish, I am a socialist after all, I'll put some of my great mates in it as well, and call it The Young Ones. Plural. Good.

I went straight home after another few pints and a donna kebab and I stayed up late writing the first series. I got through nine typewriters that night under the barrage of my relentless unstoppable fingering. They call me Mr Typewriter.

The cock crowed – ooer obviously* – and I got up the crack of Dawn (nice girl/ooer obviously again) and I got out of bed like a raging undetonated warhead and went straight off to the BBC.

"It's punk rock, it's radical, it's anarchy, it's four guys in a house together on a one way ticket to oblivion and there'll be bands – good ones – playing live and it's just a big two fingers to the establishment, and television will never be the same again. Ever." Silence. All the television executives looked at me as they sat around the table in their pastel coloured jackets and shirts.

---

* Appears courtesy of Andy de la Tour. Ooer is what you say after you've said something that might be misconstrude as rude and was famously used in the tectonic plate shifting landmark comedy pastiche "Ooer Sounds a Bit Rude" which was featured in my breakthruough situation comedy Filthy, Rich and Catflap. For further information about this please ask someone else. I'm too intense at the moment.

"I know where I've seen you before," one of them said. "Weren't you that dreadful northerner on that Kick Up the Eighties programme that no one could understand? When you were talking, you didn't make any sense. You kept going on in that ridiculous accent like you were from Lancashire or somewhere. Who on earth let you make that? Oh it was made in Scotland wasn't it? They're light years behind us. They're just a bunch of alcoholics who wear skirts. They don't know how it's done. Now, you mentioned something about having pop music in the show?"

"Yes I did."

"But that's a silly idea. Drama is drama and pop music is pop . . ."

"It's called rock 'n' roll."

"Well, whatever you silly people want to call it. You can't put your music into drama programmes. It's just not done. Now, tell me, you're not Jewish are you?"

"So what if I am. Are you some kind of racist?"

"Oh no, no no no. It's just we have to be very careful. Where do you hunt?"

"Oh this is ridiculous."

"How many bedrooms do your parents have in their house?"

"What?"

"You are Jewish aren't you?"

"Oh I've had enough of this. I'm going to prove this once and for all. Say hello to Mr Todge." And out came The Behemoth. "That's what I think of your poncey middle class attitudes," I said in my West Midlands drawl.

"Pardon," they said.

"Now listen up, I'm a hardcore socialist. I'm a man of the people. All the people are one and I am one and I am at war with the establishment and my first battle is to get something decent on TV."

But the mood had changed. There was silence in the room. They all sat there slack-jawed.

"Crikey," they said after a moment, "do you feint when you read dirty magazines?"

I saw my opening. It was now or never. "Who's in charge here?" I brooded, my manhood still unfurled like a fire hose.

"Paul Jackson."

"Okay, I want to see him. Now!" And I slammed my fist on the desk. Ow! Shit!

And out I strod. I didn't even close the door. Anarchy is my middle name. Rik Anarchy Mayall or R.A.M. to my great mates. Not in a homoey way though. Not that I've got anything against the gay – sexual equality is my middle name and I've always been a rock hard feminist and homosexualist and some of my best darkies are friends.

Cut to: Paul Jackson's office (just outside the door). SPLAM! I smashed the door open and walked into the office like a torpedo.

"Rik Anarchy Mayall here, Paul Jackson," I said but I shouldn't have bothered because he wasn't there. I waited a couple of hours outside and read a magazine. I think I had a hot chocolate as well from the drinks machine. Then he came back. I think he must have been out for lunch.

"Paul Jackson, it's Rik Mayall," I repeated.

"Rik Mayall, oh my God! I've seen you countless times at The Comedy Store and you're fabulous."

"No, Rik Anarchy Mayall here, Paul Jackson."

"Pardon," said Paul Jackson.

"Anarchy is my middle name. You can call me R.A.M. because I ram everything that moves."

"Do you mean sexually?"

"I mean anythingly. I ram everything out of the way of alternative comedy."

"Alternative comedy? What's that?"

"It's something I've just invented."

"Shit my pants, you're the guy I've been looking for. Everything at the BBC is so slack and flaccid. We need a guy like you. This is just a sad right-wing old-fashioned upper middle class flat-minded soulless organisation of victorian leftovers that needs a shock of nuclear energy like your own unique brand of originality. So please come and work for us Rik Mayall."

"Okay," I said. "Modern television is a wasteland of shit."

"You're right it is."

"I know."

"I like your balls."

"Thank you Paul Jackson, I like yours too, but we'll need some Rock 'n' Roll if we want this baby to fly. Don't you know that there are vital thrusting new bands out there that we need to get on the television like Rip Rig and Panic and other ones as well that I can't think of at the moment. They need a voice and I'm going to give it to them."

"So what's the name of the show?"

"The Young Ones."

"But that's the name of a film."

"Yes, but not just any film. It's only about the finest piece of cinema ever committed to celluloid. Comedy and pop music together – and so shall it be again. It's my mission to cure popular culture."

"My god, you've invented post-modernism," said Paul and dropped to his knees.

"No."

"No harm trying."

"Try anything and you're dead."

"Okay, sorry, but you have to do those sorts of things at the BBC in the late nineties."

"But this is the early eighties, Paul."

"Oh shit yeah, sorry Rik Mayall, I think you're great."

"Don't put me on a pedestal Paul. I'm not a god. I'm a social-ist, I'm a wide-eyed anarchist at the gates of dawn. So let's go forth and lightly entertain everybody."

"Damn right, Rik," he said and slammed his fist on the table. "Ouch."

"I've just done that one Paul. My comedy's way ahead of yours."

"Don't freak out, Rik, man. It was an homage."

"Respec Paul."

"That's early next century, Rik, man."

"Oh yeah! Oh fuck all this, let's stop all this talking and get on with the story."

"Good thinking Rik Mayall."

"I'll do the last line."

"Gotchya."

"Shut up."

"Okay."

"No! I said, I'll do the last line, now shut up!"

"Sorry."

"This is the last line of dialogue Paul, say anything after this and I'm not writing it."

See?

So I phoned all the non-entities that I knew, told them I was going to give them their first brake in showbusiness and that very afternoon, we made the first six episodes of The Young Ones. The following day I was mobbed. Things happened fast in those days.

Because of the success of The Young Ones, Channel 4 phoned me and said, "Can you invent the Comic Strip please?" It was a busy life. I went home, got some of my typewriters out, dusted off the old finger and I was at it. Then I started writing.

# CHAPTER SEVEN

## THE YOUNG ONES

I invented the word "radical." That's right. I made it up. It's no coincidence that the word radical begins with R. In fact, it is almost an anagram of Rik. It's got an R and an I in it. That's 66.6666666% reoccurring there. Which is pretty good in anyone's book. Especially mine. And what you must remember in a Rik Mayall book is never look down, never go back, never leave the boat. Just keep pushing forward into the jungle. I'm with you all the way, viewer, holding your hand and not giving you a feel up – remember my promise?

So there I was wandering in the West Midlands which is in the middle of England but which is not Middle England. Which is an interesting concept in itself. Think of all those working class people who are ignored because they are not what is considered Middle England but actually do live in the middle of England. There's a hole ethnic group right there who have been ignored and disenfranchised for years. Well, that's what alternative comedy is all about. The eighties were hard times. There were no mobile phones, no eye pods [pads?], no laptops, no speed bumps, no boy bands, and to make matters worse, there was a war going on in Vietnam.

I'd never done television on this scale before. But I was sure I could make it work. I was Rik Mayall after all – I still am – I could make anything work. I knew The Young Ones was a good idea. It was what I wanted to see on the television. That's how I knew it was a good idea. And it was produced by the Variety Department at the BBC because if you wanted music – rock 'n' roll – in your programme you had to go to the Variety Department instead of the Comedy Department. Which was great because they had more cash. And it just felt right – like The Goons who had Max Geldray in the middle. Only instead of Max Geldray, we had Motorhead.

During the filming of the second series of The Young Ones, an assassination attempt was made on my life. You might think I'm joking here. I can almost hear you viewer, laughing and saying, "Ha ha, great gag, wild one, I love you and so do all my friends – the ones that I admire anyway." But no, viewer, you're wrong. You're all wrong. It's not a joke. It's a fact. An assassination attempt was made on my life in 1983. Someone, somewhere, wanted me dead. Unseen forces within the British broadcasting establishment realised that once the show hit the television screens, the world would never be the same again. The old order was being swept away but it didn't want to go without a fight. As noble rebel leader and figurehead of the new wave of comedy genius that was coming up from the streets, I was targeted. I'll tell you what happened. Right now.

You know how people come up to you sometimes and say, "Hey Rik . . ." Actually, you probably don't but people are always coming up to me and saying, "Hey Rik, The Young Ones is the best television programme ever made." Well, they can fuck off because it's better than that. You're my public aren't you, viewer? So, if anyone comes up to you and says that to you, then punch them in the face and go into their house and meddle with their wiring. Remember, you and me are wild anarchists who live on the edge and we don't care whether we live or die. Go into their houses and do it now. Done it? Cool. Move on. You're one of mine now. Or I'm one of yours. Whichever you like better. There's no authoritarian structure in our movement. We are all equal. They are few, we are many.

So, what happened was, I had written The Young Ones, right? I wrote it and I'd like to see someone who says that I didn't because they'd be seriously big time wrong, right? Because I did and my name's at the end of it. If you go out and buy a tape or a DeeVeeDee right now from a shop – I don't know, any type of shop – you just go to the sort of shop that sells it and you put it on the tape or your telly thing – whatever kind of telly thing you've got – I don't care what type you've got – just put it on and you watch one of the episodes – whichever one you want, it's not important – just put it on and watch it and then where it says who it's written by well that's where my bloody name is, isn't it? Right? So, tell me I'm wrong. Right, so, I wrote it, okay? And I want to say here and now that I never saw the copy of the script that said that Alexei, who was playing dangerous escaped criminal madman Brian Damage Bolowski in the episode entitled Sick (correct? hardcore fans[*]), was to smash me in the face with the butt of his shotgun. This mysterious little extra piece of action was added in a covert and highly suspicious manor. There I was acting out the scene as written – or scripted as we say in the acting world – when suddenly, Alexei smashed me in the face as hard as he could, knocking me completely unconscious. It was all made to look as though it was in the script and I had just mistimed it (and the actual shot of my character Rick coming round and recovering in the episode is me coming round and recovering genuinely. This, viewer, is a fact and would make an amusing little anecdote in its own right were it not for the fact that all was not what it seemed.)

---

[*] Sometimes just referred to as Hardcores. This has nothing to do with hardcore pornography.

To this day, I am convinced that insidious elements had infiltrated us and brainwashed Alexei Sayle and the others. Earlier on that day I had just happened to see my great friend and fellow Sex Pistol of comedy, Adrian Edmondson, giving fifty quid to Alexei with the words, "as hard as you can right in the face," but this was a false trail, a smokescreen, conjured up by the shadowy forces who wanted me to think that my fellow anarchists and crazy good time compadrays had decided to have me whacked. It was an elaborate sting and from then on, I knew that I had to be careful.

Later, I decided to ask a few questions, see if I could russell a few feathers. First off, I spoke to friend and fellow cast member, Nigel Planer, about what happened when I was unconscious.

"Oh, were you unconscious?" he said.

"This afternoon, I was lying on the floor next to you."

"When was that?"

"When we were filming."

"Filming?"

"Making the television programme."

"When was I watching television?"

"You weren't watching it, you were on it."

"Did I climb on it when I was drunk?"

"No, Nige, you're an acter."

"What?"

"Nigel!"

"Who's that?"

"It's you."

"Who?"

"You."

"Who's you?"

"Your name is Nigel Planer."

"I thought I was Anne Acter."

72

"Yes you are."

"So what's my character called?"

"No, just concentrate, I'm talking to you."

"So I don't have a character?"

"No."

"Don't I have a job?"

"Yes, you're an . . . Oh God, never mind."

"So I'm not getting paid. That's a bummer. I'm going to call my agent. Oh, wait a minute."

"What?"

"What should I call him?"

"It's a woman."

"I'll call him a woman, that's a good idea."

So it wasn't Nigel who had been brainwashed, he was behaving normally. Although it was always difficult to tell with Nige.

I never did find out who was behind the attempt on my life, but what was clear was that I had to watch my back (which means be very cautious) as my work was entering a dangerous phase. I had created a legend with The Young Ones. Let's face it, you've probably got married to it. You've probably conceived to it. It has probably revolutionised your entire concept of society. You are probably wearing different clothes because of me. I, Richard Mayall, had televised the revolution. I was in danger, but I had arrived.

Bob Geldof
Basement Flat
126b Kilburn High Road
London NW8


26th November 1984


Dear Bob,

Love you work – or I did until I turned up yesterday at Air
Studios to do my bit for Band Aid. What in the name of
sweet Fanny fucking Nightingale is going on? All I wanted
to do was join my pier group of international stars from
the world of pop and rock and record a simple tune
which might bring much needed food and provisions
to the starving in Africa. But oh no. No, no, no, no, no.
Absolutely ruddy bloomin' well not.

Picture the scene. That's the one. There I am walking
towards Air Studios just as that Phil Collins is going in. I
called to him but he pretended not to hear me. Between
you and me Bob, I've never liked him. There's something
a bit seedy about him. Something not quite right. And
those bloody awful records. Anyway, I was on my way in
after him when this enormous bloke in a bomber jacket
blocked my passage. Ooer I thought but figured this was
probably just some sort of joke dreamt up by one of my
great popstar mates like Francis Rossi or Kool from Kool

and the Gang. The bloke said, "We don't want your sort
around here." I laughed knowingly but he was deadly
serious. I told him to go and tell you that I had arrived
and that I had come to do my bit. When he came back a
few minutes later, he lied and said that he had spoken to
you and you had told him to tell me to fuck off.

It was then that Simon Le Bon arrived with his all-girl
backing band. I called across to him and told him there
had been a horrible mix up but he pretended he didn't
recognise me. What is wrong with these people? So then
I spoke to the big bloke in the bomber jacket again and it
was then that he beat me up. Yes Bob, perhaps you
should read that sentence again. That's right, I was beaten
up at a charity recording. Your charity recording. How's
that make you feel?

So there I was lying on the pavement when a limo pulls
up next to me and out climbs Boy George with George
Michael and Bananarama and they all definitely
recognised me as they stepped over me and went inside,
even though they pretended that they didn't. You can just
tell.

Undeterred (no offence), I went around to the back of the
building where I managed to find a window that was ajar.
I climbed through it and imagine my horror when I fell
head first into a toilet bowl. Now you know me Bob,
I'm well known for not swallowing, but on this occasion
I had been taken by surprise and I managed to swallow
about half a gallon of toilet water and something that
I can only describe as "solid". This made me feel sick but

I decided I would press on and I managed to make my way through to the studio. I'll say this for you Bob, you got some big stars there: Boneo, Paul Wella, Chris Cross - it was wall-to-ceiling talent and just as I was taking in the sheer enormity of it all and chatting star-to-star with various top rock legends like Paul Young, I overheard you tell the security guard to "Get that twat with the shit in his hair out of here." All I can presume is that this was a joke on your part that backfired because the security guard in question did actually throw me out.

Obviously if this is all a great-mates-together music biz joke that you're all playing on me then I want you to know that I'm completely comfortable with that and love everyone as though they were my brother – or sister. But if it isn't, then you're all a bunch of jealous talentless fuck-holes.

And another thing – you should seriously consider re-routing some of the funds from Ethiopia in order to get yourself some proper professional celebrity endorsement from light entertainment giants like me. You'd make much more money in the long run but you're probably too mean and spiteful to realise it.

Anyway Bob, get back to me. Soon. Say "hi" to Midge,

Rik.

## APRIL 16TH 2005: 2.55AM

I'm troubled. There are some things I don't understand and haven't been able to understand since they first happened, and part of me is afraid of knowing what they mean. As I write this, it's blowing a gale outside. The glass is rattling in the window pane and I can taste the saltwash on the air as the wind blows in off the Cornish coast. There are thick black clouds rising above me. They are a bit like bruises, as though the sky has taken a good kicking, and every so often a flash of lightning lights up the raindrops that streak across the glass. And I'm sitting here alone in the middle of the night while my family sleep in other rooms in the farmhouse. I suppose I should be asleep too but something keeps me here at my typewriter. I need to get this off my chest. Some secrets are meant to be told. And this is a secret I have never told anyone before. Until now.

When I was a little boy, I went to bed one night and in the morning I woke up weeping. I had never woken up crying before. It scared me. In the coming days, memories of a dream began to come back to me bit by bit until the dream was complete or as complete as my waking mind would allow. This is what it was: I was in a field and it was kind of dusky. There was another person there. But I couldn't see their face because the person wore a hood. I was certain it was a man. A human-like man. Up ahead maybe ten or fifteen paces, there was a rise in the field as though there might be something the other side of it like a canal or something. I don't know what was the other side – I never got to find out. The man turned to me but still I couldn't see his face and he beckoned me. He wanted me to follow him. But I didn't follow him. I didn't want to. I don't know why, I just didn't. Then he started to beckon me more urgently as if to say, "Come on! Come on!" I don't know where he wanted me to go or why he wanted me to go there but one thing was for sure – I wasn't going to go with him. And for some reason which I can't fathom, it made me terribly sad. Terribly sad that I wasn't going to go with him. That's what made me cry so much. Don't ask me why.

Sometimes, but not very often, I have what seem like flashbacks of this dream. It's unnerving. Sometimes, usually when I'm driving, I catch a fleeting glimpse of a field through the car window as I drive past and it looks just like the field in my dream. But I don't have the chance to stop. It's always like that. But if I could stop I don't know that I would. Although I often wonder what would happen if I did. What would happen if I did find the field? What would happen if I confronted that man from my dream?

I don't know how many times in my life – maybe five, maybe eight times, I don't know – I dream the whole of the dream again. And I want to know what the end is and I try to dream it but I can't. It always ends in the same place, like a finite piece of film. And I always wake up crying. Always-ish, sometimes it makes me scared. Or angry. Or something. I don't know what it is.

Other times, very rarely but quite unexpectedly, I catch a kind of echo of the dream, a feeling, like an emotion with no apparent trigger. Like I say, it's very rare but when it comes, fear and sadness come at me for no apparent reason at all. Anywhere – in a lift, on the bog, on Kate Moss. Sorry, this is a serious bit – it doesn't last very long and I always hide it but it leaves me wondering, what is this? Then sometimes I try to think when it was that I first ever had the dream and I can't really place it. But it's always been with me, hiding in my subconscious.

This is the first time that I have ever spoken about this, and I know that it's probably hard for you to imagine that someone like me should become anxious or frightened but this does frighten me because I don't understand it. Or, at least, I didn't. There's more to this but I'm not going to write about it now. We'll come back to this later.

Arthur Scargill
National President
N.U.M.
Huddersfield Road
Barnsley


20th September 1984


Dear Brother Scargill,

Radical socialist comedian and acter Rik Mayall here.
You've probably heard of me. First of all, congratulations
on your fabulous strike. It is really sticking it to Thatch
and the fascist pig bullyboys who do her dirty work. I
thought I would right to you to offer my services in your
fight against the Tory scum. I have seen that other pop
stars and celebrities have offered to help your cause by
putting on concerts and shows and stuff and I thought
I would like to demonstrate to you (I am always
demonstrating) that I am standing firmly alongside
you too. In fact, I am more alongside you than they are
because their shows and concerts and records are always
sometimes a bit shit, let's face it. So, Arthur, I have written
you a poem which you can have with my best wishes.
Perhaps you could put it in the N.U.M. magazine. I
presume you do have a magazine although you might
have had to stop publishing it because you don't have
any money left. Anyway, if you don't have a magazine

then feel free to sell this poem to a national newspaper who would probably give you quite a bit of money because I'm such a big star nowadays and people are always trying to get hold of my material. I have checked all this with my agent and he is happy to let me give you this work for free but a small contribution for general admin and stationery would be gratefully received.

Anyway, Arthur, here is the poem. You had better sit down for this and if Mrs Scargill is in the area, it might be an idea if she were to fan you with a copy of the Radio Times or whatever television listings magazine you happen to have to hand because my words are like jets of liquid fire and you might need to cool down a little bit.

CLASS STRUGGLE

*The pit is full of grit*
*But it*
*Is the place where it is at.*
*Every single pig*
*He doesn't dig*
*What the kids dig*
*And the miners dig*
*Which is coal*
*Not dole*
*With their children*
*And their meager wages*
*In front of a fire which is out because*
*There isn't any coal*
*For the soul.*
*Or the fire.*

Powerful words, I think you will agree Arthur. And they are
all yours. Well, I wrote them and I want everyone to know
that I did and please use this letter as proof that I have let
you use them. What I suggest is that you learn this poem
by heart and resight it when you are next on television
being interviewed on the Nine o'clock news or News at
Ten. Make sure that you do mention that I wrote it if you
do. Just refer to me as Rik Mayall, radical socialist or
something like that. Just so long as you mention the Rik
Mayall bit, that's the important part although some mention
of my socialist leanings would be good. And might I also
suggest that if you are going to do the poem on TV that
you perhaps update your image a little bit. I know that
poor working class northern people are not very
fashionable but you as their leader should perhaps make
a bit more of an effort with your "look" which means the
clothes you wear and your hair-do. Firstly, I would get rid
of the Bobby Charlton comb-over. If I was you, I would get
a pony tail to show how at one you are with your
sexuality. Alternatively (and I invented alternating), you
could turn that basketball hat that you wear so that the
peak sticks out at the back. This is very fashionable on the
other side of the pond – which means America, Arthur. This
being the revolution, I think you should also buy yourself
some jeans trousers. I don't think Shay Gavarra wore a
cheap pair of slacks from Burtons with an anorak.
Although he might have done so don't quote me on that.
You should also get yourself some cowboy boots to go
with the jeans or if those are a bit pricey for you, then
maybe some Green Flash pumps are quite happening, but
do make sure that they are dirtied up a bit. There is nothing

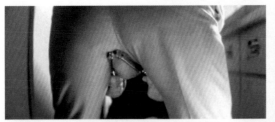

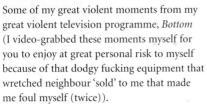

Some of my great violent moments from my great violent television programme, *Bottom* (I video-grabbed these moments myself for you to enjoy at great personal risk to myself because of that dodgy fucking equipment that wretched neighbour 'sold' to me that made me foul myself (twice)).

The greatest moment of my life.

Filthy, Rich and Catflap. No, fuck, sorry – Filthy, Catflap and Rich. That's better. No it's not. BOLLOCKS! This photo's shit. Don't use it.

Me defending the British nation when traitors in the Labour Party were trying to sell the entire country to the Germans and their banks during the Euro crisis 2002.

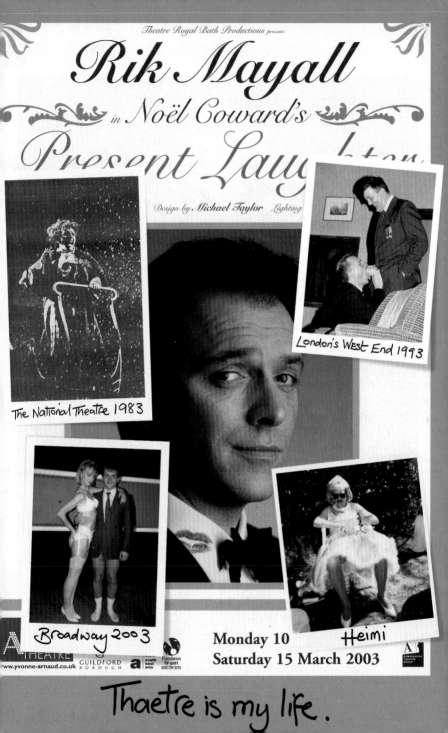

Theatre Royal Bath Productions presents

# Rik Mayall

*in* Noël Coward's

# Present Laughter

Design by *Michael Taylor* Lighting

The National Theatre 1983

London's West End 1993

Broadway 2003

Heimi

**Monday 10
Saturday 15 March 2003**

www.yvonne-arnaud.co.uk  GUILDFORD BOROUGH  south east arts  Foundation for sport and the arts

Thaetre is my life.

A bird

worse than seeing someone trying to be cool in a pair of bright wight plimsolls. If you don't feel this is the right look for you, you might like to try a daring Doctor Martin/ legwarmer "combo". It's difficult for me to picture you like this but if you fancy it I could come up to Barnsley and take a look. I would need somewhere decent to stay though and a car (not a van) there and back.

As far as that northern accent is concerned, I'm sorry to say this Arthur, but I don't think it's convincing anybody. I would just drop it. What would really swing it for you with the British public is if you put some more street slang into your diction (which means how you speak and is not a reference to anything below the waist although I am internationally renowned for my top quality lavatory gags). Maybe refer to your interviewers as "baby" and drop in a few menches (this is a showbiz word which is short for mention, Arthur) about very cutting edge pop stars like Nik Kershaw and Howard Jones. Be careful with this because if you get it a bit wrong and mention someone like Spandau Ballet, everyone will think you're a twat. Also, it's very important to remember that we're not allowed to say "cunt" anymore – it is not acceptable to our sisters the feminists – although I guess it is okay to say it about Mrs Thatch.

Anyway, Arthur, keep up the good work – although it's not really work is it, that's the whole point – so keep up the good not working.

All the pigs are racists,

Brother Rik Mayall.

# COMEDY MOSH PIT

I'd like to talk about that great performance that I gave in that thing I did that everyone talks about, but I can't because it's a secret. I'll tell you why, because when Israel was formed which was a long time ago before I was born – I wasn't involved in the formation of Israel, (if you go to anyone and ask them they'll tell you. Go up to them and say, "You know Rik Mayall?" and if they say "no," then they're just lying, so just punch them and call them a liar. That way you'll be telling the truth. They sometimes call me Rik "just punch them and call them a liar, Mayall" Mayall. But anyway, what was I talking about? Chips. No, Israel. That's weird, I've never been to a chippie in Israel. That must mean something. Things do don't they? That's what I always think whenever I go to the chip shops. I think that's enough about that subject now. Moving on.

Now, enigma codes are a thing. When I'm cracking one off*, I often think about stuff and one of the things that I'm often thinking about is my own enigma. I don't have codes to my enigma, because if someone comes up to me and says, "Hey Rik Mayall, love your work, what is it about your enigma?" What I say to

_____
* I've never known what this means – it's another of those Rik Mayall things.

them is, "Who are you? Are you a journalist?" And they usually say, "I'm sorry I don't know what you're talking about." And off I go enigmally – top lit so that it's one of those shadowy shots walking away from a big close-up opportunity. What that says to the audience is that I am a wild out of control acter and I don't need a close up. My statement has been made by my eyes and now I'm making it with the back of my shoulders as I receed down the alley into the mist. That's what really gets the gusset wet. If you went up to Jenny Agutter and said, "Hey, Jenny, have you ever seen any of Rik Mayall's stuff?" and she said, "no" then you must be asking the wrong person. So go ask someone else.

So, here I am at the typewriter, fingering away like a man possessed. But possessed with what? A question that I will leave hanging in the air. Just over there by that picture of me on the wall if you like. It's a good one. Or somewhere else. Anywhere you like. Space is ours, viewer, to float about in and be cool. Anyway, this is what I want to talk about, watch. Watch and read, obviously. One day last 1980s, to say a big kindly thank you for typing all my great material on The Young Ones, I promised that I would take Little Ben-Elton out on the road and show him how to do stand up comedy. I had already torn the nation apart with the "Kevin Turvey and the Bastard Squad featuring The Young Ones" live tour, of course, and it seemed only fair to allow Little to soak up some great comedy radiance and ride on my coat tails for a bit to learn his craft. Little was a bright boy and I knew that with my help and advice he would go far. I still think that. He just needs to knuckle down.

Wolverhampton is always a tough gig. The Germans knew that during the war and even the hardcore Nazi bombers wouldn't go there because they were too frightened. They knew they'd have a real war on their hands with the Wolves. And that's an actual fact. So they went and bombed Coventry instead.

The fans in Wolverhampton are so hard that they have a mosh pit for comedy gigs or rather, The Abattoir, as it is known locally. In a Wolverhampton axent obviously. Stage nutting, chair eating, carpet assaulting, toilet molesting, everything – you name it, the Wolverhampton fans do it. The place was jam-packed, there were people hanging from the balconies and we had managed to squeeze in an extra couple of hundred by locking the fire doors.

Little was frightened to go on but I told him that I was there if anything should go wrong – and he did well. Got a few laughs and there were only a couple of attempts to attack the stage and eat him.

Then it was my turn on stage and within a split second, the whole place was rocking*. The Master was at the mic. People were haemorrhaging they were laughing so much, bleeding from the eyes and leaking from every orifice. All the St Johns Ambulance brigades from all over the Midlands were on standby because they knew I was in town with my talent. And boy, wasn't I just. Kidneys and livers were suddenly seizing up and spontaneously imploding all over the place and people were literally trying to commit suicide because they couldn't laugh any more. And those that could were beginning to cough up their larynxes like there was no tomorrow. Which there wasn't for a lot of them. Crikey it was a good night, viewer. Never mind the Luftwaffe, this was Rik Fucking Mayall†.

I was detonating one of my legendary woofers (which means that I was telling one of my more popular anecdotes which I presumed would take the roof off the place‡ like they usually do) but I made the fundamental mistake of hinting that Wolverhampton's

---

* Which means that it was all going very well.
† This is not two people having sex, one called Rik and one called Mayall. It's me, sweary and hard.
‡ Which means it would be very well received by the audience.

greatest sons, Slade, were slightly not hard. And BLAM! Suddenly it was as though time had stopped. The earth had been switched off.

"What's wrong with that?" I asked. Silence. And that's when it turned nasty. There was a whistling through the air followed by an ugly thud. It was a severed head. And after that, they threw everything they had at me. They even threw their unfashionable flared trousers. Some of them were still in them. I was dodging all these terrifying blood-drenched missiles until I was hit by a security guard. I don't mean I was hit by security guard as in he thumped me, I mean he was one of the things that was thrown at me. He hit me at Mac 4. He had been thrown from the back of the stalls. And he was still in his chair. I looked down at his twitching, spasming body.

"Save yourself, Rik," he said with his dying breath. "You've got to get out of here now."

"I never surrender," I said.

"Oh and Rik? I hope you don't my mind my saying –"

"What is it? What is it? Hurry up and do the line, I'm busy dodging body parts."

"Love your work."

"Thanks."

The crowd was like a heaving churning maelstrom of fury. I decided I'd better get the hell out of there.

"Thank you Wolverhampton. You've been marvellous. See you next time. Be good." But when I looked around, I saw that the exits were barricaded as more furiously psychotic Slade fans slathered and howled for my blood. It was me against the world. I was moments from death. A disembowelled usherette hit the stage in front of me. There was ice cream and ribs everywhere. It was either think quick or die, so I decided to think quick. What shall I think about I thought. I didn't have much time. Whatever it is, I'd better do it quickly. I know, I thought. Well what is it then? I thought back. I'll tell you, I thought. Well go on then, what is it? I thought back again. I'll tell you. Go on then. I'll seduce them with my comedy. Nice thinking. And it was.

It was a comedy miracle. Just like something out of the Bible. I stole one of Ben Elton's jokes and got a laugh.

"A funny thing happened to me on the way to the theatre, tonight," I thrilled. "I was walking past an Elizabethan Horse Shop and the farrier said, "Hello Rik Mayall, big fan, lots of love, can I interest you in a horse?" and I said to him, "nay.""

I was saved. The blood-drenched hell-pit was mine once again. I had prevailed. Next night of the tour – Broadmoor. Easy.

The thing is viewer, I have always been great and I have always loved appearing live. It's like I'm appearing live all the time but I do find it's best with a live audience. Every town is different and has its own personality and I treat them all in a different way. I'm clever that way, clever but careing. On the south coast, for example, wherever that is, I find the audiences tend to be a lot older and it takes a lot longer to get them going[*]. But after an hour in the company of The Master (me) they're usually boffing each other in the aisles and snorting crack off each others genitals with joy. I've always been able to knock them dead in the retirement homes. In other places, like Glasgow, they appreciate more physical comedy. One time, when I was on Tour with Andy de la Tour (no relation), I got a nine minute standing ovation when a fan ran on stage and I battered him to death with a tyre iron. But wherever it is that I go, one thing's for certain, I'm always dangerous. I am a comedy outlaw, a punk icon. To this day, people still spit at me in the street.

---

[*] Be careful though, in Eastbourne the smell of urine can take the enamel off your teeth. Never smile at the stalls on the south coast. (Rik's tip.) Noel Coward told me that.

# [AMUSING CHAPTER TITLE HERE]

While I was storming the ramparts of the British establishment, tearing up the rule book and sticking it to the squares*, Peter "Peter Richardson" Richardson was becoming the greatest film directer of his generation. I used to like to give "Peter Richardson" (as I like to call him) a hand which I did by starring in all of "Peter Richardson"'s landmark productions such as War, Beat Generation, Summer School, Dirty Movie, A Fistful of Travellers Cheques, Gino, Bad News etc, etc, etc, – there's so many I could talk about – which I could if I felt like it but I won't right now. It's just another one of my things. But the only down side of my breakthruogh performances in these films was that I showed up a lot of the other members of the cast for their poor acting abilities. That is why so many of "Peter Richardson"'s films didn't have me in them. We thought we would give the others a chance to shine too. I'll mention no names†. Let's just say that the history of light entertainment has not been as kind to others as it

---

* Squares are people who are not hip. Hip means cool. If you stick it to the squares, it means that you stick two fingers up to them. I don't know why it isn't sticking them to the squares – it's just one of those things. I don't make the rules. I just break them.

† I'm a mentioning no names kind of a guy.

has been to me, and it's not fair to kick a man or a woman when they're down. Although there was that time with that nasty little Scottish shit in that awful late nineties pile of drivel that I somehow got involved with. I know you're supposed to be nice to disabled people but there are some times in life when you just have to push people down staircases. Teeth and claret* all over the floor of the Celebrity Squares set. How we laughed. If only the cameras had recorded it, we could have shared the moment. Although, thinking about it, maybe it was Blankety Blank? Oh who gives a toss. Let's just go to another paragraph.

I remember it so clearly, as clearly as if it was yesterday which is amazing really because it wasn't yesterday. It was a long time ago. I can't remember exactly when, but I do know that it wasn't yesterday although I can remember it like it was. I can do things like that. I've probably already told you. I can't remember. I'm like that. You just can't stop me when I'm off and running, so get your brain around this anecdote for a mother. One day, back in the mid-eighties, I was sitting in this cool place, or somewhere else, it doesn't really matter. I can't remember. Anyway, it suddenly came to me SLAM! and it was there in front of me. An idea. It was time to create another landmark BBC situation comedy vehicle for me and my show business cohorts. So, I called up Little Ben-Elton and told him to get his typewriter out and went to see Paul Jackson, the head of the BBC, and told him I was putting the old team back together again to finish off the last remnants of the fetid diseased art form that was family entertainment.

"Good idea, Rik Mayall," he said and we were on†.

---

* This is cockney gangster talk for teeth and blood. It works because claret is red wine and blood is red. Although that might just be a coincidence.

† Which means that he wanted to make the show. It does not mean anything untoward [check meaning].

While Little typed up my great gags and tried to pass them off as his own, I went looking for Nigel Planer who played Neil in The Young Ones, a powerful individual acter of stupendous insight and vision who would help me take British television by the scruff of the neck and shout "Hey Britain, wake the fucking crikey up!" in its face.

I found him sitting on a park bench.

"Hey Nige, it's Rik!"

"Who?"

"Rik Mayall, your great mate and fellow comedy colossus."

"Hello."

"I need you for my breakthuogh new situation comedy idea."

"Great."

"I've got a really big one here and I'm not talking about my penis – although it is enormous."

"Who did you say you were?"

"Look, Nige, stop messing around, I know you're an amusing guy but this is serious. I need you to do a job."

"But I don't need to go."

"Great gag but no, now listen to me for a moment, we need to finish off the last dregs of the old guard of comedy. Think of me like Karl Marx – only with better hair. This show will be like a death camp for old-style light entertainment. When we have finished, art will be purified, refreshed and blonde."

"Radical man."

"Exactly. You've hit the nail right on the head which means that you're absolutely right."

"Great."

"It'll be like old times – only better."

"Who did you say you were again?"

Suddenly, my mobile telephone rang. This being the mid-eighties, I kept it in a supermarket trolley because it was too heavy to carry, and I heaved it out – almost slipping a disc in the process – and held it up to my ear. It was my talented and better looking comedy partner Adrian Edmondson.

"Have you got the cunt yet?"

"Yes I think so, Adrian, thank you for calling."

"Good, get him to sign the contract, I need his money."

"Yes yes, Adrian, of course, great idea, I'm doing it now."

"Hey queer, don't you owe me some money?"

"How much would you like, Adrian?"

"Another fifty grand or it's the other kneecap."

"Oh Christ, Adrian, that's fine, fifty grand, no problem. And hey, great mate, can I have some my children back now?"

"No."

"You said that after the last instalment, I could have some back."

"No I didn't."

"I'm sorry."

"Just shut your fucking mouth and send me the cheque, and remember, you've never said or done anything funny in your life, got it?"

"Yes, sorry sir."

"Shut up your blabbering. You know it makes me vomit. Listen, I want the money by sun down or you'll hear another one of your children squealing on the phone."

"Okay, great idea, no problem."

And that, viewer, is how I came to make Filthy, Rich and Catflap which became a huge gaping cult. The critics hated it though. Bastards. The thing is you see, it wasn't The Young Ones and the "critics" were so stuck in the early eighties – and this was the <u>mid</u>-eighties. I was so way ahead of them, you see – it's not that the show was a pile of bollocks, it's just that I was screaming forward like one of those Japanese bullet trains that go about two hundred miles an hour, only this one was on fire with heavy metal pop music playing at full blast on the in-Japanese-bullet-train-that's-on-fire stereo hi-fi system. I should have slowed down to let the critics catch up but you know what I'm like. Anyway, I know that Filthy, Rich and Catflap was great and you know it was great – and that's all that matters. Never mind what the critics say. They're all utter utter utter bastards*.

---

* No offence great critic mates - I have always held you in the greatest esteem and love all your work both individually and collectively and anythingly really. Don't worry about it, the cheque's in the post. I've got cash too.

# HOW TO CREATE EDGE CUTTING
# TELEVISION PROGRAMMES

One day, on a dark elevenses Wednesday, I was just finishing explaining to the Worcester Police (who are terrifically good and always on my case) that I had nothing to do with the fire at Worcester Cathedral twenty years ago. I was a bit hungry but I didn't have any food in so I went off to Sainsbury's (but before I went I thought I'd put on my Australian underwear because I didn't want to take any chances) and that's when it happened. I saw this tree and I thought, "God isn't that interesting – nature. I know, I'll go on holiday." And I did and it was while I was there that I thought to myself how sick and tired of racism I was. Especially racism in light entertainment. It makes me furious. I have been trying to get Lenny Henry banned for years.

Anyway, there I was on the beach with a cigarette in one hand, banana dakiri in the other and I'd got my "I fucked Greg Dyke" T shirt on because I like to be controversial wherever I go – even though no one had heard of Greg Dyke then – this was years ago. I was just sitting there watching all the people wandering past me thinking, "Fucking hell, that's The Rik Mayall on the beach," and then they formed into small delegations that would come forward to me and ask for my autograph and I would engage them in conversation for a moment, offer them sex and see if they had any drugs on them (which I don't take and anyway they always say they haven't got any. Little shits. It's heart lifting moments like this that are always just like my old friend whose name escapes me used to say . . . oh let's not bother with that, it's not very good.)

Anyway, I want to stop the book here and now to tell you my great anecdote about the theatre director and big impresario type, Richard Eyre. It's very good, but first things first, some background information. The Government Inspector is a play written by some Russian twat or other called Nikolai Gogol. God knows how he thought up that name. And it's all about pre-revolutionary Russia, (if you can believe anybody in their right mind would be interested in a play about that! No one would want to see bollocks like that especially at the National Theatre – mind you, no one goes to that shit hole anyway.) So Richard Eyre's thinking, I've got a pile of bollocks to show to acres of no one in a shit hole. What am I going to do? I know, I'll get Rik Mayall. He's a problem solver. He's a curse lifter. I can see it now, jam packed bars, fabulous reviews, but most importantly bums on seats. (Pervert.)

Clever man, Richard Eyre. Good director. Good lay as well. I never said that. Quick get out of here to the next paragraph. Fuck.

Anyway this arse-faced play's all about these poshos and aristos who wander around with canes and groovy hair and this twat comes to town called Klestakov (that's me – fucking good too) and he is mistaken for the government inspector and he ponces about and everybody sucks his cock (metaphorically speaking) because they think he's the government inspector even though he isn't. That's the basic gag. See what I mean? What a pile of bollocks. And Richard Eyre was the director, right? And he came to all the rehearsals, right, but then he didn't even bother to come on stage for the performance! I was on stage every night for three months and he didn't come on once! I only ever saw him off stage, giving notes, advising people and, you know, helping. It's a nice angle and I don't think he ever got caught once. Nice one, Rich, respect. See what I mean? He had a good life. He didn't have to put on his costume. He didn't have to do his make up. He didn't even have to fuck any of the extras! Bit of a miscalculation actually. Some of them were quite tasty (but not Marian Farley – I don't want to imply there was anything wrong with her twadge but she tasted FOUL. Take it from Rikky, DON'T GO THERE.) Anyway, I've got this brilliant story about him. And it's true. So it's more than just a story, it's a hot news item – a showbusiness nugget of golden truth, if you will. Or if you won't. I don't fucking care.

I want you to know here and now that I'm not bitter about bad reviews when I very occasionally get them. Lesser talents get spiteful and angry. I turn the other cheek. It's like water off a duck's back – not that I do things like that with ducks. I'm just not like that. Anyway, let's walk away from this. It's turning ugly and I don't do ugly. I can feel a cloud hanging over my typewriter, a cloud that screams, "I smell death and I want it now – I want my veins to burst so that rivulets of blood stream down my arms as I howl for release from seven types of agony." Kind of thing. You know typewriters. Let's just forget about it.

So there I was at The Nash. I like to call it The Nash. I don't really know why. Whatever. They have three stages there – two little ones and one that's named after that acter. He's dead now. But don't feel sorry for him because he's dead. I never actually met him and that's the same with an awful lot of people. There's a lot of people that I haven't met. It's just the way life is.

Now if you were to ask Jim "Hello mate, how are you?" Broadbent who was the best actor in that production, The Government Inspector, he's going to say that it was me because it was. Jim was in it – bless him – I don't know why I should bless him, it's not like he sneezed or anything that would require blessing. We're just wildcats, us acters. We just do shit like that. But anyway, I could phone Jim whenever I want to because I've got his phone number. So there. My dear friend Peter somebody-or other was also in it – lovely bloke – at least I think he was a bloke. I never checked.

Some of the cast[*] were frightened because the Nash is so big. But I wasn't because I'd just played the Liverpool Empire which is three times the size and rammed full of scousers. Shame we hadn't sold any of the tickets.

Being in a play in London is great for having sex in the afternoon. You wouldn't do it for any other reason. The pay is shit. It's an actual fact that I had sex with seven different people (women) during my time at the National. I was known as Hot Cock at the Nash. But a word of advice for you, viewer, if you're going to have sex with actresses, you must always bag up (which means wear a johnny) and when you've finished, take off your johnny, tie a knot in it and write the actresses' name on it (don't use a sharp Biro for obvious reasons) and keep it for at least a year and a half in a brief case with all the others and put it somewhere that your wife won't find it and don't write "Johnny Bank" on it (like you might want to) because she might see this and become suspicious. So, that way, when the actress says she's pregnant, you go down the police station with your "Johnny Bank" briefcase and you tell them that it couldn't have been you because – and you get out the johnny with her name written on it. Quid Pro Quo, as the Romans used to say. Along with stuff like, "Let's go and watch some gladiators having a fight," or, "Let's invade England," or, "Why do we have

---

[*] The cast of a play is the collective expression for all the people who are in the play but not including all the people who don't go onto the stage and walk around and pretend to do stuff and say things. So, what I'm saying is that the people who do do all those things (go onto the stage and walk around and pretend etc) are the cast. Got it? Christ, it's not difficult.

to wear togas all the time – I've been wearing this toga for years and it's getting pretty wiffy. It can stand up and walk around on its own. Oh no, that's with me in it, sorry. Come on, let's go and watch some more Christians being eaten by lions. It's a bit shit this conversation, isn't it? In fact, it's a bit shit being Roman really, isn't it? I wish we had some telly. But not late twentieth century telly which is all such nob dribble apart from The Young Ones. Which is great. I'm a huge fan. God I wish it was 1981 – have you seen that Rik Mayall bloke? He's great. That's what all us Romans say. Only another two thousand years to go."

So, right, my Richard Eyre anecdote, right? So, there's me, right? You know me. I'm Rik Mayall. You're reading my book. You got it. So there I am one day at the Nash. That's the National Theatre, remember? We call it the Nash – well, you know all this already – but if you don't then go back a few lines and I'll wait for you here. Because I'm a nice guy. Okay? Done it? Cool. Told you I was. Let's do it now then. There's me right, you know me, and there I am, right, walking down one of the corridors at the Nash and Richard Eyre is coming the other way.

"Hi Rik Mayall," he says.

"Hello Richard Eyre," I say.

"Hey, are those your jeans?" he says.

"Yeah," I say.

"Oh right."

"Why, did you think they were someone else's?"

"No, I was just asking. Did you know that Jim's had a bit of flu?"

"Yes."

Stuff like that happened all the time. Loads of other stuff happened as well. It was great. I'm sure stuff like that happens at the Nash to this day but I wouldn't know personally because I haven't been asked back there since. Not since the restraining order which is all a load of shit anyway because I never touched her.

Heimi Fingelstein
Top Bollocks Management
PO Box 4372
Bermondsey
London SE16


21st November 1986

Dear Heimi,

I thought I would try and write you a letter because
my last few attempts to telephone you have been
unsuccessful. I tried all last week but each time the phone
was picked up and I said who I was, the line went dead.
Perhaps Big Joan is on holiday? And then, the last time I
phoned, someone answered – I could have sworn it was
you but maybe I'm mistaken – and said, "Mad Keith?"
and before I could reply, this person on the line –
whoever it was (it really did sound like you) – said, "Have
you whacked that fucker Mayall yet?" I want you to know
that if this was you joking with me that I totally get the
joke and find it highly amusing. Anyway, what I wanted to
talk to you about which I will write down here – because
writing's not really talking is it (although I'm good at both)
– is that I was wondering whether you could find me
some voice-over work. I see that other acters and
comedians – far less talented ones than me – are using
their voices on television and radio commercials and I
hear that there is a lot of money to be made.

I presume that the best way to go about this is for me
to contact companies with ideas for adverts that feature
me in them. This is not a problem because even though
I am a radical hardcore socialist, and a communist even
sometimes, I am also "in bed" with capitalism. I am
after all, part of the international currency of talent.
I am a showbusiness Wall Street in my own right. I
do not see a problem in combining socialism and
capitalism together. For example, if I was to do a radio
voice over for cough sweets, I could knock off a few
quid because it's winter and I am worried about what
my people are sucking. (I am not being disgusting.) That
way, everyone is happy – the cough sweet company,
my people, me, and you as well Heimi, after you have
taken your 90% commission.

The way I see it is that it isn't called showbusiness for
nothing. It's not all blockbuster movies, top television
light entertainment formats, sell out West End runs and
comedy tours, there is also international trade and
industry to think about. I see myself as more than just
another celebrity with a great voice who can speak on
commercials, I can also be an advisor to companies on
how best to create edge cutting advertising campaigns.

For example, I was in Tesco's the other day. I sometimes
go to Sainsbury's but I didn't this day because I had to
return some books to the library and if I go to the library
I walk past Tesco's and if I was to go Sainsbury's, it
would mean walking about another half a mile and I've
been having trouble with my big toe recently – Doctor
Dunwoody thinks it might be an ingrowing toe nail but

he's just a fascist pig and he once made up a story
about me having a scrotal rash just so he could get my
trousers down. Anyway, none of that is important. I was
in Tesco's and I was buying some toothpaste and I saw
that there was a new mouthwash on special promotion
called Country Mouth. I took one of the leaflets from
the leaflet dispenser thing and I thought that because I
didn't have to get back straight away (I had already been
to the library) I would read about this new mouthwash.
I can't remember what it said word for word but it
basically said stuff about how the mouthwash – Country
Mouth – would leave your mouth smelling like a fresh
woodland glade. Now this is all well and good, Heimi,
and I appreciate that Country Mouth is a more snappy
(that's a media expression) name than Woodland Glade
Mouth but even so, I think the company behind this
product is making a big fundamental errer. I know that
us leading acters and entertainers can speak properly
but a lot of ordinaries (especially the really poor ones)
can't and their pronunciation of Country Mouth could
represent something of an accident black spot, media-
wise. So, what I was thinking was that you might get me
a meeting with the manufacturers of Country Mouth and
I can go in there and have a brainstorm (this is a new
marketing expression, Heimi, that means everybody sits
around a table – a glass topped one preferably – and
talks about lots of ideas and stuff) with their marketing
top brass. I could say to them, "Now listen, guys, I like
all the running through the pastures and all that but
think about your radio commercials. You're only an
"R" away from being deeply offensive. From where I'm
sitting, it's screaming vagina in my face and I think with

an oral hygiene product, it's best to have a vagina-free playing field." So, with me, not only would the manufacturers of Country Mouth be getting a top quality acter's voice and intonation but also even topper quality advice about the product itself. Everyone's a winner – and I don't mean that song by Hot Chocolate. But if I did, I would.

I hope I can talk to you soon about all this and we can get our heads together on this one (another great marketing expression) and work out a strategy.

I look forward to hearing from you soon.

Best wishes,

Rik Mayall (your star client A.K.A. "the cash machine").

P.S. I think there might be some money owing to me from all the work I've done over the past couple of years. I've been working like a dog. I know that you and my great friend Adrian have split all the money from Consuela, Private Enterprise, Eat the Rich, Whoops Apocalypse and Filthy, Rich and Catflap but there is plenty of other stuff that I've done like my Australian tour with Little Ben-Elton (those theatres looked pretty full to me), and Bad News. They must have earned something, not that I am questioning your honesty in any way Heimi – I want to make that clear – but you definitely said that you would probably be able to cream off a few grand from the Comic Relief work. Obviously, if you can sort this out I'd be much obliged but it must never leak out. If people were to find out that Comic Relief is a front for organ harvesting, drug dealing and global child prostitution, there'd be a hell of a stink. The papers would be all over us. And Cliff must never get found out.

Anyway, whatever you can do on the money front would be great. I'm still on the run after the last palimony sting so I need cash to keep moving. All I've received from you recently was that mysterious package with the wires sticking out of it.

# ANOTHER BIT OF MY PART IN THE DESTINY OF THE NATION (BRITAIN/BRINGING DOWN THATCH* (PART ONE†)

British showbusiness has two high points above all others: the two Elizabethan periods. The first Elizabethans had no electricity. They had no microphones or photo opportunities, so it was always at 2pm that the curtain went up in their theatres. And so it was that at 2pm on the afternoon of the 21st May 1587 that Christopher Marlow (good play writer)'s new play "Tamberlain the Great" opened at the Carlsberg Hammersmith Apollo Theatre in the heart of London's Hammersmith. It was an instant smash hit – it had everything – violence, sex, words, good acting and some plot, and it shat all over Shakespeare (not hot)'s bollocks. And it was two hundred years later to the minute in 1987 in the age of us the second Elizabethans, the new Elizabethans (our queen is called Elizabeth too so it all works) that Paul Jackson, the head of the BBC, took me to a TV conference and A THING HAPPENED.

I know loads of stuff about historical stuff. They call me Rik knows-loads-about-historical-stuff Mayall. Doesn't exactly roll off the tongue, but you know what they're like, some people.

---

* If you're reading this Thatch, big fan, no hard feelings. It was a great ride together in the cavalry of destiny.
† Please note, viewer, there is no part two. Now that is what I call anarchy.

They've just got crap tongues. There's loads of people out there and I know because I've been out there. Let me tell you about some of the time I've spent out there. But not now, right, because I'm right in the middle of a chapter. I don't fuck about, viewer. Nuff said (which means enuff although it's spelt differently). Now, where was I? Oh yeah, I went to a TV conference in the north of England with Paul Jackson, the head of the BBC. Now I'm a caring guy especially with northerners who I love and adore massively in everything they do or think, even though they are all indescribably ignorant and need all the help they can get. Some of them can't even speak you know. Well, I mean, they try but you can't understand a word they say if speaking is what they're trying to do. I've been to their towns – some of them more than once. I don't mind having the inoculations although the smell can be really quite overpowering. It's their diet I think – when they can actually get something to eat – hence the fact they are all so ugly and small. But that's the working class for you. Born and raised in the north of England. They love me up there. I can speak to them and they treat me like a Christ figure. That's why I decided I would bring down Thatcher for them after all that she did to them, like making it illegal for them to work in their holes which is where they get the coal to light their little fires.

So anyway, A THING HAPPENED (this is the same thing not a separate one).

"Meet these guys," Paul said.

And it happened. I met them.

Marlow would have written one of his plays about it.

"Hello," I said, "who are you?"

"We're comedy writers called Lawrence Marks and Maurice Gran."

The room went quiet.

"We're big fans," said the guys, "we love your work." (People always say this to me but I don't put it in books.) "We've got a great idea for a television programme."

"What is it?"

"It's you."

"Fucking hell that is a great idea."

"You can use swear words as well."

"What's it called?"

"It's called Jackanory."

"It's called what?"

"Jackanory – you can read stories in that special way that only you can."

"That's rubbish, it's been done. I invented the programme, you twerps. Haven't you seen George's Marvellous Medicine?"

"Oh Gosh, sorry about that, the great Rik Mayall."

"That's okay, but I tell you what fellas, I've got a great idea that you can write for me and pretend that you thought it up your-selves."

"That's very kind."

"Don't mention it. How about someone called Alan B'stard who is a cunning and handsome young Tory MP and we can make it so damn good, make the satire so needle sharp and I can act the part so convincingly that we'll bring down the government."

The room went quiet. Again.

"You can call it The New Statesman," I said. Lawrence and Maurice sat there slack-jawed. That was when the face of Great Britain changed forever.

Crikey oh blimey, I really threw myself into the role when I played Alan B'Stard. That doesn't mean I jumped off something or committed suicide or anything like that, it means that I really worked hard on learning my lines (that means words) properly and put my costume on the right way round and made sure my flies were done up and stuff.

Role is what they call the name for the person you're pretending to be in a film or a play or something on the telly, sorry, damn, the TV. No one has ever known why it's called a role – that's just another one of the mystiques (that's not a spelling mistake) of the film industry making business. It's not that they are stupid although a lot are and I know who they are and I could say their names anytime I felt like it but I won't because I'm not like that. I think it's probably got something to do with breakfast but I don't show off that I know this, I just know it quietly like in that one with Yul Brinner (who I respect).

I would like to ask you one question, viewer, and it is this: What other light entertainer that you can mention has actually changed the government? I'll leave that question hanging in the air, right next to that other one from earlier. It's not that I can't think of anything else to say – it's just very poignant [check meaning].

Orson Wells
118118 Sunset Boulevard
Hollywood
California
USA


22nd October 1986

Dear Orson,

Big fan, love your work. Now you know me, I don't
mess about and I've decided that being the inventor of
alternative comedy in the UK (or this side of the pond as
you yanks like to call it) is all well and good but there's
not much money in it. So I've thought up something
which I thought you might be interested in having a think
about too.

Now I've seen you on the television advertising that
Domestos Double Century – "a full blooded aloroso" as
you call it with your deep balls-like-billiards voice and
I figure that there's room for two big name stars to enter
the sherry arena, make a killing and clean up. Now
obviously I don't want to muscle in on your scene – not
a man of your kaliber – so I wondered if you would mind
me having a pop at scooping the Emva Creme account.

I kind of figure that with two giant behemoths of western
popular culture standing astride the sherry market, we

might be able to form a united front and move on to other brands like Harvey's Bristol Creme and Crufts Original. I reckon that in no time at all we could have the sherry industry in a headlock/stranglehold arrangement and we'll be able to ask our price when other brands come a-knocking. We'll be like a sort of global sherry advertising consortium kind of thing.

Something else that springs to mind is that we might consider developing a "lo-cal" sherry option and thought you might be up for doing a before and after type campaign where we show you as you are now (i.e. a bit of a bloater – no disrespect Orson) and then show you after you've been drinking the Mayall/Wells lo-cal option and all the punters can see the startling difference. We can do something with trick photography I'm sure. No one will ever know.

Anyway, get back to me as soon as possible and maybe drop in[*] next time you're in town (but please call ahead if you're planning to so I can get the toilet reinforced and the house underpinned).

Cheers! Mine's a double (or a large one or whatever they call it with sherry),

Rik Mayall (acter, comedian and top British phenom)

---

[*] This means walk through the door unexpectedly not fall suddenly through the roof.

Mark Rogers
EMI Records
46 Brook Green
London W6


3rd March 1988

Yo Mark man,

Was it you that had the heart attack? Anyway, never mind
about that, I'm told you're the guy to talk to about rock.
And that's fucking cool with me. Man. (Sorry I nearly
forgot.) Because I am rock. And I'm just hanging here
with some chicks, blowing on a few joints, drinking some
Jack Daniels with my shirt buttons open to the waist and
I'm thinking about getting another hurty tattoo done. Not
sure whether to go for a snake design or a topless lady on
a motorbike. You do know that when I say topless lady,
I don't mean a woman who's just driven her Harley
Davidson at 100 m.p.h. under an unexpectedly low
bridge. Or maybe I'll just go for both designs or even
combine the two so that the topless lady on the
motorbike is wearing the snake around her neck like a
scarf. It's all the same to me because I don't care. I'm too
busy chilling out with my chicks here and listening to
heavy rock pop music like I do most days at this time of
the afternoon in Stourbridge. It's really loud as well.

Anyway, Mark man, the thing is that now that the legendary greatest band ever, Bad News, have finally ridden their Harley Davidsons into the byss (like on that Bat Out Of Hell record cover), I thought it was time to throw down (meaning record) a few cuts (songs) for my first ever solo concept album, AN UNEXPECTED SPURT OF EVIL, which is enclosed (which means it's in the envelope marked PLEASE DON'T NICK – IT'S VERY VALUABLE AND DON'T THINK ABOUT DOING IT BECAUSE I KNOW WHERE YOU LIVE WHOEVER YOU ARE AND THAT'S NOT A LIE SO JUST DON'T DO IT, OKAY?). So that's where the tape is, Mark, 'kay? You'll see that it's a C90 tape and it's nearly full up so I think that means that it is practically a whole double album which is great because then we can have one of those gatefold sleeves with a big band photograph or a big fantasy illustration of me on a motorbike with a chick, driving really fast whilst I'm drinking some whisky and smoking lots of cigarettes or those little Cherillo things like Clint. Everyone'll rave about it and think that I'm great. And they can show it to their girlfriends too whilst they listen to me rock.

At the moment, all the tracks (the tunes on the tape) are just hard raw recordings of me singing the songs and playing my acoustic guitar, so you'll have to imagine what they will sound like when I've got the band together and there are some really heavy drums and good guitar solos. Also, once I'm in the studio, man, with the guys and a top producer, I will be able to sing much louder. On the tape, I don't sing very loudly because it distorts a bit on the cassette player and the neighbours complained quite a lot this time. Obviously, the full album will be an awful lot longer – maybe even a triple album – because I would really like – sorry, dig – to have some massively long guitar and drum solos if at all poss (means possible). Thank you.

The concept behind this concept album is really important to me, man, and is something that I think I could talk about for a long time in interviews like in my favourite magazine, Kerrang. The concept is that other rock music is either really heavy and shouty or really loving and tender but (you're gonna like this Mark baby – maybe skin yourself up a J (this means roll a cigarette with marijuana in it)), this album is going to be really heavy AND loving and tender. I reckon that with some clever marketing (which is where you dudes come in) we could unite the two Heavy Rock factions.

Anyway, before we go any further, it's probably best if you actually listen to the album and see what you think. If I were you, I would stretch out on a couch (preferably leather) with your shirt off and your hair down, smoke a few more Js and drink some bourbon and let the music drift over you. A few blondes with their jugs out sitting around on motorbikes would also be good but it's up to you. Anyway, here goes . . .

So hey man, like, what do you think? Pretty powerful I think you will agree. (You have listened to it all the way through haven't you? If not, then make sure you do.) Good, now, as far as the band's name is concerned, I have given this a lot of thought and I have decided that

I want to call it, MEPHISTOFELES HAS RISEN. Maybe we could put a couple of dots over the "O" in Mephistopheles like Motorhead do. As for the image, I'm thinking epic and Nordic is the way we should go. I would also like the members of the band to have kind of viking stage names like Fjord Rockstack, Adolf Car-Accident and Thor Arse – stuff like that. Rock is a serious business. There are Monsters of Rock and there are Monsters of Light Entertainment and I am one of both.

So, I'll leave it with you, man. I know it's a lot to take in all in one go (which is what a lot of chicks say to me when I'm doing my good loving on them).

Take it easy man,

The Rik "Rock is my middle name" Mayall, A.K.A. Colin G. Grigson.

S.C. Johnson Ltd
Frimley Green
Camberley
Surrey

23rd November 1988

Dear Shake 'n' Vac,

Actually, forget about it. It was just a thought. It doesn't matter.

Keep up the good work.

Yours etc,

Rik Mayall, The (Mr)

# SEX[*]

A question for you viewer: what do you do when a jealous
husband catches you red-handed with his wife and you've got a
pork pie up your arse? It's questions like this that international
celebrities like me are faced with perpetually. And I ask you this
question in my own special way, thinking on my feet, unless I'm
lying down, which I always don't, but picture the scene right, a
top posh bird's flat somewhere in the south of England or wherever's special to you – wherever that is, that's exactly where it was.
Ouch! Stuff about Rik coming atchya[†]. That's synchronicity that
is. Anyway, this story is true this is, it really is, listen. What happened is that I had just been to see that movie with Mickey
Rooney in it, you know, that incredibly great film Nine and a Half
Weeks. If you've seen the movie (and if you haven't there's very
little point reading this chapter so you might as well move on to
the next one because all the following stuff is big boys hot-time
stuff for real men and ladies from the dark side. So you'd better
finish up your Ribena and get out of town because we're going in.)
Now you'll remember that Mickey Rooney and that blonde bird

---

[*] Back in the stable, Geoffrey, I don't mean that saucy tea-time table book
with loads of nudey pictures of Maradonna in it.
[†] Bless you.

115

Kim Wild get down to some breakthruough cinematic erotica on the kitchen floor by the fridge and Mickey Rooney starts putting loads of groceries all over Kim Wild and then they have it off. Well, I think they have it off – I missed the second half of that scene when I went to see it at the cinema because I had to pop out for a wee at that point actually and not for any other revolting ignoble reason as the security guards claimed when they caught me in the Ladies and had me thrown out of the cinema. And the only reason I've got a subscription to Readers Wives, Razzle and Big Ones International is because I am interested in all forms of media – which is newspapers and magazines and comics and television and stuff – and don't want to feel that there are any gaps in my knowledge. I also have a subscription to Radio Times but it doesn't mean I masturbate over it, does it?

Anyway, I was in this posh bird's flat and I said to her in my alluring way, "Do you want some food, love?"

And she said: "No thanks Rik Mayall, I thought we were going to do some having it off?"

"That's what I meant, bird. We can do some having it off with food on top."

"Oh crikey, blimey, you top acters are so [fill in word that means louche and Risk A]."

So I went to the fridge like a nuclear submarine, opened it up and stood there with my six pack glistening, my biceps trembling and my calves flexing. But the fridge was empty! My Mickey Rooney/Kim Wild shagging with food concept lay in ruins on the kitchen floor.

"Bird, get your coat, we're going to my secret West End apartment which I rent in order to have somewhere to do hot romancing on actresses without my wives and families finding out[*]."

---

[*] You never read this, viewer.

"Great, Rik Mayall, let's go now." And we did, straight out of the door (we put some clothes on first obviously – I'm not a naturalist – although I am very natural. Which is curious really. Maybe I'll come back to this later.) We went straight across the pavement and caught a bus to where my secret flat is (if you're reading this Selina, it's all made up – I don't really have a flat – it's just a joke*) and when we got inside, my bird took all her clothes off and got onto the kitchen floor. I took all my clothes off and went to the fridge, opened the door and stood there with my six pack glistening, my biceps trembling and my – never mind, I've done that bit. I looked inside the fridge and the first thing that caught my eye was a piece of Edam cheese. Now, a word of advice for you viewer. Cheese and sex are not happy bed fellows. It's like coco-pops and dangleberries – you'll never know whether it is a dangleberry or a coco-pop until it's stuck in your teeth and then it's too late. If you find yourself in a situation like this and you've only got brown food to play with (like HP sauce) then I suggest you keep your reading glasses on and keep a flashlight handy under the duvet. It's tricky to tell what's what in the darkness and I'm not talking about that rubbish band either. Curry sauce is another one that you should avoid at all costs, especially if it's Vindaloo – it'll sting for weeks.

Anyway, I thought "no fucking way!" in my great way to the Edam and looked for something else. Next to the Edam was a pot of crab paste [print carefully]. Fish products are another bad idea for obvious reasons so I continued my search until I found the only other food product in the fridge – which was a pork pie. I stood there erotically for a moment and thought to myself, "What would Mickey Rooney do?" And that's when it hit me like an out of

---

* Or maybe it isn't. Who's to know? I've got enigmatic motherfucker written all over my face. But you know that. No you don't. Oh bollocks, this is shit. Don't print this bit.

control petrol tanker that is rolling down a cliff on fire. "Slice it," came back the reply. Good reply I reckoned butchly, and that's what I did. I sliced up the pork pie and inserted it between the cheeks of my arse to bring it to body temperature which is a highly respected advanced food love technique, especially when you're moving backwards towards the bird to show off the slices of pork pie to arouse her. I have always been a highly considerate lover.

"Hurry up Rik Mayall," said the bird. "I've been waiting here for half an hour for you to infuse me with your sensational love making and all you've been doing is squatting over a mirror trying to bloo tak slices of pork pie to the inside of your buttocks. It just doesn't give me the horn."

And then out of the blue after another fifteen minutes, she said, "Oh bollocks to this, I'm going back to Keith Chegwin." Ha! So what, what did I care? Less is more, as I say to so many birds as I fold my pants at the foot of their beds next to my trousers giving them a side shot of my torso[*]. I've always been known as "Catnip to Women[†]" which means that I am to women what catnip is to cats which means that they go bonkers and can't get enough of me (the women not the cats). I could make a pussy joke here but I'm not that sort of comedian and if you're looking for that sort of gag[‡] then you're in the wrong book. That is bad comedy. And you ought to know by now that Rik Mayall doesn't do bad comedy. La bad comedie, ce n'est pas moi (which is French for something or other. It fucking is. Look it up if you don't believe me.)

---

[*] Rik Tip for the middle-aged bloke. Always try to hide your tummy from the lady. Apparently there's a sex position called "taking from behind" and if you do it, she'll never see your tummy. Unfortunately though, rumour has it that this position is known as "doggy" in some circles. So it's a tricky one to suggest. Especially if she's got a dog. Saying things like, "Do you fancy doing doggy tonight?" can get you quite savagely beaten up.

[†] Copyright Trudy Kamester, Northants.

[‡] This is show business for joke.

Mohammered L. Fayed
Harrods
Shop
Nightsbridge
In London


14th December 1990

Dear Mohammered L.,

Shut up and listen. I've got a fucking great idea for your pre-Christmas sales drive. If you give me five hundred thousand quid, I'll come into your store twice a week for a month and wander around buying lots of stuff and saying how great it is. I can say all this in one of my trademark loud voices that I'm so good at. You could do with some proper slebrity endorsement. What do you reckon? Are we on? Please forward cheque and it's a deal.

Keep up the good work. Job done.

Yours with, erm, whatever it is that they say at the end of letters like this,

The Rik Mayall (hi-profile acter and stand-up icon)

## CONDOM MEMORANDUM

TO: Derek Henderson
C.E.O. Jureck Condoms

FROM: The Rik Mayall
Showbusiness phenomenon

February 20th 1991

Dear Derek,

My agent Heimi Fingelstein has just called me – that was
him on the phone just now, you can dial 1471 and do
ringback if you don't believe me (and I don't fuck about
and talk bollocks so you'd better believe me) – and he
said that you want me to endorse your new range of
Maximum Warrior condoms. I wanted to write and tell
you that this is fucking great. No, seriously, it's fucking
really fucking great and I've got tons and tons of solid
workable ideas about ad campaigns and scripts and stuff
involving me and condoms and birds and nobbing and
stuff and already I can see that this is shaping up to be
another Mattahorn in my great career. See how I did a lot
of swearing back there a few sentences ago, well that's
me all over because I live on the edge, the cutting edge –
they call me The Edge Cutter.

You know about me and capitalism, Derek, and if you don't then you really bloody well ought to because me and the capitalists are extremely in bed together hardcore style which is the thing which makes your wanger-anorak advertisement concept such a total cock-ripping baby-maker in my opinion and that's the one that really counts in showbusiness – which is what everyone in showbusiness says except maybe some people who don't but hey Derek, let's get real, they're just cunts anyhow so just forget I ever said it. It didn't happen. I'm not here. Walk away. Job done. Goodbye.

Hey Derek, got you right between the eyes there. I'm not actually finishing the memo there as you might have thought, I'm just being dramatic which is kind of what you pay for when you hire the showbusiness Schlieffen Plan which is what I am. I mean yes, some people say that my memos are too long but hey, get out of Denver, baby, they're just wrong. Wrong. That's all I ever say. Wrong. That's the only word I use. Wrong. There, I just did it again. Anyhow, first off – and I've been thinking about this a lot for lots of reasons which I'll get to in a moment – I'm not one hundred per cent comfortable with the name. Mmm, big one, isn't it. If you want me to be the face of your condoms (not literally of course – although it's a thought) for the next twenty years then you should listen up because this is important. Maximum Warrior Condoms – the Maximum and Condoms bits are great but are you sure about the Warrior part? There are other warriors – some big and some small. For example (E.G.), Samurai warriors are Japs and we don't want people thinking that our brave boys have got Jap-sized nobs. The British warrior has historically always had an apocalyptic nob. Hey, this is a time of war after all and any suggestion that our Tommies have small cocks is just NOT GOOD FOR morale. (Do you see the thinking behind that there? Passion, right? Correct. Read on.) Well get this Der, this is going to work – how about Maximum Chieftain Tank Condoms? Or Flying Fortress Condoms? How about Aircraft Carrier Condoms? It's got a good ring to it and I'm not making a joke there. Blitzkrieg or Firestorm condoms would also look good on the shelves in the chemists. These are all concepts that we need to slalom around in our media dune buggy, you know like those great ones that bounce about the place in the sand looking hard. You could have me in one with a suntan and an obligatory bird. That's going to sell a lot of rubber johnnies, my friend.

But hey hey hey Derek, hold everything, I don't want us to fall out about the name here or anything. I mean, you've probably got quite a big cock yourself. I mean, working for Maximum Warrior like you do you're bound to and there's no way that I want to cast aspersions on it or in it or whatever you do with them (the aspersions, not your cock obviously). I mean I've hardly got to know you. But I bet Mrs Henderson's a bit of a top bollocks bird, isn't she? I don't want you to feel that I'm hitting on Mrs Henderson, Dickie, if I may call you Dickie. It's just that who knows? Maybe when we get to know each other better we might like to get into a bit of wife swapping. Obviously I'd have to check her out first or maybe you could send a photograph. I can't promise anything but so long as she's up to scratch and jugged up then you're on. At the moment I've got myself a Japanese wife and you know what they say about it going from side to side, well it's <u>not true</u>.

Anyway, supposing that we stay with the Maximum Warrior name as opposed to Maximum anything else (like Field-Marshall perhaps) – here's a few fabulous cutting edge ideas that I've come up with as part of your marketing campaign.

You know how like everybody knows that I'm a great lover and know lots about shagging and all that kind of stuff, right? Anyhow, so the thing is, I thought I could write to the newspapers and tell them about the advertising campaign I'm going to do for you. That'll get them going right from the off. If we treat the media like a top bird and get it all horned up about me and your condoms then you'll sell loads of them and maybe you can consider increasing my fee from the usual £63 per day (and don't forget that nothing is signed at the moment – everything's still open to negosheashon – so don't foul your seat just yet or whatever the current euphemism is for shitting your pants). Bish bosh, I slip you and you slip me, my agent gets his usual ninety per cent, the press are on board, and everyone's on a beach snorting coke (apart from me because I don't do that) and shagging people they shouldn't be. It's a win win win win win win win situation. In fact, I haven't got enough ink to say win enough, everyone's winning so much. Am I the guy with the top hairy bollocks or what (if you know what I mean). (That's a poetry thing.)

Firstly, (I like to do things in order because that's the kind of guy I am) I think we should think about print ads. These are the kind of ones they have on posters and in newspapers and magazines and stuff like that. You know, here's something – wherever I go in Media Land people are always looking at me and talking about me and saying, "Who the fucking hell is that guy – he must know what he's talking about." So it's worth listening to me Dickie and maybe even taking notes. You should probably photocopy this as well and distribute it throughout the Jureck marketing department. It'll also be good practice for when we really get into bed and start rubbing up against each other. That's not a pervy thing – that's a top media advertising buzz expression – you know, like the ones they use on the television about advertising agencies and stuff.

So, weld your eyeballs open, in we go, hold on tight, fingers on the trigger, straight into the big one. The image for the advertisement, Dickie, the image. You've got to get it by the throat. The image should be very simple – "clean" as us media gurus call it. Just think, Dickie, picture the scene. You're driving along the M4 coming into town in your big flash car. Obviously, it doesn't have to be the M4 – not if you don't live anywhere near it or are coming from somewhere else but go with it Dickie, just for a moment – you're in safe hands. So, you're going along the M4, maybe Mrs Henderson is in the passenger seat stroking your thigh (it's up to you) and you look up from the road to see a fuck off huge billboard on the side of a building. On it is Rik Mayall (i.e. me), smiling and looking really great. Next to me is an internationally respected glamour model and she's glazed in sweat with her hair all over the place like I've just given her an extremely major having it off. And that's where the fist of advertising hits the general public right in the face and breaks all their noses in such a really cool metaphorical sense. Hey! We're really moving aren't we? (Not house.)

Being such a top acter and writer, I can create a character that you can use in all your campaigns. I've given this a lot of thought so run with it. I reckon we should call him Chick Nailer, because it sounds a little bit like Rik Mayall and it shows that I can do a lot of birds. It's clever isn't it? Chick Nailer, Rik Mayall, it rhymes and everything and if we play this right, there could be all sorts of spin-off opportunities and maybe he could even have his own line of condoms named after him. So, perhaps you could have a Maximum Warrior Chick Nailer Special Edition for rock hard studs. Anyway, I digress. (I can do all sorts of stuff – just ask Heimi for a price list.)

So there you are on the M4 or somewhere else that's quite hard and beneath the picture of me with the glamour model who looks as though I've just given her a right good, er, whatevering, you can run the strap line. Don't be afraid Dickie, I'm not talking bondage here. That's just another media buzz phrase (stick with me and you'll learn plenty) and it means "some writing" (i.e. words). And the strap line can read:

*Maximum Warrior Condoms* (or something bigger as I've already mentioned – obviously this bit in between the brackets wouldn't go on the poster. That would be dangerous because by the time you'd read all this, you'd

have crashed on that sharp bend on the elevated section
– I've got an anecdote about that) – anyway, here's the
rest of the slogan. Actually, forget that. Let me start again.
You're driving into town in your big bastard car with Mrs
H stroking your scrotes and you look up and see me with
a cracking bit of babe mounted on my fully loaded
wanger anorak and the slogan reads: *Maximum Warrior
Condoms for guys with savage cock attitude.*

What do you reckon? I can be standing there smiling –
not too much of course, we don't want to be crass – and
it will be a very powerful image (another good marketing
expression) which will stick in people's heads as they
drive past so that when they next go to the chemists to
stock up on johnnies, they'll think, "I remember seeing
Rik Mayall/Chick Nailer on that poster and he'd just
shagged a top bird with a Maximum Warrior condom so
I'd better get some so I can be like him." It's all about
identification with top stars like me. That's how it works,
Dickie. Trust me, I'm a professional. (Not like a prostitute
or anything. Although if the price was right I'd give it a
whirl if the bird was nice. Imagine getting all that jug and
twadge action and being paid for it! That's a job made in
heaven. In fact there might be a movie in that with me
having to shag lots of people in order to raise money for
a children's hospice or something hard like a war.)

In magazines and newspapers, we can have even bigger
adverts with more writing on them. And we can vary the
strap lines (you've remembered what strap lines means
haven't you Dickie? Because that's what I was talking about
a bit earlier, right, when I was doing some of my great

126

explaining to you and I could explain it again but if you look a few paragraphs back you'll see what it says. Okay? Sorted? Or not? Or what? Look, we don't have to sort it out now Dickie, we can do it at another time in one of our other great memos to you. Anyhow, on with the subject matter.) So, what was I talking about? Oh yeah, so you can vary the strap lines if you want (meaning you can say different things) so that on some of them it might read: *Chick Nailer says, "Put a Maximum Warrior helmet on your helmet",* and on others it might read: *"I smell twadge, there's work to be done"* or even something like, *"Hey Geoff! Get it on, get it in."* (Just think how many people there are called Geoff – that's a few lorry loads sold already. I'm unbelievable when I get at it. Okay, let's continue.)

Now, at this point, and I know you're probably all horned up at the prospect of this, but we need to put our feet on the brake for a moment. This is where my knowledge of media stuff and marketing will really come into its own because what we need to do is taylor our strap lines for each of the magazines and newspapers. Are you getting this Dickie? I really feel we're rock solid, locked together, and I don't mean that in a sexual way. We are just rolling around together and thrusting conceptually. So, for example, in a high quality jizz rag like Razzle[*], you might be able to put, *Clench your teeth baby, I'm coming in on a wing and a Warrior,* but for something more

---

[*] I've got my own Razzle archive in plastic easy wipe covers and I've arranged them in leather ring binder things like they have on the Marshall Cavendish adverts. I've annotated them all myself, repeatedly. You're very welcome to come and take a peek Dickie. Probably best not bring the wife.

middle-of-the-road and steady-as-she-goes like The Radio
Times which is read by the elderly, it might be something
tasteful like: *Maximum Warrior – a tough well-worn helmet
for the old soldier.* Or maybe: *Old Birds! Get a Grandad in
your trench.* In the chicks-with-their-clothes-on magazines,
you can appeal to today's modern woman with a powerful
in-your-face message like: *Sophisticated birds! You haven't
been shagged until your man's worn you with a Warrior.*
And in tabloid newspapers, it might be: *Cock! Get some in
a Warrior.* As you can see, these are fully formed ideas with
"green light" written all over them and they're falling
straight into your lap here, Dickie.

Now, we need to think about TV and radio spots and I'm
not talking acne and blackheads here – it's yet another
one of my happening expressions. So don't get strung out
about it. Or is it strung up? Or hung up? Hanging up?
Out? Shake it all about? Whatever. But listen, this is big.
This is where using a big showbiz star like me with lots of
great ideas will really come into its own. Now first of all
we must think lengths and I'm not making a funny joke
there about cock size although I could if I wanted to but
I'd probably have to charge you something. Once again,
I'm speaking media language here and talking about the
length of the commercials. So, with this in mind, Dickie,
and in trouser – that *was* a joke – just a little one but you
can have it on me, here are some Maximum Warrior
radio commercials I've brainstormed and written down
on a piece of paper. We are at the cutting edge of radio
voice-over work here. Believe me, this strategy is going
to reach out to the British people and yell "happening!"
in their faces until their eye sockets bleed cash.

## **Maximum Warrior Radio Commercials**

Written by The Rik Mayall – top Maximum
Warrior commercials writer.

Dramatis Personae (i.e. names of acters)
(i.e. means, "this means"), (they don't
usually put brackets like this in radio
scripts – crazy out of control
motherfucker – that's me), (although
that's not my name, it's a way of
describing myself – which is what I was
doing just then.)

Dramatis Personae: (again, but not with
the other stuff.)

   1.  Rik Mayall as Chick Nailer[*]
   2.  Various top birds

**10 second spot:**
*Sounds of what it must sound like when
you're having it off (bird sounds only).*

CHICK NAILER:   *In a butch sort of war
                 movie hero type of voice*
                 Maximum Warrior Condoms for
                 precision having it off.

---

[*] The thing about Chick Nailer is that it sounds like I'm a bit
of a chick nailer which is cool – and I am anyway. Ask
anyone, Dickie, they'll tell you.

**20 second spot:**

*The sound of proper full on dirty love doing. Lots of heavy breathing, squeaks and gasps. Lots of bird going "ooh ooh ooh."*

CHICK NAILER: Hi, I'm Chick Nailer and I say, "Maximum Warrior Condoms – girls like it when you've got one on your penis*."

**30 second spot:**

CHICK NAILER: Hi.

A BIRD:      Just shag me now.

*A thundering clusterbomb of shagging (both bottoms, front and back – it's okay, this is radio), screaming, slapping, shouting and head cracking against bedstead (but bird not minding) throughout.*

CHICK NAILER: I'm Chick Nailer.

A BIRD:      God you're fabulous.

CHICK NAILER: I know, well spotted and that's why I say, "Maximum Warrior Condoms.
*Pause*
For serious battle-formation cock attack."

---

\* Maybe something more snappy here. (It's just a work in progress, Dickie.)

```
A BIRD:        Good grief, it's like a
               French loaf!

CHICK NAILER:  Yes it is, or should I say -
               [Insert something French
               and amusing here]
```

Do you see how this works now, Dickie? This isn't just some top showbiz bloke giving you the low down here. I'm a media scientist – I know what I'm doing and we're talking synergy here. Synergy. Look it up if you don't know what it means. It can't be hard to find.

With TV and cinema commercials, this is where your advertising campaign will really come alive. Not only are you getting great vocals with me and a gargantuan screen presence but you're getting high quality acting as well. Just think, if I get my break, or rather when I get another great break to make another great film, people will think, "Fucking hell, there's The Rik Mayall and he has suggested the concept of going out and buying Maximum Warrior condoms. I'm doing it. Count me in and I mean every birds' fanny in the pub." It's a circular concept of capitalism – they'll buy your condoms and they'll go and see the film with me in it. Everyone's "juiced" as my loads of American friends who work in Hollywood always say when we're chatting like good mates on the phone which we do all the time.

Anyway, here is the script for the TV and cinema commercial overleaf*.

* That's Oxford / Cambridge publishing talk for turn over the page. (Cunts.)

## __M A X I M U M   W A R R I O R__
## __(Insurgency Range)__

"A-poke-in-the-lips Now" Campaign

Television and cinema commercial (length TBC)

Devised, workshopped, written by and starring
The Rik Mayall as Chick Nailer

Directed by Francis Ford Coppola[*]


FADE IN:

EXT. RIVER WINDING THROUGH THE JUNGLE LIKE A SNAKE[†] – DAY

*The boat goes upriver moodily with smoke everywhere and Japs on the riverbank holding spears and looking hard.*

*CHICK NAILER (27) leans against the bulkhead (check terminology). He is dressed in military green and beige slacks with cool boots and those bullet belt things stretched across his toned pectorals and oiled six-pack. He has*

---

[*] Maybe check availability (mention me).
[†] A cunning subliminal message. We're talking Dickie here Dickie.

*loads of make up on his face – I mean
camouflage. He eyes the Japs with his
inexscrutable tortured eyes which you
can't actually see because he's wearing
Ray Ban Aviator shades (nothing wrong
with a bit of extra product placement
here Dickie, all the other big Hollywood
stars are at it – I just run with the
pack.) Jimmy Hendrix plays his guitar
throughout (I know he's dead but we can
use one of his recordings, he won't
mind).*

*The boat docks at a large stone
headquarters in the jungle with loads and
loads of well-thought-of oriental glamour
models hanging around in G-strings and
lashings of that special oil stuff that
makes it look like you're a bit sweaty.*

*Chick steps from the boat and makes his
way majestically through the crowds of
birds who watch him, hungry with desire.*

INT. ORSON BRANDO'S JUNGLE HEADQUARTERS –
ELEVENSES

*ORSON BRANDO, a middle-aged bald man
sits next to an absolute top notch hit-
the-jackpot type of oriental bird. He
looks sad. His girlfriend strokes his
arm.*

*Suddenly, the door is kicked open and in
strides Chick with the grace of a*

*startled alley cat. (That's a cool thing not shit writing). He eyes the bald man ferociously.*

CHICK:        Eddie Catflap what the
              fucking hell are you doing
              here?

ORSON:        The horror...the horror...

CHICK:        Never mind the horror
              Orson, you're surrounded by
              fabulous jugged up birds
              who are all extremely
              thumbs-up for a bit of
              naughty. You should be in
              heaven.

ORSON:        The horror...the horror...

CHICK:        All right, easy does it.
              How can I help?

TOP JAP BIRD: He hasn't got any johnnies.

CHICK:        Fuck my old boots, that's
              terrible. Six months up the
              Yangtse with all these
              birds and no spermicidally-
              lubricated rubber sheaths
              made from the highest
              quality products. Absolute
              bloody horror there Orson,
              you're not wrong, but fear
              not because I've got just
              what you need.

*Chick reaches moodily into one of those big pockets they have on the side of battle trousers where they keep bullets and grenades and stuff like that and he pulls out a bumper pack of Maximum Warrior condoms and passes them to Orson.*

CHICK: Here you are, buddy, whap one of these Maximum Warrior condoms for heavy-duty jungle war film nob and twadge protection on your wanger. Should keep you going for a couple of days.

ORSON: Not the horror...not the horror...

TOP JAP BIRD: What he means is, do you fancy a threesome with me and him by way of saying thanks? You can toss a coin for who goes front or back bottom.

CHICK: Thanks but I've got work to do.

*Chick goes to the door and sees a scene that looks like a ladies' sixth form college on laundry day (in*

> *Japan obviously). What a
> girlfriend competition for
> Chick to judge!*

CHICK: I'm just going outside, I
may be some time.

TOP JAP BIRD: What a guy.

> *Chick winks to camera and
> strides off looking
> magnificent and ready to get
> down to some private
> gentleman's business.*

FADE OUT.

It's just a first draft although actually it's fine and maybe just needs a tweak here and there to round off the sharp edges of my hard-hitting proase. We're talking homage here not pastiche – whatever that means.

Obviously, this is just the short version of the commercial but it could be that if you wanted a longer version for the cinema or Channel Four or Five where it's only about a tenner a spot (because no one's watching) then you could have the commercial continue for a full ninety minutes of a feature film. Big adverts for big guys for big products for big audiences for big profits for sounds of people saying, "smashing idea, Rik Mayall." (That's the kind of sound I like to hear, Dickie, as I'm sure you do. Except of course they'll change the name to your name when they say it.)

Now Dickie, in addition to my advertising and marketing conceptual nuggets, I've got a radical idea here which could land us with a No Bell prize or a marketing award of some sort at least which could also – if we play it right and be proper sensitive about it – unite the men and women of the world. Are you sitting down for this? Because I think you should be. And if you are sitting down then might I suggest that you loosen your tie and clear your desk of sharp objects that you might fall forward on to and have your eye out – or your other eye for that matter too because this is big trousers time. Are you ready, my friend? Because I don't do big memos. This is really hot stuff – so deep breaths and read it slowly. In fact, might I suggest that you read it out loud as well so you get the full impact. So, here we go – hold on tight – because this baby's coming at you and it's going to run and run. Well maybe not run and run because babies don't do they? But maybe it could crawl and crawl – you get my meaning anyway. You see what I'm doing here, Dickie? I'm building you up into a lather of pre-brilliant-concept expectation. Are you ready? Call me. Oh no you can't, that's stupid. Ignore that. Okay, here goes. I'm just going to come out with it now and give it to you straight. Here it is. New paragraph for maximum impact. And here it is:

Non-gay and gay condoms.

So, what do you reckon, Dickie?

I know, I know, you're probably trying to scoop your bowels back in, but just hang in there (I'm talking metaphorically). So here's the deal: your non-gay condoms won't work on arses (apart from birds' arses of course – I'm all inclusive) and your gay condoms won't work on birds' front bottoms. Now you're probably thinking, "Yeah yeah yeah, Rikster – love your idea (and everything else you do) but the whole gay/non-gay concept is unenforceable." And this is where I'm going to turn around (not literally because I'm sitting down although I could maybe swivel if I had a swivel chair) and hit you with the double whammy because not only have I developed this radical new contraceptive formula but I've also thought of how you could ensure that gays don't use non-gay condoms and non-gays don't use gay condoms. I don't want to come over all authoritarian and I know we all like to go crazy and writhe like rabid beasts in a warm drizzle of blood and semen when we're sinking giant boreholes of nob gristle, but there have to be rules. You and I know that Dickie, we're civilised men of the world – but the younger people, well, don't get me started on them – apart from the young female jugged up ones in which case do get me started on them (that's another little joke for you there. Let's not make anything of it.) What you need to do is install a small bleeper like a modified car alarm on the teet that you squeeze between thumb and forefinger as you roll it down your shaft*. Now I'm no product designer (although I probably could have been one if I hadn't gone and failed my bloody Art "O" level – that was a travesty if ever there was one. Aren't some people just felchers of

* Probably glistening.

the Devil's ringpiece, eh Dickie?) but a small self-
lubing micro-chip might work for the alarm or failing
that, a small backpack could be provided with the
condoms which would contain the alarm and have a
wire that runs around the man's arse crack (in a small
length of coving perhaps), bissecting the testicles and
running in tandem with the blue vein along the old
todger. As you can see, this isn't just some off the wrist
idea that I've scribbled down but a fully operational
solution that could revolutionise contraception
throughout the world. And not only will it ensure that
rules are enforced but the alarm will also act as a
warning to blokes who might be a bit drunk and end
up with one of those lady boys in Bangkok. I've got a
very long and painful anecdote about that.

Jesus, I'm on fire here, Dickie! Because another idea has
just popped into my head like an exocet missile of pure
crystalline genius. We could develop a special
"genocide" version of the Maximum Warrior which could
be sold to terrorists. And instead of the modified car
alarm on the teet (that you squeeze between thumb and
forefinger) you could have a small explosive charge that
would explode as the wearer reached climax thereby
killing the nasty bastard and whichever loser was
curtseying on his toolkit. It's hot – this is counter over-
the-counter counter terrorism. Terrorism that works for
us, the good guys. Terrorism-nice. Got a ring to it, hasn't
it? (Possibly a ringtone too – I'll dance around with that
one for a while and get back to you.) I've always fancied
myself. As a UN ambassador. Anyway, that's another
memo.

So, Dickie, that just about raps it up. I look forward to hearing from you soon and keep up the good work.

Yours etc,

The Rik.

PS: I've copywrote all my great ideas and concepts herein and patents are pending and applied for or whatever the expression is, so don't think you can take them and use them with some other Hollywood star instead of me. I have lawyers. I have my "people" and they are everywhere. No man is in Ireland.

# DROP DEAD FRED

Hello again, viewer. Here's a living fact that I want to share with you. Breakthruogh movies don't just come along like that. They're not just ten-a-penny. And Drop Dead Fred was another one just not like that. I remember it well which must mean something because remembering things well doesn't always happen to remarkably unusual special people who are soon to have profoundly shocking life-threatening beyond death other side type experiences, like meeting God and learning things about stuff – so it matters. I remember it so well . . .

It was Christmas Eve and the rain was falling in that grim London way that only London rain can. It fell outside the sash windowpanes of my comfortable well-furnished enviable (actually) London home. I could smell chestnuts roasting. I was sitting a bit too close to the fire*. I wasn't actually, I was sitting broodily by the fire like in a film, an art film, because I don't do shit films. Some people call me Rik "doesn't do shit films" Mayall. Anyway, the fire crackled warmly casting its Christmas lines on my children playing

---

* I am contractually bound to make that joke because chestnuts are what people sometimes call their bollocks. Some of you might not be comedians. But that's okay. I dig that. I'm down with you.

on the latest-styled carpet. My wife and friends were all laughing and were happy. But something was wrong. I just knew it. I concealed a tear from those I had paid for and cared for and given most of my money to and gazed out intelligently at the rain. What was it? What was this unnamed emotion that whispered at my sensitivity? Charity work? Another best-selling blockbuster smash hit West End play with lots of serious acting in it? Which one of these many things could it be I pondered as they wrestled together in my skull.

Ring.

I jerked*. The phone! Just leave it Rik Mayall, I thought, don't let your cared-for-ones see that lonely tear. Just think what it would do to them you fool. Keep your emotions to yourself man†.

It was as if it was an instant later – which it was – that there was a tugging at my cardigan. It was one of my many children. I won't say which one. It's not because I can't remember his name, it's because I respect the privacy of people within my rarefied orbit.

"Daddy," said the little tot, "there are two hugely successful Hollywood film screenwriters on the phone for you who want you to make a smash hit film for them. Shall I fuck them off?"

"What are their names, baby [fill in name]?" I interrogated.

"It's Carlos Davis and Tony Fingleton, the hugely respected movie industry titans with countless blockbusters to their names. Shall I say that you're whacked out on methadone as usual and why don't they try Harry Enfield?"

"No, not this time, baby," and a piece of well-honed stagecraft had that tear gone in the whisper of an eyelash. "You'd better tell them Daddy's home. This might be something to give the nineteen nineties some meaning."

I turned to the light.

---

* I don't do that often. Jerking in the living room is not one of my things.
† I'm not usually like this. Everyone knows me as the hard man of light entertainment – which I am. See page 72.

"God I love you Daddy," said baby as I strode purposefully towards the telephone which I snatched up like a power drill.

"Rik Mayall here, what's the problem?"

"Rik Mayall, I can't believe it. Rik Mayall whoah – this shit is coming down big time man! We got a situ-fuckin-ation here man – it's one motherfucker of a scene! We're like out of our arse-eating minds here, Rik Mayall – we need someone who can act!"

"I think you've got the right number," I breathed using one of my trademark top drawer knife-edge English accents that in Hollywood they call Saville Row. "If it's a top screen acter you're looking for then you obviously know the right place to look."

"But Rik Mayall, it's like, you know, like now man!"

"Relax gentlemen. All you need to do is give me a script with all the words and the other acters' names in it and I'll give you a smash. Like what you Americans say, I can act it up like a shit-eating motherfucker of a bitch."

"Like wow man, we love you," they said.

"And if this is going to be a Rik Mayall film then you'd better start writing your award acceptance speeches."

I turned to the wife like a nuclear warhead.

"Get my chopper out Belinda [check name] and give it a wipe because I'm going to L.A. and the rest is history yet to be written."

She dropped to her knees.

"No, no, the helicopter," I smiled forgivingly.

"Oh Rik Mayall, you and your top quality cock puns," she laughed happily with tears rolling down her face. "So you're really going to Hollywood?"

"Yes."

"Is there time for a . . ."

"No babe, let it wait. Besides, the children are in the room and I've got to go." I scooped her into my arms in a top-lit two-shot. Our lips met again and again.

"I'll be back in the spring," I breathed huskily.

"Your helmet, Rik Mayall!" urged Hilary [really must check name].

I didn't take the bait. Self control Rik Mayall, I thought.

I looked back at her and purred, "Keep it warm, baby."

And in the blur of a flash I was away like a speeding bullet, roaring away on my hog*. Then I set off. Straight around the corner, down Carnaby Street, over the Kings Road, full throttle jumping the gap across Tower Bridge as it opened, screaming past the Houses of Parliament, twice around the dome, up Whitehall, over Westminster Bridge, round St Pauls, past Westminster Abbey, collar up down Fleet Street – I didn't want any journalists to smell my intention on this breakthruogh movie – roaring along the Embankment avoiding pedestrians coming out of the National Theatre shouting, "Cor blimey, God bless the Queen Mum, apples and pears, it's the Rik Mayall phenomenon! Now I've seen it all. You're one of Britain's top light entertainers. Stop your motorbike, we want to tell you how much we respec your work." I slalomed around them signing autographs.

Three chords of action music and there I was in extreme close up at the desk at Heathrow.

"Passport please," said the woman behind the desk.

"My face is my passport," I growled. Her huge innocent blue eyes lifted up from the desk and puckered.

"I'm so sorry, Mr The Rik Mayall," she blanched, clutching for support as she fouled herself. Her life was ruined.

"It's all the same to me, bird," I said kissing her on the face cheek. (Careful viewer – always get your cheeks right.)

I gave her a wink and boarded the plane like an exocet.

---

* This is what top quality Hells Angels call their motorcycles. Tip: it's currently fashionable to say motorbike instead of motorcycle.

An air hostess who looked like that BBC weather girl who looks like she might be a bit dirty – you know the one – met me at the door to the plane and said, "This way please, Mr The Rik Mayall. Straight into First Class."

"First Class? But I'm a socialist."

"We know that and we love you for it but this situation must override your heartfelt beliefs in humanity's equality and your lifelong championing of human rights. Added to which, the captain of the plane loves your work (as do we all)," she bracketed, "so you've got your own First Class Showbusiness The Rik Mayall Suite."

I cupped her chin in my hand and whispered, "I respect women as well."

"Oh I knew that a long time ago," she heaved, her breasts engorging. She struggled to maintain consciousness such was the electro-static charge of attraction between us. I did one of my smouldering eye looks and breathed past her in one of my great suits.

She showed me into the Rik Mayall suite and unbuttoned her blouse.

"I've got something here for you," she said.

I did that enigmatic thing that I do with my forehead.

"Jesus Christ, you're enigmatic," she intoned.

"There are three types of people in this life. There's you, there's me and there's everyone else and I like your attitude young lady." There was a moment and then it was gone. "Now, what have you got for me?"

"This," she said and there it was. She unbuttoned another button on her blouse and she pulled out a big one. WHAP! And there it was in my lap, fat heavy and thick – the Drop Dead Fred script.

"Thanks Candice," I said intuitively.

"That's all right, The Rik Mayall. I'm just doing my job. If there's anything else you need, I'm here for you. Maybe you'd like to join the Mile High Club?"

"I'm already a member. In fact, I'm the chairman. In fact again, even more factually, I'm the founder member."

She turned to go and then she turned back. "Oh, and the captain loves your work," she said. "Did I say that already?"

"Yeah baby."

"I beg your pardon."

"I mean, yes dear."

"Oh right, sorry."

And with that, my head hit the back of the seat. The government had obviously authorised an emergency take off for me. This was serious. The country, it's people and showbusiness itself were at steak.

A voice came over the intercom: "Would all passengers please fasten their safety belts, unless you're Rik Mayall, you can make up your own mind because you're a free spirit roaming the globe like a high planes drifter."

I allowed myself a wry smile.

"Thanks very much," I said.

"That's all right. You can have as many wry smiles as you like. Have one on me."

"I am me."

Safety belt or no safety belt, I was going to America.

Once I had changed my mind about Candice and the hot toilet action and then sunk a large one, I settled down to read the Drop Dead Fred script. The words quite literally jumped off the page and into my head where I memorialised them, verbatim, word for word. I finished it in the twinkling of an eye. I must get that looked at when we land, I thought. And I did. And it wasn't. So I shouldn't have. Forget it. Move on.

The plane screeched in with a howl of brakes leaving a trail of burning rubber and screaming ground crew in its wake.

Candice said, "This way Mr The Rik Mayall, good luck with the film."

"No," I said. "I'll never leave a plane first. I insist, orphans first."

"No, Rik Mayall," said the orphans, "you go first. You are the man."

"Thanks Orphans," I said, "love your work."

I threw – no not threw, tossed careingly – a fistful of autographed cash to them and I was out of there like a mushroom cloud.

"Clear the area! Incoming!" someone shouted as I strode like an inter-continental ballistic missile across the tarmac towards the airport. Only slimmer.

Whoah! I thought as I entered the building. What are all these flashing lights and sounds? I must have changed movie. This is America.

"Shit my Grandmother's shit out of my own ass!" yelled an American voice as I approached. "It's Rik fuckin' Mayall! Hey guy, I love your motherfuckin' work, man. I mean, are you for real? I'm like whoah! Hot shit diggety doo, my eyes is seeing you in unison man. I'm going out of my goddamn mind. You're killing me bro."

"Hello," I exhaled with typical British restraint.

"May I see your passport please motherfucker?" said the customs man with a smile.

"Certainly," I said.

"Maximum apology for this Rik-baby, you internationally acclaimed globe-trotting showbusiness phenomenon, but I got to ask you a question, man. What is the purpose of your visit?"

"I'm here to save the global entertainment industry with a breakthruogh new pre-award winning movie called Drop Dead Fred," I said not immodestly.

"That's some seriously dangerous shit Rik Mayall man. No popular light entertainer from the U-motherfuckin'-K has ever survived out here. Are you crazy or what?"

"Stand aside, I'm goin' in or rather, excuse me, stand aside, I'm going in."

"Eat my fatherfuckin' ass breasts. Hold it there Rik fuckin' Mayall, this is America man, it will eat you up and spit you out in little bits. You is gonna die boy! You can't make the film Drop Dead Fred and put Working Title films back into the black by playing an invisible character. Nobody can. You're out of your goddamn mind. You is a crazy motherfucker. You is gonna die screamin'. I don't know where you think you English guys come from."

"I'm not one of the English guys, I am THE English guy. Now, that's enough chit chat extra, I'm a man on a mission."

He looked a bit frightened of me.

"Okay, you mad mother."

"Do you even know where England is?"

"No I don't."

"Well that's why I'm making this film, friend, I need to put it on the map." I span around and looked him in the eye. There was a beat. "Where do I go for the anal search?"

"No need man, I can see you're clean."

"No, I insist. I want to keep America safe. One day you will thank me for this when the war on terror is invented and everyone wants to kill all you Americans. Anyway, I've brought my own torch and Anusalve."

Four hours later, I was allowed out of the cubicle. They used everything they had on me but I was as clean as a whistle. I walked out a proud man. Well, waddled a bit. No, not waddled, limped, but only a bit, although I leaked rather a lot. Even so, because I'm hard, I still think that four hours of fisting is a sensible security procedure.

Victory. I was through customs. My foot touched the good earth of the land of the free. This was America.

Someone shouted, "Eat lead and die, motherfucker!" as I walked across the airport concourse. A shot rang out and a body fell four blocks from a window and landed at my feet. I gave it an autograph and moved on.

SLAM! It was straight into the limo. There were lights flashing, motorcycle outriders, drive-by shootings, hi-velocity snipers' bullets pinging off the bullet-proof windscreen of President Bush's limo, and it was straight ahead to wherever these good people were needing me.

Rubber was burning, people were diving out of their cars to get out of my way as we screamed along the interstate highway towards what me and the Americans call The Dream Factory.

I swatted the door open like a big fly that was in my way a bit in the door frame, and was made of door, and walked into wardrobe where I stood and looked around the room in a medium shot. I was panting like someone quite out of breath and mildly perspiring which I hid with my acting technique.

There was a silence.

"Are you the guy?"

"I'm the guy."

Carlos and Tony, the big swinging screenwriting gods who had phoned me in London, stepped out of the shadows. Big, white, New York, guns. We high fived. We upper four B'ed. We middle sixthed. We went to see the headmaster. We rusticated each other and we nearly got expelled.

"Are you packing, Rik Mayall?"

"No, my pants are too tight."

They slipped me a piece. They gave me a gun as well. But I refused it.

"You'll have to learn the script," they said, as one.

"I've learnt it already," I said as one as well.

"Shit man, we knew you were a top acter but to learn the whole script in a two hour flight, that's blown our goddamn fucking minds," they said high fiving the furniture.

"Cool it guys," I said, "Daddy's here. Now, send in the wardrobe people\*."

In they came.

"Green," I said, "with red hair."

"Sure thing, Rik Mayall," said the wardrobe people and they went away immediately muttering, "he looks very good for twenty. He's lost a lot of weight. Great muscle tone as well. If I was a chick I'd fancy him."

"I am and I do," said a chick.

"I'm going for a sex change," said one of the guys.

"So are we," said the others. And they did.

I didn't hear any of this conversation and I went to work, making subtle rewrites to the script with one hand and discussing Drop Dead Fred Two with the other†.

Double crikey with lots of gosh – this script is a work of genius, I thought broodily to myself playing my cards close to my chest. All it needed was someone to realise it and make it live and breath. Now I understood the telephone call. There wasn't an acter alive or dead in America who could begin to wonder how to cope with beginning to think about the concept of how to commence the first glimmer of an entrée into the dark pulsating heartbeat of this gargantuan figure, Drop Dead Fred, who was going to dominate the now-closing century. Thank God

---

\* "People" is Hollywood slang for people.
† My instinct knew there was Jimmy Carrey ten paces behind me, snapping at my heels (career-wise – I don't mean he was lying on the floor trying to bite my shoes). And I respect him. If you're reading this, Jimmy, love your work. Unless you don't like being called Jimmy in which case, Jim (we're great mates).

Olivier was dead. Not because he was better than me and would have taken the part from me and played it himself and I would have had to walk away and watch him bankrupt Working Title Films*. No, far from it. It was because poor Lawrence was too old and decrepit to play a part like Fred and he would have had to try and hang himself with his arthritic old fingers. I couldn't live with that. I'm a nice guy. I don't say unpleasant things about that cunt.

Even Orson couldn't have done it. Orson couldn't fly. They certainly didn't have a crane that could lift him. There was indeed only one man in the world who could bring this to life. This piece of cinema was going to overshadow everything that had gone before in the artform and was going to bring the century of film to a shuddering climax. I would be the coda.

"This movie will save the film industry," I said quietly in case someone stole these words and put them on posters for their films. Nothing is private aboard the Hollywood love machine.

As soon as I was on the set and the news got out, other top quality film acters came to watch me work. It was like an acting masterclass. There were over two hundred and fifty top name Hollywood stars gathered around the camera. I don't want to say their names because I'd rather protect their identities and in no way wish to demean their craft. But I'll say here and now that the fat one was there, that nasty one with the skin problem, and the really absurd one with the ridiculous haircut. All of them watched me from their own auditorium which they had designed for them by a top designer whose name I also won't mention. Thankfully, I am never more at home than in a theatrical environment. So rather than being intimidated, I was infused. As you probably already know, viewer, they call me Mr Theatre.

---

* Could have been a good shot though.

The director, Ate De Jong, said "Turn Over*" which I did. Then I got up again. Everybody loves that joke and they all howled with laughter. A good joke like this always puts people at their ease on a first day's shooting. As the raucous laughter echoed around the set, I noted the looks of joy upon the faces of the sound department as they realised how important sound is to me.

People tried to give me flowers.

"No," I staged a tantrum, "no adulation on set. We're working here." The audience backed off respectfully, putting their awards they were going to shower me with back into their handbags.

Silence. All you could hear was my heart bumping.

"Sound, turn over and . . . action!"

I moved my head slightly to the left into the light.

"Cut! That's beautiful," said Ate.

More applause. I was beginning to worry about my ears. Ate fell to his knees, weeping: "We've already got two seconds in the can and it's still spring."

My co-star Phoebe Cates was the most beautiful woman I had ever seen. There must have been a reason why God had made me marry before I met Phoebe. And then I saw Kevin Kline and I knew that God had saved Phoebe for Kevin. God knows, I'm not an adulterer – I don't even know the meaning of the word. I don't even know that it means having it off with loads of birds that aren't your wife. Kevin is Mr America and I am Mr Europe or maybe Mr Rest-of-the-world – only time will tell. I am history in the making and it's a historical fact that my Andrex commercials have been heard all over the world. You name it – Zanzibar, Wales, my Bottom has been seen in Croatia.

What was extraordinary about the film was that everyone was beautiful – not just Phoebe. For those of you who were in it and

---

* "Turn over" is Hollywood speak for "press the button on the camera".

are reading this, read that first line of this paragraph again because it's good. But what I brought to the set was all the class-lessness and quality and love that is so English to American sensibilities. I was a whole new concept for them. They basked in my making-them-feel-nice. The cast were always telling me how happy I made them – as did the accountants because of all the money that the global cinema audience was about to shower upon them.

The shoot* was near Chicago, and the thing is that no one was murdered in Chicago whilst I was there. In fact, there was no crime at all. A whole new love had descended on the land. This was not a wishy washy hippy love. This was a true Judeo-Christian-Moslem non-denominational love. The chief of police from Chicago came to the set with some prostitutes who wanted to meet me. They were out of work and hungry because all the crime had stopped. At first, they tried to attack me and threw sachets of heroin at me because they were no longer employed. But then I spoke to them and all the other criminals who came to meet me and made them all realise that they should look for more worthwhile employment, and I made them smile for the first time in their lives. Because of my words, everywhere you looked, there were prostitutes that hadn't been slept with, guns that hadn't been fired and drugs that hadn't been taken (especially not by me). It was as though the sun had come out. It was a very happy time for America and I'm sure this helped make Drop Dead Fred the best-selling movie of the nineties. That's what we call films in America – movies. It's short for "moving," which is what my films usually are. And this one was very moving.

---

* This is an American word they use for when they make films and you all sit around in chairs near a camera. You can also do it with a gun but not in this context. A waste disposal chute is something different. And is spelt differently as you can see. As in parachute. Although it sounds the same.

It wasn't until I realised how big an American film set is and the amount that a talented acter can bring financially to such a large body of people that I realised how much prosperity I would bring to a vast swathe of the global entertainment industry. Even Britain with all its heart-breakingly bad films would have a knock on effect from this, recouping all the money that had been lost to the nation and making the industry appear profitable and worthwhile.

As you know, truth is the big word in my life. It is *the* word. It's the only word I know. Actually. That's why it's heavy – a heavy job for me to tell you, viewer, how things came about. But it's a fact that I am the man who saved the British film industry. And there are millions of talentless people in the British film industry that don't accept that – or even know it. No one has ever said thank you. Not that I expect thanking. It's not in the British cultural make up to want people to say thank you to you. But in other countries all over the world, people come up to me with Drop Dead Fred posters asking me to sign them and then they thank me for what I have done and give me things. Some of the things they give me are shit but what do you expect from Eastern Europe?

The thing about Drop Dead Fred is that I gave myself to the film. You know that scene where my head was squashed – the really powerful dramatic one that makes people go "Fucking hell, look at that"? Well get this, that was no special effect. I did the whole thing with my own head. And that's why (although only one reason) it became more than just a film. It became a bible for film makers and film enjoyers and film watchers and film critics*

---

* I did it for the film critics more than anyone. Those poor guys. They get so much abuse and disrespect from entertainment workers. They've got a job to do and they do it very well. I've always admired all the critics in the British film industry. They should be paid so much more. They should be respected and decorated. Let me say here in print – and I promised myself that I would never say this – but I am the only acter on the planet who adores every critic that ever lived. I don't see them as equals – they are far above me. I'm just a

and anything associated with the art that is pointing a camera at a bunch of acters and filming them. At last, the film industry had discovered how to make films. I had shown them.

And it all started with just a telephone call on Christmas Eve* and it went on to become an international showbiz phenomem-inem, no, global, no, trans-global, nay again, universal. In fact, it was outside the universe. It was trans-universal. The world had changed and I was at the vanguard of the change. Not that I talk about this. I practically find it impossible to blow my own trumpet. And that's the truth and if you don't believe me then fuck off. No offence.

---

cog in the wheel of entertainment. But they are the machine itself and the driver as well and the Godhead. I only got into the entertainment industry to help the critics earn money. That's why I'm here. That's why I do it. Yes there are other reasons, but these are the primary ones. The critics bring meaning to what we all do. I love their work. And I love them. Book critics are even better.

* Is this how it was for Mary when her waters did break?

# MORE GREAT STUFF

Picture the scene, viewer. No, not that one, you disgusting fuck-hole. If that's what you're looking for then you're in the wrong book. Made me feel quite ill. Anyway, picture this scene: Cows with horns, circling vultures, a bit of that twig stuff sticking out of the corner of my mouth, cowboy boots on a chair and I'm wearing them sitting on another chair next to that chair and I'm looking out at the horizon. This is me in my hotel sweet on Sunset Boulevard. Films stars coming here and there. Chicks in those really short skirts that look as though someone's just put some gaffer tape around their arses. Just hanging out. Me that is, not the chicks arses. Although they might be. And good luck to them if they are.

And that's when it happened. I heard a voice through the door: "Shit man, I can't like motherfuckin' believe it man. It's like whoah! – I've got a friggin' letter for you man."

It was the postman.

"Wait a minute, Mr Postman," said I, "it's just like being in that Carpenters' song."

I opened the door like a cluster bomb of early evening television comedy formats. The postman looked at me in that American way as if to say, "That's the best joke I ever heard."

"Have a nice fuckin' day, motherfucker," said Postie as he walked off whistling and muttering, "shit man, I ain't never fuckin' whistled before."

I tore the letter open like a battering ram. "Dear Rik," it said. Nice start, I thought. I can't tell you what else it said because it's confidential and has to remain in the national archives until it is de-classified in fifty years time. But I can paraphrase a bit. Basically it said, "Dear Rik, love your work, you are an inspiration to me. Great idea getting into bed with the Americans. All the best, Tony Blair, M.P."

Tony Blair, M.P.? I mused in a brooding close up. I've heard of Tony Blair. He's that good looking young M.P. that I've been keeping my eye on (which is not a gay thing although I've got nothing against them). And M.P. means Member of Parliament – that's good, I thought he'd end up there.

It was like a tap on the shoulder from fate telling me that there was work to be done back in Blighty, or on the other side of the "love gulf" as I like to call the Pacific. This very letter – the contents of which I cannot divulge – made me feel the tug of my homeland. Like every Englishman worth his salt (not that I take very much) I decided to save my love for the people who sprang from the same sod* as I. It was a turning point in my life. It was time to shrug off my accursed modesty like a used chrysalis. Was this a new maturity? All I knew then was that I must concentrate one hundred per cent on what was so important in mine and so many other people's lives – me.

And so began my relationship with Tony and Cherie. We met. We talked. We bonded. Now I've met a lot of famous people in my life especially in voice-over work but none that I have felt so

---

* Meaning earth. It has nothing to do with sodomy. I have nothing else to say on this subject.

at one with, instantly. It was as though we had been friends since childhood. But with Cherie, there was something else. Something more than friendship. And so it was that we grew closer.

Every man has a crucifix to hide and I am no exception. I will never openly discuss the love that Cherie and I have made because of the damage that it will do not only to Tony and Cherie themselves, but also to the British people. It's not as though I'm going to reveal in print that Cherie and I have been on/off lovers for a long time now, or passionate pillow-biting adultarees as I like to think of us. And, believe me, she can bite a lot of pillow with a mouth like that. I've always adored Till Death Us Do Part. Alf Garnett is a huge inspiration to me.

The way I like to look at it is that I was doing a service for the country. Tony was a very busy man. He couldn't apply himself to the task of satisfying his wife sexually while at the same time trying to rid the country of the working class and help the Americans to eradicate the Middle East. He needed help, which is where I came in. My award-winning lovemaking ensured that Cherie was a better Prime Minister's wife and therefore Tony was a better Prime Minister*. Consequently, it's a better world that we live in today. And our children – Cherie's and mine – are lucky to have my genes and not their assumed father's, because although Tony is beyond question in all political, moral and spiritual stuff, he wouldn't have given them their brooding Heathcliff-like individuality and accomplished close-up abilities like I could.

Anyway, I'm not the sort of guy who puts things like that in books.

---

* I let him take the credit too – five times a night! Someone had got to do it. Imagine being the first British Prime Minister ever to have no penis. I know I can count on you to keep a secret, viewer, and not spread it.

# HOW I DESTROYED BRITISH TELEVISION

The Young Ones destroyed rock 'n' roll; Filthy, Rich and Catflap butchered light entertainment; The New Statesman brought down the Thatcher administration and Bottom was an all-out attack on existence itself. These are true words, viewer, read them and weep. Done it? Good. Now dry your eyes because there are important things to be told and no one – I repeat – no one, is innocent*.

I remember that day so well. The Soho pavements were lightly drizzled with rain. That's why I had my raincoat on with the deep pockets. And I was walking along with my great friend Adrian Edmondson (who I love like a brother and is a much better acter than me). We had important business to attend to – show business. We were researching something, although I can't remember exactly what it was. Not because my brain's fucked because of all the years of drinking which I haven't done or the fact that I fell off my quad hog. Let's just say we were desperately not looking for drugs. We were spreading our large S and before we knew what had happened we found ourselves in a peep show. Now, the only reason that we had gone into the peep show was that we both find

---

* Not even if some twat in a wig in a courtroom somewhere tells you that you are innocent. Even then, you're not. All right?

them very sexist (although Adrian finds them more sexist than I do because he is much more morally sound than I am) and we wanted to find out just how sexist the peep show was so that we could tell on it and have it closed down. And that's where we met Paul Jackson, the Head of the BBC.

"Fucking hell, I mean, shit, hi Paul, what are you doing here in this one man cubicle?" I enquired.

"I've got a bit of a cold so I'm looking for some tissues that someone might have left in here."

"That's a coincidence," I said, "so am I."

There was an awkward silence. I don't know why, because we were both telling the truth.

"Anyway," I said, "I've just had a great idea for a television series."

"Oh great," said Paul, "that's why I'm in here just in case you might come in here saying something like that. Is that why your trousers have come down?"

"Yes that's right, isn't it Adrian?"

"Shut up, I'm not here," said Ade and he wasn't actually in the next cubicle masturbating because he doesn't do that sort of thing. He must have been projecting his voice from a nearby charity organisation that he was donating money to.

"So why have your trousers come down?" asked Paul.

"Because that's the title of my new great comedy show – I mean, ours, mine and Adrian Edmondson who isn't here. It's called Wanking erm, no, it's called Used Tissues, no, no, it's called 50 pence slots, no, erm, it's called Paul Jackson, no, forget all that, it's called Adrian Edmondson is not in the next cubicle masturbating."

"Shut up fuck pig!" Adrian didn't shout from the next cubicle.

"No," I said thinking on my feet, "it's called Bottom."

"What's it about?"

"It's about me and Adrian Edmondson being brilliant on

television and it'll Ghana lots and lots of awards and bring the country to its knees with amusement."

"You're on," said Paul zipping up and running.

"Phew that's a relief, Ade," I said.

"Shut up," he said, "I'm trying to pull this bird."

"What, through the slot?"

"Yeah, I've already got half her head through."

"Nice one. Is it because you're offended by the sexism of it all?"

"Yeah, I've just got to get my hands on her and get her home."

"Great. Can I help?"

"No, fuck off."

"Good gag, great mate."

So, we took her back to my place where she beat us both up and left. So we had nothing to show for our day's work but an idea for an award-winning TV series. All we had to do was write it. Which is no bother if you're a legendary duo of dangerous gorilla humorists. Ade did the typing and he allowed me to go to the off licence to buy all the drinks. And what I really enjoyed about writing with Ade was that having your legs broken can be great fun and very funny.

But when we sent our dark and subversive scripts to the BBC, that's when the trouble started. First of all they said that it wasn't possible for just the two of us to sustain a whole show alone. But we reminded them that Hancock and Sid James did an entire show together. They'd forgotten about that because they were all so busy being morally sound and politically correct but when they realised we were right, they said, "Oh er, right, er . . . daddio or whatever it is you working classes say. You're on. You can have a television series."

So we got it! Fantastic! We were in, and we started work. But as soon as we started filming, we hit problems. We were told that we had to talk differently because we weren't allowed to speak on television like we could in the theatre. It's the same nowadays. No one really speaks like they do on television. Well, this was the beginning of that. There was a quota in those days. You were allowed three Bloodies per programme – no Fucks and absolutely no Cunts – you would be expelled from the country if you said "cunt" and it still is a very rude word and I never use the word cunt myself. Sometimes there would be huge fist fights with the BBC executives that came to the set. But even though there were about twenty of them, me and Big Ade (sorry, slim attractive Ade), took them on and won. It was savage and brutal and all just because we wanted to say "bloody hell" in our show. Sometimes we went over our "bloody hell" quota and they would tell us that we had to say things like "crikey" and "blimey" instead.

"I used those words in The Young Ones," I said, "and now you want me to say them again so that I'll turn into a has-been. Next, you'll be asking me to use a slight speech impediment on my Rs."

Sometimes it was like that movie Zulu with all the BBC executives on the horizon and we took them on over the word "bugger", It was a battle for freedom of speech, part of my ongoing war against the insidious forces of censorship. Take George Orwell. He wrote books. He's dead now. Nuff said. If you're reading this George, well, I don't really know what to say. Hi. I suppose.

We fought those battles on behalf of all those comedy giants who had come before us, like all the greats: Brucey, Tarby, Lynchy, Tommy O'Connory. We didn't want them to feel that all the blood that they had spilled was in vein. We were part of the bloodline of British light entertainment. The baton was being passed from one generation to the next.

Some of the BBC executives even tried to make out that the show was sexist. But as I pointed out to them at the time, if they hadn't insisted on us cutting out the nineteen bird-shagging scenes that we wrote into each episode then there would have been

The Lemmy, The Rik and that twat from *Holby City* having a soft drink and looking like a girl.

Me, top bird and Kate Moss.

# BOTTOM
## LIVE 2003
### WEAPONS GRADE Y-FRONTS TOUR

**ALL DATES COMPLETELY SOLD OUT**

**OCTOBER**

| | | | |
|---|---|---|---|
| Fri | 03 | GLASGOW Clyde Auditorium | 0870 040 4000 |
| Mon | 06 | PLYMOUTH Pavilions | 01752 229 922 |
| Tue | 07 | PLYMOUTH Pavilions | 01752 229 922 |
| Wed | 08 | PORTSMOUTH Guildhall | 023 9282 4355 |
| Fri | 10 | BOURNEMOUTH BIC | 01202 456 456 |
| Sun | 12 | CROYDON Fairfield Hall | 020 8688 9291 |
| Mon | 13 | CROYDON Fairfield Hall | 020 8688 9291 |
| Wed | 15 | NOTTINGHAM Royal Centre | 0115 989 5555 |
| Thu | 16 | NOTTINGHAM Royal Centre | 0115 989 5555 |
| Fri | 17 | NOTTINGHAM Royal Centre | 0115 989 5555 |
| Sat | 18 | NOTTINGHAM Royal Centre | 0115 989 5555 |
| Mon | 20 | LEEDS Grand Opera House | |
| Tue | 21 | LEEDS Grand Opera House | |
| Wed | 22 | LEEDS Grand Opera House | |
| Thu | 23 | LEEDS Grand Opera House | |
| Fri | 24 | LEEDS | 0113 222 6222 |
| Sat | 25 | | 029 2022 4488 |
| Sun | 26 | | 01923 445 000 |
| Tue | 28 | SOUTHEND Cliffs Pavilion | 01702 351 135 |
| Wed | 29 | SOUTHEND Cliffs Pavilion | 01702 351 135 |
| Thu | 30 | SOUTHEND Cliffs Pavilion | 01702 351 135 |
| Fri | 31 | BRIGHTON Brighton Centre | 0870 900 9100 |

**NOVEMBER**

| | | | |
|---|---|---|---|
| Mon | 03 | MANCHESTER Carling Apollo | 0870 401 8000 |
| Tue | 04 | SHEFFIELD City Hall | 0114 2789 789 |
| Wed | 05 | SHEFFIELD City Hall | 0114 2789 789 |
| Thu | 06 | WOLVERHAMPTON Civic Hall | 01902 552 121 |
| Fri | 07 | SUNDERLAND Empire | 0191 514 2517 |
| Sat | 08 | MANCHESTER Carling Apollo | 0870 401 8000 |
| Sun | 09 | IPSWICH Regent Theatre | 01473 433 100 |
| Tue | 11 | NEWCASTLE City Hall | 0191 261 2606 |
| Wed | 12 | BLACKBURN King George's Hall | 01254 582 582 |
| Fri | 14 | LLANDUDNO Theatre for N.Wales | 01492 872 000 |
| Sat | 15 | BLACKPOOL Opera House | 253 292 029 |
| Sun | 16 | OXFORD New Theatre | 0 606 3500 |
| Mon | 17 | OXFORD New | 0 606 3500 |
| Wed | 19 | BIRMINGHAM Academy at the NIA | 0870 607 7500 |
| | | Theatre | 0870 607 7500 |
| | | | 0870 909 4144 |
| | | BIRMINGHAM Academy at the NIA | 0870 909 4144 |
| Tue | 25 | LIVERPOOL Empire Theatre | 0870 606 3536 |
| Wed | 26 | LIVERPOOL Empire Theatre | 0870 606 3536 |
| Thu | 27 | LONDON Carling Apollo Hammersmith | 0870 606 3400 |
| Fri | 28 | LONDON Carling Apollo Hammersmith | 0870 606 3400 |
| Sun | 30 | LONDON Carling Apollo Hammersmith | 0870 606 3400 |

**DECEMBER**

| | | | |
|---|---|---|---|
| Mon | 01 | LEICESTER De Montford Hall | 0116 233 3111 |
| Tue | 02 | LEICESTER De Montford Hall | 0116 233 3111 |
| Fri | 05 | DUBLIN The Point | 1890 925 100 |
| Sat | 06 | BELFAST Odyssey Arena | 028 9073 9074 |
| Mon | 08 | IPSWICH Regent Theatre | 01473 433 100 |
| Tue | 09 | IPSWICH Regent Theatre | 01473 433 100 |
| Wed | 10 | NEWCASTLE City Hall | 0191 261 2606 |
| Thu | 11 | WOLVERHAMPTON Civic Hall | 01902 552 121 |

**National CC hotline: 0870 011 2626**

A McIntyre Entertainment Presentation

7 November 1981    US $1.95 (by air)    30p

ISSN 0028 6362

NEW
MUSICAL
EXPRESS

ADAM LP
POLICE DATES
DANCIN' MASTER
CASSETTE OFFER

THE BEAT
ASSOCIATES
KOOL

CRASS
IN COLOUR
DEFUNKT

LOOKING
THROUGH
KEVIN
TURVEY'S EYES
LAUGHTER WITH MENACES p.25

GARAGELAND VIDEO
LEGAL PIRATE RADIO

EYEBALL CONTACT WITH RICK MAYALL ALIAS KEVIN TURVEY PIC: ANTON CORBIJN

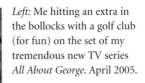

*Left:* Me hitting an extra in the bollocks with a golf club (for fun) on the set of my tremendous new TV series *All About George*. April 2005.

*Left:* Extra clutching his head wound while I have him sacked for being so shit at being hit in the bollocks with a golf club.

*Below:* Extra not giving me drugs hidden inside my mobile in order to get his job back.

*Left:* Me being great.

plenty of women in it. We even put in a couple of lesbian scenes but they wouldn't allow us those either. We were only trying to be all-inclusive (which is one of my middle names). How hypocritical is that?

Anyway, Bottom was great and it ran for five series and everyone loved it. And when Richie and Eddie had done every gag possible in that format, we decided we needed a bigger arena. We felt constrained by rules and regulations. We knew that the BBC was beginning to corrode, to buckle, petrify, rot and lose its vision. Its eyes were beginning to dim and its teeth were beginning to decay. Its skin was beginning to flake and it gave off a rank stench as its bowels gave out and it became flaccid and flatulent. The great Adrian Edmondson and I had invented reality television (which is really all about drinking a lot and squabbling unpleasantly) but now it was time for action. It was time to by-pass cosy middle-class reactionary BBC sensibilities and show our Bottom to the masses.

Chapter ends for maximum effect.

# PRE-AWARD-WINNING GUEST CHAPTER
# WRITTEN BY KEVIN TURVEY

Dear Bloke who's reading this book – unless you'm a lady who's reading this book of course – or maybe someone who doesn't know yet, or both, or neither, or all three, or somebody else completely, or something. But whoever it may concern, or even whoever it may not concern – in case you're someone who's reading this book by accident – in fact anyone at all: Good Evening. I'm Kevin Turvey. That's my name as well. You know how people ask you to put a bit in a book. Well, I don't. This is a first for me. You know that bloke Rik Mayall? Well, I know him as well. So that's quite a thing, isn't it? Because you know him and I know him as well. So that's like two of us. Well, it's not like two of us, actually, it is two of us, except there might be more of us. You know how I don't know you and I don't know how many of you is reading this, or am reading this – that's writing that is – it depends on what I'm trying to say really what words I use. I mean, I do know what words I want to say but I don't know which one's the right one at the moment so when I say "am" or maybe "is" then just imagine, or think, or do something like that with your brain which makes it all right and then I can tell you the rest of the sentence. Okay? So that's what I'm going to do now, right? I'll start with the starting bit again so we all know where we am: you know that bloke Rik Mayall? He's the one who's in them things on the telly. You know the telly? That box in the corner of your room? Well, that's the telly. I mean, you might keep it somewhere else. Like a table. Or somewhere else that's like a table but isn't – a supermarket trolley that's accidentally not stolen and makes the news look like it's in prison or something – but wherever it is that you keep it, you go up to it and you press the button on it, right, and the telly comes on and if it's a programme with Rik Mayall in it, well, that's the bloke I'm talking about. He's the one in those programmes with Rik Mayall in. I think there might be some videos that he's in as well. I know there's video packets because I rent them from the corner shop although there aren't always videos in them. I'm not saying they're crap but all the ones that I rent from my video shop aren't very good cos when you open up the packet, there's nothing in it. Anyway that's Rik Mayall and he's the bloke that I'm talking about. Cos last month, right, I think it was the – no, I'm not going to tell you the date because that's not important. It might have been the 9th of December but it might not, you know, it might have been another date like the 15th of August. That's one that it might not have been or there are loads and loads of other dates that it might not have been but I'm not going to go on about it here cos that would be a waste of time. So that's what I'm not going to do, right? So, anyway, you know that Rik Mayall? He's that bloke on the telly and you know how sometimes you've got to go out and you've got to put on a rain-coat in case it's raining. Well, that's exactly what I didn't do, right? Because it wasn't raining. Well, it might have been raining but it wasn't raining on the place where I came out of my front door because that was the place where it wasn't raining. If you went down the street, it might have been raining but the thing is, I wasn't there. I was back where my house is. So the whole thing about the raincoat is that it's not important because – you know everything that I've just said, right, well forget that because it's not important either, okay? So, there's me right, not here where I am now, I mean there where I was then – and I was just going out of my door and then I was just walking down the street like you do, well, like I do anyway, or like I did that day, whenever it was, and I was walking down the street and I realised that I'd forgotten something, right? I wasn't esactly quite sure what it was that I'd forgotten but I thought better safe than sorry and decided to go back for it. But when I got home I realised that I hadn't forgotten anything, so I didn't really need to go back home at all. So it was a bit crap. Escept that in actualness it wasn't really crap. Because if I hadn't remembered that I hadn't forgotten anything at all then I would have had to spend ages and ages and maybe even more ages in my house looking for something that wasn't there. And that's what would have been crap. Which it wasn't, because it didn't happen, which is a thing that's great isn't it? Although it wasn't really like that at the time, because I didn't think any of those things. I just thought, oh great, and went away again. Anyway, I went out to have a look at the bus stop. Cos someone told me there was a new bus stop. So I went to look at it. It's a great bus stop. It's got a pole and you know, one of those sticky-out things with a picture of a bus on it and the number 144 cos that's the number of the bus that goes past it. They put that there cos if it was another number it'd be wrong and people would be waiting there for the wrong bus and that's crap. That's why they don't do that kind of thing unless it might be an accident. But that's the thing about this bus stop, it's got the right number on it and loads of other things. It's got a shelter, a bit of kerb, a litter bin – I didn't have time to look at what was in the litter bin although I do sometimes, and it had got a little notice on it that said, "Looking for a good time? Try Worcester 3089." I didn't try it cos it must have been put up for someone else. And there was a different sign and it was quite old and a bit falling off and it said Don't Drop Litter and there was a picture of a green bloke with only one arm dropping litter, so you've got to watch out for him. So then I did some waiting for the bus cos you know, it's great. And then I came home again. And that's when it happened. The phone went. It just got up and ran away. Just like that. Actually, that's not true. It's a joke I made up. You know with jokes how they're not true? Well this is one of the ones that isn't as well. So, I picked up the phone – not all of it obviously – just the bit I needed to speak into like, cos if I spoke into the bit I didn't need to speak into then the person on the other end of the line wouldn't be able to hear what I was saying. So I spoke into the phone properly like I always do so you don't have to worry about that bit. I said, "hello," friendly, like they do in movies although thems just actors so it's not true. Well, some of them are not very good at acting so thems not actors, or it might be that someone has wandered into the film and isn't an actor at all. But what I'm trying to tell you is that it was Rik Mayall on the phone and he told me to write a chapter for his book. He said I was the Lord Lucan of light entertainment and I didn't know that. He said he'd found my number off the card I've got up in the grocer's window advertising my hoover part. See, my hoover broke down so I sent off for a new part but by the time the new part arrived I'd mended the old one with some glue. You know, that superglue stuff. It's very good but you don't want to get it in your hair. It's terrible. I don't mean it's crap, superglue – it's great. The getting it in your hair bit is what's crap about it. So anyway, I mended the broken hoover part which meant that I had a spare hoover part so I thought, waste not want not, so I put an advert up for it in the grocer's window. No one's bought the hoover part yet so if anyone would like it, please send a letter to where I live which is the third one along the row behind that bit where the fence is broken by a lamp post with "fuck off" written on it, the one with the green door – number 13 at the moment unless the 3 has fallen off again in which case number 1 unless it's the other way around or maybe someone's fixed it on the wrong way and made it 31 which is what happens if you put a 3 in front of a 1 – so it might be that but if it doesn't have a green door then it really is number 31 so don't post it there cos it's not Kevin Turvey's house, Calcott Drive, Redditch, Worcestershire. Okay? Anyway, none of that's important, unless you want the hoover part in which case it is. So, Rik Mayall is on the phone right. The bloke off the telly. It's 85p by the way, if you want the part – it's the bit that goes at the top of the nozzle that looks a bit like one of them hammerhead sharks except that it's not, you know, cos it's not big enough and anyway it's not a shark is it? But that Rik Mayall bloke says he's doing a book right and would I write a chapter for it and he says, "If you don't I'm going to kick your fucking head in Kevin Turvey. I know where you live and I'm going to torch your house." I don't know why he said that. I've already got a torch. And then he slams the phone down. So I thought, well I'd better make a start, so I made a cup of tea, got my biro and my pad that I use for writing things on and sat down. Then I thought I'd better get a biscuit. And you know that thing with them biscuits you can get where like the top of it – not the biscuits, I mean the top of the packet that they all come in, cos you know how biscuits all come in packets, well they have a bit at the top which they call the top cos that's where it is on the packet, right, and you get this bit of plastic on the top and you get it with your finger and pull it all around the top and pull the top off the packet and that's where all the biscuits are. Well that's what my packet of biscuits had on them. So I got hold of the piece of plastic on my packet of biscuits with my fingers right, just two of them, not five or eight of them or something like that cos that would be the wrong number of fingers right so that's what I didn't do, I just used two of my fingers, not somebody else's, and opened the biscuits up and took one out and put it on one of my plates which I use for carrying biscuits around the place with and walked back to the cupboard which is where I keep my biscuits when I'm not eating them right, and put the packet of biscuits that I've been telling you about just now back into the cupboard and closed the cupboard door right and walked over to my table with the biscuit on my plate for carrying biscuits about the place on and sat down on my chair that I use for sitting down on – it was the yellow one that used to have a rip on it but now it's got some sellotape on as well as the rip – and that's esactly the time that the doorbell started ringing like it does when someone presses on it and that's what was happening. So I thought, that must be someone pressing the doorbell. Which people do with their fingers when they want you to open the door for them. So I lifted up the biscuits in my hand – I think it was my left, but that's not the thrust of the story at the moment – and I went down the hall to the front door at the edge of my house where I keep it and answered it and it was Teresa Kelly. My girlfriend. We're in the love. She said, "Hello Kevin Turvey." I said, "Hello Teresa Kelly." She said, "Is that your biscuit?" And I said, "yeah." And she said, "Can I have it?" And I said, "yeah," and so I gave it to her and she went away. She said, "Thanks Kevin," and I said, "That's all right." Then I said, "I love you Teresa Kelly," but she'd gone by then. So I closed my front door with one of my hands and thought to myself in my head, like you do, I haven't got a biscuit anymore. I can't write a chapter for that Rik Mayall bloke's book if I haven't got a biscuit. I'd better get some biscuits from that bloke in the corner shop who sells biscuits, not the one who rents videos not very well, and that's when I started to think about whether or not I needed to put a raincoat on, a bit like the time I already told you about a bit earlier in the story. You know, about when I didn't know whether to put on a raincoat or not. That's the one. Anyway, that's not important right now cos I suddenly twigged the grate thing that I had them biscuits in the cupboard which was really lucky thinking and I could always get another one whenever I needed. So I got another one nearly quite exactly the same way as I got the last one so I won't tell you about it right now, put it on one of my plates for carrying biscuits around the place cos I've got loads and I started writing the chapter for Rik Mayall with my yellow chair and my biro and my biscuit and everything I needed for the job. It was a hard job but I did it. And that was it. Good evening. Kevin Turvey.

Leonardo Spinetti
Guchi UK Ltd
Bond Street
London W1


7th June 1994

Dear Leonardo,

You remember me, I'm in loads of great sitcoms and
you also had me thrown out of your barbecue last summer.
Sorry about that. How's the wife and the kids and all that
bollocks? You do have a few – kids I mean – you're wopping
away all afternoon you Italians, aren't you? Anyway, I've got
a deal for you. If you give me lots of clothes I'll wander
around in them and people will think, fucking hell! There's
The Rik Mayall in a load of top bollocks Guchi gear! I'd be
like a live Guchi advert masculining up and down Bond
Street every few days. Plus I can go up to people and
say, "Hey you! You look like a shit cake. You ought to be
wearing my kind of clothes." And then walk off like
nothing's happened. I don't care, I'll say it to anyone –
even Kate Moss (that's a yes in case you're wondering).

So what do you think? Fucking good, eh? Have a think
about it and send me some money.

I hope you are well,

Rik Mayall (acter) (fuck, sorry, top acter) (yes I am) (cunt)

# SECRETS I WILL NEVER DIVULGE FROM THE BLOOD-SPATTERED TRENCHES OF THE SHOWBUSINESS FRONT LINE

Let's face it viewer, a nob gag is a nob gag*. Fashions in comedy come and go but the nob gag will always be with us. I remember as though it was yesterday hanging out† with the two Littles – Little Ben-Elton and Little Richard – at the launch of my other great noval, Bachelor Boys: The Young Ones book. Now Little Richard is a great hero of mine and a vast towering leviathan of rock 'n' roll genius and he told me his philosophy of live performance which will stay with me for all of my life.

"Lemme tell you somethin' here, Rik," he said (this really truly happened and you absolutely have to do it in a Little Richard accent to make it work). "You gotta keep the audience waiting before you get on that stage. This gets the audience high. And when the audience cain't get no higher, you git on that stage and you take 'em higher. You take 'em higher and higher til they cain't

---

* A nob gag is a joke about a man's nob. You're with the whirlwind here, don't forget.
† Hanging out is street slang for standing around exchanging pleasantries.

git no higher. And when you git 'em as high as they can go [slight pause], that's when you get off that stage*."

Listening to Little Richard's advice was a momentous moment for me for many reasons. The success of Kevin Turvey opening most of my shows from an offstage mic a good five minutes before I got on was all down to Little Richard. Now that's rock 'n' roll.

Anyway.

I like to think of live stand-up comedy like a flying fortress aeroplane. They call me the Dresden firestorm of light entertainment. Rik "Dresden firestorm of light entertainment" Mayall is my middle name. You swoop down low when you first come on stage and the nose gunner opens up with a couple of tweeters (small "warm up" jokes) like howling violent abuse at the audience, getting into a serious fight with the microphone or completely and utterly losing your temper with everything and committing suicide by throwing yourself into the orchestra pit. And then you open up your bomb bay doors and you hit the audience right between the eyes with your first woofer (the really heavy stuff, a "biggie". Hilarity immediately prevails causing major spinal trauma from laughing-related whiplash injuries and spontaneous bowel eruptions). You might be pretending that you've forgotten to do your flies up and then when you do your flies up, you pretend that you've caught your nob in them. BANG! Off comes the roof and the audience are in the palm of your hand, fouling themselves with mirth and television executives are queuing up at the stage door waving cheque books. All of which reminds me of the night I found myself in a bar. It was not a strip bar – I want to make that perfectly clear. Even though it was in Soho and was called GIRLS

---

* It's very important for this last sentence to have its full effect that Little Richard says it to you quite loudly with his eyeballs stretched wide two inches from yours.

GIRLS GIRLS and the waitresses weren't wearing much – that's because it was a bar for hardcore feminists like me – and a place where women could be respected properly. Right sisters?

Anyway, there I was sitting there just being Rik Mayall, you know, being great and drinking some beer and doing some really good pub chat like I do with some great mates whose names escape me when BLAM! The door came in. Actually, it didn't, it opened. Outwards. Or inwards, it depends where you were standing. Anyway, it was a moody day and the wind was lashing. The door opened and a man in full BBC uniform came in. It was Paul Jackson.

"Hello Rik Mayall."

"Hello Paul Jackson," I acknowledged selflessly. "Hey Paul?" I decided to hit him with a diamond bullet of a line just to show him my love and respect. What you have to remember, viewer, is that Paul Jackson was the Head of the BBC. He had great woofers and tweeters chucked at him all day long by comedy greats and didn't even crack a smile.

"What is it Rik Mayall?"

"Have you let rip? Because I think I can smell one." Paul collapsed to the floor in hysterics spraying the room with bodily fluids like those sprinkler things that people have on their lawns when it's been sunny and the ground is a bit dry.

"Great one Rik Mayall, another one of your cutting edge lavatorial gags."

"Just keeping it real and living the dream, Paul."

"What's all this I hear from Britney about you working for ITV?"

It went quiet. There was a chill. Everyone in the pub looked at me. And then they looked at Paul. And then they looked at me again, and then at Paul again, and it went on like this for a few seconds. It was like one of those spaghetti western moments –

with great music and lots of close ups obviously. Actually, it was better than that. I did one of my moodies and took out a cigarette. I lit it and took a drag broodily – didn't cough – and moved my eyes into the light. It was a good shot. I took a deep breath ready to say something meaningful and plot-laden when BANG! The door came in again – only it was a different door [check pub]. New paragraph.

Here we are. The door came in. It was Andy Harries, the Head of ITV.

"Fucking hell, it's The Rik Mayall, blazing qasar of light entertainment," he said in a northern accent (ITV). "I thought I'd find you here."

"Hello, Andy Harries, trouble at t'mill?" I quipped with a satirical nod to the regional stereotyping of old fashioned comedians.

"Is that Paul Jackson, head of the BBC?" Andy asked.

"It sure is," I breathed like Clint in that other one with the guy with the big horse.

Andy Harries blanched.

"Eeeurgh!" gasped Paul Jackson. "Are you blanching at me? There's only room for one broadcasting behemoth in this adult cocktail porno lounge*. Step outside."

"I don't step outside," said Andy Harries. "I step inside."

"So do I," said Paul Jackson.

"In that case, I step all over the place," said Andy Harries.

"Well you don't step where I step," said Paul Jackson.

"Oh get on with it," I said.

"Okay Rik Mayall," they said as one.

"Look guys, we can do this," I said, "we're the big three here. We can sort this out."

---

* It wasn't really, it was just a normal everyday London pub. I don't know why he said that.

Let me give you some backstory, viewer[*]. Andy Harries wanted me to go to ITV to make a series of dramatic films under the title Rik Mayall Presents . . . You probably know them. They were great. But Paul Jackson wanted me to do more comedy at the BBC. It was shaping up to be another Waterloo.

"Please don't fight," shouted a bottomless barman.

"The Rik Mayall is more than just a white knuckle ride of early evening comedy television formats," said Andy Harries. "He can also tear up[†] serious acting like a freshly napalmed jungle. There are so many more quivers to his arsenal than just his comedy genius. He can act the shit out of a sewer."

"But this guy is the nob gag supremo," retorted Paul Jackson. "You can't tame him with serious films."

"Damn right I can," said Andy Harries. "Just look at the co-stars who have waged brutal bloody wars to work with him. We've got Helena Bonham Carter, Martin Clunes, Saffron Burrows, Phil Daniels, Amanda Donohoe, Lee Evans, Frances Barber, Michael Kitchen, Eleanor Bron, Peter Capaldi, Michael Maloney and Stuart Hall from It's a Knockout[‡]. You guys just can't compete."

Paul was stunned. "I can't do this. This is too big for me. I'm walking."

"Not so fast," said Andy Harries.

"Okay then," said Paul Jackson and slowed down. Then he stopped and turned round. "No, I've changed my mind. This ends here."

---

[*] Backstory is a script writing term which means background information which you will need to know about a story otherwise you won't know what's going on.

[†] Tear up is a light entertainment colloquialism for do something really well. Which I do.

[‡] That's yes no yes no yes no yes no yes no no and don't be ridiculous.

They squared up to each other. Then they triangulated. And then, when it looked as though it was going to turn real hardcore ugly, I thought I had better break it up. But something stopped me.

"Stand back Rik Mayall," it said. "Let them fight. It's better for the whole of the British nation's broadcasting impasse this way."

"Thanks," I said.

"Don't mention it," it said.

"I just did," I said.

"Oh don't start on that one again."

I didn't. We were cool.

But right there in front of me, right then and there, it was like a TV executive slaughter house: blood, teeth, filofaxes, hair pieces, surgical supports, clip boards, boots with zips up the sides, tie clips, cuff links, enormous portable telephones (this was 1992), widely flared ties, white jeans, designer framed glasses that are dark at the top and not at the bottom, button-down shirts, and T-shirts with ironic slogans on the front – for the weekend. Everywhere. A member of the public tried to intervene and suddenly the whole place had erupted. There was a blizzard of objects: Sony Walkmans (with cassettes), Wayne's World videos, Madonna Sex Books, Take That albums, Big Breakfast calendars, Femidoms, You've Been Tango'ed adverts, Los Angeles riots and lots and lots of tissues.

Then, suddenly, CRASH! The door was caved in in an explosion of splinters and a vast shadow filled the frame. It was Robbie Coltrane. (Handy hint: If you ever get into a game of "my showbiz mates are harder than your showbiz mates" then you will always win if you say that Robbie Coltrane is your showbiz mate. But only say this if he genuinely is your showbiz mate because if he isn't and he finds out, he'll have you alive. I saw him eat a table once.) The fighting ceased in the blink of an eye. Everyone returned to their seats and pretended that nothing had happened as Robbie strode across the room like a colossus and ordered himself a bottle of whisky.

"Hello Robbie Coltrane," said I.

"Hello Rik Mayall," said Robbie (in a Scottish accent obviously). Then he picked me up affectionately and sat me on his shoulder. "Now then," he said, "what's the problem, big man?"

"Top telly executives are fighting over me again. What can I do?"

"It's tough a one, Rik, but you've got to follow your heart. They've been fighting over me too. But I've made a decision – I'm going to ITV to do Cracker. You should do the same."

"Surely they wouldn't want the two of us to play the part, Rob."

"No, I mean, you should go to ITV, it's where all the top guys are going now."

"Nice one Rob, I think you're right. It's time I spread my talent far and wide."

"Not a problem wee Richie."

"Thanks very much Robbie, although it's a bit scary up here on your shoulder, can you put me down now?" And he sat me kindly on his favourite ashtray.

"Don't mention it," said Robbie as he stubbed out his Guards cigarette on my head, ate the empty whisky bottle and left.

And so it was. We were both now working for the great ITV, Robbie making Cracker and me making Rik Mayall Presents. This had nothing to do with the fact that ITV pays sixteen times more money than the BBC.

Rik Mayall Presents was a series of six movies. Movies is what you go and see when you go and see telly at the cinema. It's like telly only bigger. Only what was good about doing them on ITV was that they were on the telly (the one at home) and my viewers could go to the toilet during the commercial breaks. Consideration is my middle name. They were huge artistic successes that would have conquered America if they had been released on the telly at cinemas there, but hey, I can't do everything can I? I was too busy attending all those award ceremonies and prize receivings, accepting all the countless tropheys, awards, cups, plaque, medals, bar bills, maybe that should have been plaques back there, film offers and plaudits (which I do know how to spell. See "unexplained death of English teacher" section of whichever chapter it's in*.)

---

* His death was not my fault. I wasn't there. So don't even suggest that it was me who held his head under the – never mind. I've got a cast iron alibi. I was with Debbie Kirkpatrick and she's dead anyway – and I had nothing to do with that either so I am beyond recrimination. And I can spell that as well. Subject closed. So don't go back to that chapter. My lawyers are watching. And my people. And these are extreme people, not any old people. They are full on, take no prisoners people – don't fuck people I like to call them – so don't mess. This does not mean foul yourelf. Unless you have in which case it does and I respect you for it. Go and get yourself cleaned up. Foul person.

# THE GREAT COVENT GARDEN BLOODBATH

It was a Tuesday afternoon. I remember it so well. I was sitting in my exclusive private members' club in Soho with a young actress. You know her name and you know her face but let's call her X for legal reasons. She won't mind me saying that because you'll never guess. So there I was in my Soho Club and all was well in my world. It was 1988 and I had just received showers of critical acclaim for the Bad News album, the first New Statesman series, my sold out tour of Australia with Little Ben-Elton, and feature films like Eat The Rich, Strike, More Bad News, Mr Jolly Lives Next Door, and my genre-displacing management training video, Managing Problem People. But the icing on the cake was my appearance in The Common Pursuit at the Phoenix Theatre in the heart of London's West End, which is like a second home to me. Actually, I've already got a second home, better make that my third home. It was a wonderful play by my great friend Simon Gray – who is now Lord Gray. Who is big mates with Harold

Pinter. And anyone who is big mates with Harold     Pinter* is all right with me. If you're

---

* Slightly smaller pause there.

reading this Simon your Lordship – big love and respect. My fellow cast members were all great and I was very happy. Johnny Sessions was in it (who I have not had sex with), John "Hello I'm John Gordon Sinclair" Gordon Sinclair (no), Paul Mooney (no), Sarah Berger (yes) and my old friend Stephen Fry (see following page – just read the bit in between first). Another great thing about the play was that I got to smoke. I've always enjoyed smoking on stage, that's why I've never done much Shakespeare.

The Common Pursuit is all about some Cambridge intellectual types who write a student magazine called The Common Pursuit. The rest of the cast was good but I ripped the face off the place – probably because I was more intelligent than the others. And it was because I was such a sensitive and brilliant acter that Lord Simon wanted me for another of his great plays.

Fast forward to 1995 and there I am at the Albery Theatre in Cell Mates with Stephen Fry. Unfortunately, when the play opened (which means when we had practised it a bit and then the critics (who I love) were invited to come and drink some free booze and write things about us) Stephen got some bad reviews. Now, I want to say here and now in my book that it's not Stephen's fault that he's not as good at acting as I am and I would never want to rape over old ground but here are some of those reviews: "Stephen Fry is shit; Rik Mayall is a much better acter than him." Daily Telegraph. "Fucking hell, I wish both parts were played by Rik Mayall because he's much better than Stephen Fry." The Times. "I've never seen such a shit performance as Stephen Fry's in all my life. But Rik Mayall is great." The Spectator.

I couldn't understand what was wrong. Maybe it was because Stephen wasn't with his usual comedy partner, Huge Lorry, or maybe it was because he felt intimidated by my great performance but, whatever it was, Stephen was upset and unhappy. So, I went to comfort him and that's when a thing happened. But unfortunately,

I'm not allowed to speak about it. And after it had happened, Stephen told me that he was pregnant and would have to leave immediately and I wasn't to tell a soul for at least ten years and preferably, not ever.

Now, you know me, viewer, I am always very considerate of my fellow celebrities' private lives and I'm not saying that Stephen ran away to Belgium because he was pregnant with our love child. There, you heard me not saying it just there. And if you didn't quite catch me not saying it, then go back and read it again and remember that I'm not saying it. Anyway, he did fuck off to Belgium and Lord Simon was so upset he fucked off to the Caribbean leaving me all on my own in the heart of London's West End – alone in the trench with the great Simon Ward (no) who took over from Stephen Fry. It was a tough gig[*] especially because I knew that the show was not shit. Every night when I was on stage doing one of my great Irish monologues in my terrific Irish brogues that I'm so good at I kept thinking to myself "this is not shit" in those very words but it still closed and absolutely no one got paid. Not even my agent, Heimi, and that's unheard of.

And it's just a coincidence that I saw a bank and happened to have a gun in my hand that day in Covent Garden. It was all a terrible misunderstanding and I'm going to take this opportunity to set the record straight. You see, the thing is, I could see a load of armed robbers heading towards the bank I was standing next to. So I ran inside the bank and said, "Stick your hands up and put all the money in here," because I happened to have a large canvas sack with me and I wanted to keep all the money safe so that the armed robbers couldn't steal it and I could give it all back to the bank. I told everyone to get on the ground and those that couldn't get down quickly enough, I shot so that they wouldn't be shot by

---

[*] This is showbusiness for it was a difficult thing to have to do.

182

the armed robbers who were fast approaching the bank now. It was philanthropy [check everything]. Once I'd got all the money, I thought it best to put it in my sack and run away screaming, "Nobody moves motherfuckers!" and that's when I accidentally kicked the bank manager in the face a couple of times and stamped on his head until he was unconscious. And when I got outside the bank, they were only warning shots that I fired at the police to let them know that the real bank robbers were getting away and I was going to chase after them. So the point is that when I got mistakenly arrested at gunpoint and was rammed face down in the gutter with policemen spitting at me and putting those nasty plasticy handcuff things on me, I selflessly gave my name to them, well, shouted it, as Stephen Fry, because it's nice to give your showbusiness chums a mention when you get the chance. But it got me such a serious three hour kicking that I won't be giving his name again. Although he might have enjoyed the enthusiastic round-the-back truncheon business.

So you see, the whole thing is a terrific misunderstanding which is so rare for the Metropolitan Police who I think are great. Especially as it wasn't me. In fact, I wasn't there. Ever. I've never been to Covent Garden in my life. And fuck off if you don't believe me. Oh I've had enough of this.

Harvey Winestain
Mirrormax Films
5th Avenue
New York
New York
U.S.A.


January 2nd 1995

Dear Harv,

I don't fuck about – you know that. I'll come straight to the point. We're both men of the world. We're big men, both culturally and in your case, for real (no offence you fat cunt – we're the kind of guys who like to rip the shit out of each other aren't we?). So we don't need to pussy feet around here – let's just talk plainly and frankly like two big epoch-sculpturing overlords of the global entertainment industry which is what we are. I know we've both been admiring each other's work for some time now but I thought I'd take the bull by the horn and make the big gesture here to break the ice. What I want you to know Harv is that there is room in the film-movie-making industry for both of us. I want you to think of this letter as the well-washed hand of friendship. There is no point the two of us being giants in our respective areas of genius when we could join forces and advance man's artistic endeavours in one vast triple-jump-like leap forward. I think both of us know that together, we are capable of reaching a new milestone in the history of human endeavour. So that's what I think we should do. Right now.

What I'm thinking here (and what I've been brain-tornadoing for weeks now) is a film that will totally blow the critics away but also give the punters the raging horn too. Pulp Fiction was good, I'll give you that. In fact, you might want to get Quentin on the phone and read this bit of the letter to him out loud because it concerns him too. You see, the thing is Harv, I've got this film idea and it's hot. In fact the word hot doesn't do it justice. It's totally on fire like a fireball careering towards earth like a meteorite – in fact it's a mother of a meteorite, Harv, and it's heading straight at you so you'd better duck or this baby'll smash you right in the face big time.

Hi Quentin if you're there, love your work (you have called him haven't you, Harv?). Now what was good in Pulp Fiction was how like you took an old gangster movie kind of film and messed about with it and made it really happening and edge cutting with cool talking about cheeseburgers and foot massages. So what I propose with my blockbuster-in-the-making is that we take another old type of film like maybe a disaster film and play around with that too. It's got green light written all over it already has it not. Obviously it hasn't literally but don't worry Harv, you're in safe hands here.

Now you and me both know that it's only the real men that survive in the blood-spattered abattoir that is modern-day film-moviemaking these days and interlectual fraud can be a big crime problem. So, in case someone has opened this letter before it's got to you Harv, I just want to say to them that they shouldn't even think about trying to steal my film idea because I'm going to the Photo-Me booth outside Ladbroke Grove Tube station right now to have a photograph taken of me holding up this letter in one hand with a copy of today's newspaper in the other to prove that it's mine. Got that? Job done. You really don't want to fuck with me because I'm pretty hard and Harvey Winestain who this letter is addressed to is a bit gangster-like himself and would probably have you dumped in the river in a pair of concrete wellies if you fucked him. That's gangster terminology and not what you think it is although I've got nothing against gay movies although they haven't got any birds in them and they're all shit. Not that I've seen any. Walk away. Like a hard guy. Which I am. Not that I've got a stiffy or anything because I've just said gay because I haven't. Although I could have if I wanted. I can get a stiffy whenever I want. Ask anyone. Except Beatrice Campbell. She's dead now. Not that I had anything to do with it. Anyway, it's a metaphor. So nothing actually happened. Oh bollocks to all this anyway. How did this happen? Oh fuck everything. Give me a new paragraph.

Okay Harv, so now we've got the threats to potential ideas thieves out of the way, let's press on. We've got a lot of ground to cover and you look like you tire easily, fat boy. No you don't. Fuck! I'm typing too fast. Don't read that last bit Harv. I dig you and you're thin. All right Quentin? Fine. No – cool, or some word like that. Shoulders back, we're going in . . .

**TITLE: NAME OF RIK MAYALL'S GREAT NEW FILM**
(This has got to be good, Harv – V. imp)
By The Rik Mayall

(getting wet yet?)

IMAGINE THE SCENE . . .

*A Cinema. Audience. Popcorn. Everyone looking at curtains (ooer obviously). Check no one is looking. Open flies. Get nob out. Stick it through hole in bottom of medium-sized packet of popcorn. Nudge bird (not mate. And especially not mate's bird), breath to bird, "Would you like to have a piece of my popcorn, bird/love (optional)?" Bird takes firm grip. Bird thinks it's large piece of popcorn, starts pulling on it. Result. Nice work Thomas Edison. Then curtains open (ooer obviously again).*

*Film starts. Audience of ordinaries sit silently agape, transformed into mindless receivers of meaningless information in exchange for their cash. The sting is done. We're on.*

*It's a big sexy fuck off American airport. Cool, happening and wow! Fuck me blind, here comes a tall good looking stranger (27) striding through the duty free with a strong hairline and all his own teeth. It's THE RIK MAYALL!*

*Bird's grip on todger suddenly relaxes and she completely loses interest. But no problem, would actually rather watch this great film than get wristed off by bird.*

*The Rik is actering the edge-menacing, confident, currently available leading hard man, RIP STUFF. This is a blinder of a movie already. Look, Rip Stuff's waiting for a ticket in the ticket queue. And there are lots of ordinary people wandering around meaninglessly buying tickets and duty-free things and being ordinary.*

*Rip broods his way through baggage control and waits for a while in a transit lounge. Maybe reads a book or something. (But not a complicated one, right, in case he alienates his audience. Cinema audiences are all usually iliterate don't forget.)*

*This is where it starts to get good because what happens is that Rip gets onto a plane with a load of gangsters. In fact, only him and the pilot (someone not much but noticeably older than Rik and carrying a little too much weight) and the air hostess (Uma Thermon) are not gangsters.*

*For the next hour or so, there will be lots of snappy dialogue between all the gangsters you know, like they always do in films and you know, they do stuff and talk about loads of stuff like pop music and chicks they fancy and then harder more scary things like shooting people in the face. And then, irony of ironies in the bollocks, one of them does end up accidentally shooting the pilot in the face when he gets caught in the crossfire in a heated argument on his way to the toilet. This really hots things up Harv, I thought of this myself, because Rip Stuff has to take the controls and fly the plane. I forgot to mention earlier on that Rip has a basic knowledge of flying planes because he was in the R.A.F. Cadets at school. So I had thought of that. This is also when Uma Thermon starts getting really turned on by Rip's brooding good looks and plane driving but he doesn't give her one just yet because he's got to fly the plane. Then lots of other really good stuff happens before Rip has to hand over the controls to Uma while he goes back to tell off all the gangsters who have now all really fallen out extremely big time and are standing there all of them pointing their guns at each other whilst doing really snappy dialogue. One of them might say something like, "Don't fuck with me you fucking fuck, or I'll stick my gun up your fucking trousers and blow your brains out of your fucking eyeballs, got it?" and things like that. And another one of them does some random unconnected swearing, and all of it is totally natural and film-like. But Rip is as cool as ice and tells them just to ruddy well shut up and stop making such a frightful racket whilst he's trying to drive the plane. This is the most God-awful shitter though cos the gangsters don't like being told off and they don't give a toss so they throw Rip out of the plane. But get this, Rip doesn't die! That's right! And you can hear the audience going, "Fucking blimey mates, I was going to go home then, but now I won't, I'm going to continue to be interested in this film now. What clever film makers, they really foxed me with that one." That's good film writing that is, Harv. I don't miss a truck. You see, because, what Rip does is that he suddenly lands on a hot air balloon which just happens to be flying past (underneath obviously) and survives by using his great free-falling technique (which I'm good at). But it's a motherfucker! (That's Oedipal,*

*Harv) because the hot air balloon is full of insurgents (we could make out that this is somewhere in the middle east but let's not go there, it's ghastly). And one of the insurgents has a rocket launcher hidden inside the balloon's tidy box which Rip wrestles off him, spins round and fires broodily (or broodingly, or maybe broodishly – oh fuck this, check that, oh you can't, this is a letter, OH CUNTS!, (ignore that bit Harv)) at the aeroplane but making sure just to nick the wing rather than blowing it up completely because we've still got Uma Thermon inside, remember, and her and Rip are still powerfully in love and still haven't had it off yet.*

*So, now it's had its wings nicked, the plane goes neeeeeeeeeeeooooooooeeeiiiiiiieeeeeeeeaaaaaaarrrrrrgghhfuc- kingcrash into the desert but luckily not far from where Rip is being great in the hot air balloon. So quickly, Rip makes friends with the insurgents who are actually really nice guys and good at insurging and disapprove of gangsters (which is quite clever Herv because it means that all the cinemas showing our feature film won't get car-bombed by insurgents or their relatives). So, then the gangsters all fire their guns at Rip when they see him in his balloon, and Rip and his new insurging chums land the balloon and attack the gangsters and have the greatest desert battle that's ever been seen in the cinemas including that one with that bloke, what's-his-name, you know, the one who used to drink too much. And the audience all go crikey at the amazingness of the film,*
 *(or maybe, motherfucking crikey depending on which country they're in because this is an international smash hit, don't forget). We're talking ultra-violent, Harv. Are*

*you still there Quent? We're talking bullets flying
everywhere and blood and bits of flesh and bones all
over the place and swearing and Uma Thermon in just
her pants because her clothes were all ripped off when
the plane crashed. There will be loads of slow motion
shots of bullets actually going straight through the
gangsters' heads with their teeth and eyeballs exploding
out of them in all directions. It will be a whole new bench
marker in violent stuff generally and at the end, though
wounded and dripping blood, Rip will beat the gangsters
and end up doing some top drawer having it off with
Uma. THE END. So that's it audience – get your coats,
wipe the popcorn and love juice off your cardigans and
fuck off out of the cinema happily making room for a
whole other load of completely innocent audience
people who won't know what the fuck is going to
happen to them. Actually that's a good point, maybe
there should be a big sign at the end of the film saying,
"Don't you fucking dare tell anyone what you have just
seen because it'll give the plot away and fuck everything
up. So just don't, okay? We know where you live and
stuff like that so just fucking don't. We're serieos people."*

So Harv and Quent – what do you reckon? Personally, I
think it's got the lot: sex, violence, snappy dialogue, lots
of swearing and I haven't even mentioned the soundtrack.
You know I don't need to do that because, as you know,
I'm <u>so</u> in with THE MAN. That's right, THE MAN. I don't
even need to tell you that I, Rik Mayall, am very very
very tight with Cliff and that's not a reference to holes.
That's the sort of thing that happening dudes say about
being friends with somebody – you do know what I'm

talking about don't you Quent? Good. THE MAN has spoken. About THE other MAN. Or maybe the other way round – or not, or whatever, I don't care, I'm a high planes drifter who lives on the hedge.

So, you get us the money Harv, and Quent, why don't you look into casting? (But keep it cool though Quent. Hey, I don't need to tell you what. You're THE MAN. Oh no you're not, that's someone else. Well, maybe you're ANOTHER MAN. I don't know. Maybe you're SOMEBODY ELSE. There's a lot of men around in capital letters, aren't there? It doesn't matter GUYS, we know who everybody is because we're cool. No, WE'RE cool. Shit! No, we'RE cool. Fuck! No, no, no! WE're cool. That's the one. Next paragraph.)

I'll drop Uma a line separately just to break the ice. Do you know if she's seeing anyone at the moment? Actually, it doesn't matter really because my on-set chemistry can tame a vicious furious hurtling lesbian rhino, especially under the hot lights. So I think Uma's and my rapport is as good as nailed to the floor with "fuck me" written on it in peuce spray paint.

Anyroadup, see you soon. I hope you are well.

Here's to the Palm Door,

Rik.
x x

# MAVIS WENT TO MOSCOW

Iron curtains, ladies' curtains, you name them, I've got behind them and parted them. Rik "he's quite good at parting curtains" Mayall as I am often referred to by birds. I have tentacles everywhere. My cock looks like an octopus. No, get rid of that. It doesn't work*. Anyway, what I wanted to tell you about, viewer, was the axis-tilting landmark moment in international cinema, Bring Me the Head of Mavis Davis, in which I starred as Marty Starr alongside Jane Horrocks (fabulous actress, yes) who played Mavis. Two important things that you need to know about this film Mavis Davis, viewer, is that firstly, I looked a lot like Bruce Willis in it. People were often stopping me in the street and saying, "Hey Bruce Willis, love your work, did you know that you look a lot like Rik Mayall?" And the second important thing is that it defined the direction of British pop music for the next decade. It was more than just a film. It was a cultural revolution in its own

---

* Note to self: Maybe save great house-storming woofers like this that don't quite work and have a book of outtakes. Maybe stake out role as Dennis Nordern of gags that didn't quite work properly. No, fuck off Rik, that's a shit idea. All right you fat has-been, keep your trousers on. Euurgh – you're talking to yourself now aren't you, loony? No I'm not. You are. No I'm not, I'm not here. Yes you are. You're the loony. Oh, go and have another ride on     your quad bike, arse head.

right. I have never met anyone who hasn't seen Mavis Davis. The world is divided into two camps, those who have seen Mavis Davis and those who haven't.

I was so good at acting my part of Marty Starr in the film that I was nominated for Best Acter at the San Remo film festival and won! Yes, that's right, I fucking won. And then I was nominated for Best Acter at the Moscow Film Festival. Yes! I fucking was. Really. Me! Nominated for Best Acter at the Moscow Film Festival. Maybe this was some sort of destiny? Maybe Drop Dead Fred had conquered the west and now Mavis Davis would conquer the east. Perhaps it was my calling to help the communists. Morally, spiritually, emotionally, and above all, showbusily. Now was the time. The Eastern Block needed an icon. And that's true. You know me, I don't fuck about when I write books. As I jetted off to Russia, I felt very Bob Geldof-like, only with better hair and singing voice (and I'm better friends with Tony B than he is).

Now, you know me, viewer, I've never had a drink problem. That's never, okay? I'm Rik Mayall. Now, you need to understand that vodka is a complicated drink because it looks a lot like water and you can drink a whole pint of it without realising. Plus it does take five minutes or so to set in and I had had about five pints that breakfast because I was so thirsty and in a hurry to get to an important social function. That's why I was pissed for the entire day. Anyway, I turned up at this enormous 15,000 seater cinema in Moscow for the film festival and I had to make a speech in front of hordes and hordes of people. I don't know why. I can't actually remember what the speech was meant to be about. I can't remember very much at all about that period but I can remember that it didn't go very well. I'd written down what I was going to say on a piece of paper and when I got on stage, I couldn't find the piece of paper. I think I might have eaten it or something. So, I just did some talking, like you do. Well, I do, or did that day in Moscow on stage. And when I was finished I encouraged the audience to clap. 15,000 of them. But they didn't. Not one of them. 15,000 people not clapping at the end of a ten minute "amusing and entertaining" speech which they hadn't laughed at once is a bit of a bummer for a wild cat of comedy. And then, when I tried to leave the stage I went the wrong way and fell off it. Then some bird came up to me and escorted me to my seat which I mistook for a hotel room and tried to get it on with her which she encouraged me not to do because there were 15,000 people there and they were all watching us on cameras. I can't remember her name. It might have been Ivan but basically she was a bird. Very nice too. Whatever her name was. I remember her black dress which was very difficult to get off and when I kept trying to get it off, she kept hitting me. And she was extremely good at hitting as well. And accurate.

Anyway, I had to sit through loads of speeches and bits of films, none of which had me in them so it was all a bit pointless, and then suddenly, there was me – Rik Mayall – you know, and there I am on the enormous mile-wide Russian telly on the wall. And someone was reading out the winner of the Golden Kalashnikov or whatever it was, and I knew for a certainty that I'd won it! So I stood up and started running towards the stage, waving at everybody (because it's a big honour, winning). And some bloke or bird – I can't remember – said, "And the winner is . . ." (in Russian, obviously), "Robert D*. Niro." But because I was quite drunk, I couldn't stop running. And there's Bobby D getting up to accept his prize, and there's me heading towards the stage as well, thinking, "Shit! I've made a fool of myself." But luckily, I fell over and smashed my face on the floor quite badly which drew stares from a couple of thousand of the Russians nearby who were

---

* It's probably David.

clearly thinking, "This man is a complete arsehole," in Russian, obviously (again). That's when I stood up and shouted, "I'm not Robert D. Niro, I'm Rik Mayall and I'm going to the toilet."

Nobody seemed to get the joke.

So then I shouted, "It's a gag! I don't think I've won the prize, I'm just going for a piss!" Nobody laughed. So I continued, "What's so not funny about an Englishman going for a piss?" Still nobody laughed. I even got my cock out but even that didn't work! So I went back to my seat and sat down and blushed like a beetroot. Although beetroots can't blush but I can't think of anything better to say for the time being. Anyway, it was while I was blushing that I felt a soggy warmth down my leg and realised that I should have gone to the toilet all along and I had only gone and pissed myself. And that does not mean laughing.

So, there I was, sitting there with piss down my legs with fifteen thousand Russians and Robert D. Niro thinking that I'm a twat, and I'm thinking, well, at least things can't get any worse than this. And then they did. Suddenly I buckled forward and vomited into my lap. I'll ask you this one question: how many stars that you can think of have made total arses of themselves at award ceremonies and then pissed and vomited over themselves? I'll leave it hanging there. I think I've made my point. Actually, it reminds me of another story – oh sorry, wrong chapter.

Anyway, Mavis Davis was a big film. It was important. And apart from anything else, it was good. Now, good is a four letter word that we use in the acting world. Especially I. I don't mean there is an I in good – there are two "O"s as everyone knows. They look like a couple of jugs right in the middle of a really heavyweight word. And if you take out one of the jugs, you've got God (or a bird with a knocker hanging out – big gag in the seventies that, kids) and if you add one in you've got God with two tits. And they're big ones and they're pointing straight atchya. Nuff said. Period. Sorry. (Why do Americans have to be so foul at the end of sentences?)

The thing is, all that "O" stuff isn't really important. Unless you're God. Or a bird with good "double O" jugs. What is really important is learning words and getting into bed with ideas. Then getting out of bed and straight into wardrobe, which is what we call the place where you put your clothes on in films. But I am also very good – look at the jugs on that word – at getting into wardrobes when husbands return home unexpectedly. But I don't want to get into that at the moment – the topic not the wardrobe – although I could if you wanted me to but it would break the flow of my proase so I won't. There are other places for everything. And this is one of them.

What I'm really trying to say to you is that when you go into wardrobe when you're making a film, it's important that you get yourself a good wardrobe bird because you get a lot of good zip action in movies. Top flight wardrobe action is essential in my game. You've got to get your kit off while your wardrobe bird gets your kit on. And if you're good, you'll be able to get it on with the wardrobe bird whilst she's getting yours off. These are complicated words but you need to know them. So, you get into wardrobe, get it on with the wardrobe bird while she's getting it on while she's getting it off, then you get 'em back on, get out, get down, give it some, throw it down, get out, get back in again, get 'em off, get it on with her again (if you're quick), get out, go home. This is top class showbiz talk for changing your clothes. But not always though. Actually, it's really complicated this, because when you're doing nudey porno, costume is a whole different ball game. Oh well fucking bollocks then! You may as well forget all the above and forget you ever read it. Shit, shit, FUCKING SHIT!!! Oh just go and see some other bit of fucking writing somewhere else. Go on. Forget everything. I'm going to have a lie down.

## **MEMO**

TO: Ursula Goodson
Publisher-in-chief, Global Magazines Ltd

FROM: The Rik Mayall
Showbusiness Behemoth

RE: JIZZ MAGAZINE

12$^{th}$ July 1997

Dear Ursula,

You know me, I'm in loads of great sitcoms and stuff. In a
multi-tasking kind of modern media way, I've now got a
great idea for a new magazine. I've called a few times to
tell you all about it but your assistant keeps telling me
that you're in a meeting or you've gone home for the day.
Maybe she doesn't believe it's me. Her loss. (Sounds like
hair loss – I won't make a joke – I could – because I'm
great – like balding saggy flappy-titted witch – but I won't
– I'm not like that – I'm a feminist – always have been.
But enough about me.) Anyway, what I've got in mind is
a hybrid of two different types of magazines. Now
everyone knows that porn mags are very popular
especially with blokes and broad minded birds; and
women's magazines are popular with women who don't
like porn mags. So after lots of brainstorming and lateral
thinkage, I've come up with a revolutionary concept.

You don't suffer from stress incontinence do you Ursula? I know a lot of women your age do and if you do then might I suggest that you put a pad down your pants before you read this next bit. Ready? Okay, here it comes. How about a magazine, called JIZZ! both for men who like porn and for women who don't? That way you're going to have twice as many people reading it and it'll definitely become a best sellar.

Ouch! What's that noise? Sounds to me like rival magazine publishers blowing their brains out because they didn't get the Rik Mayall magazine idea first. But you did, Urse. How it works is this: on one page you have a picture of some bird or other wearing nothing but a thin drizzle of baby oil and maybe a bit of string or something, right? And on the opposite page you can have something that birds are interested in. You know, a bit of something or other or whatever, you know, so do you see how this works Urse? It's such a happening take-it-to-the-bridge media concept (this is guys talk Urse that is rockin' all the way to the singles bar). So all that it needs to kiss hello to a cultural Nagasaki (no offence) is to have me in charge. So long as I have plenty of assistants (subject to my approval) I think I could probably edit the magazine at the same time as continuing with all my television, film, stage and voice-over work. I mean, how hard can it be? I would also want a really top office in your building where I can approve all the "copy" (remember your Media Studies A-level, Urse?) and brainsteam project ideas with my creative team (also subject to my approval).

Yeah and check this too, Urse, this could give a
Yorkshireman the horn, because as a free introductory
offer with the first issue, we could do a charity calendar.
It's just so now. And people will think we're being really
nice to poor people and we'll make a killing. I've thought
about the birds we should have on it and here's the list.
As you can see here Urse, there's something for everyone.

| | |
|---|---|
| January: | Siân Lloyd |
| February: | Siân Lloyd again |
| March: | Jane Mansfield (outrageous head) |
| April: | Siân Lloyd eating a boiled egg in the nude (Easter) |
| May: | Condoleeza Rice. Bush optional |
| June: | Dot Common in an incontinence thong (one for the grandads there) |
| July: | Siân Lloyd looking fabulously alluring again with something Welsh |
| August: | Siân Lloyd outside a bank in the nude (August Bank Holiday) |
| September: | Jenny Bond with a strap on |
| October: | Siân Lloyd not wearing a witch's costume (Halloween) |
| November: | Siân Lloyd holding a box of matches provocatively, looking fabulous (bonfire night) |
| December: | Siân Lloyd locked in a hotel bedroom with Rik for three weeks and the photographer can't get in (but he has to pay the bill) |

So, what do you reckon Urse? Are we in bed together on
this one? I mean that purely in a strictly trousers on,

seriously sensible, media kind of way and imply nothing untoward as regards any potential face to face meetings we might have where you might find yourself lonely for male company. I know that in your job people like yourself do get lonely so maybe we could take ourselves off to a hotel for a night (perhaps on company expenses or something) and go via a sex shop and stock up on some romantic love things like vibrators and handcuffs and a couple of copies of Razzle in case we're looking for imaginative love ideas. So, Urse baby, if that thought interests you, then get in touch, although obviously I ought to see a photograph of you first – you might be a dog. I mean, you can't be too careful, can you?

So, it's love and business now, Ursey Wursey – our secret – and when it comes to business, I've got the Midas Touch, there's no two ways about it. So, please forward something for me to sign and don't think you can make out that you never saw this letter and then go ahead and publish Jizz Magazine and cut me out of the deal because I know some serious people – people you wouldn't want calling round at your house late at night – if you get my drift, and I think you do. We understand each other don't we, Urse?

Anyway, keep up the good work. Oh, and I love you and all that.

I hope you are well.

The Rik Mayall.

# GOING DOWN ON THE* BILL†

There used to be a shit programme on the telly called The Bill. And I was in it once. I know you don't believe me but it's true. I can do everything. And there's no point doing everything if you can't be great. And I am great. So that's why I did it. And now I have done it, I'm going to tell you about it and include it in my great book. Not least because working with me was probably one of the most extraordinary experiences of the cast and crew's lives. It was an important social event. It was a phenomerama actually. Which means it was a biggie. And that's not toilet stuff.

Picture the year, 1997, got it in one. It had been a busy year. I'd been working like a Japanese prisoner of war. Which means that I was busy, not thin and nearly dead. Although I was quite slim. I still am. Anyway, I'd just done Jack and the Beanstalk on Jackanory along with now iconic voice overs for Beatrix Potter's

---

* Note to printer: please ensure that you print the word "the" otherwise it'll look like I'm going down on a bloke called Bill and as you may or may not be aware, "going down" on someone means that you put their toilet equipment in your mouth. That I do not do. Although I don't have a problem with people who do do. I've always been a radical socialist feminist icon.
† I'm almost certain that's what it's called. It's the one with all the policemen in it.

classic revenge thriller The Tale of Two Bad Mice and Johnny Town Mouse and my award-blizzarding portrayal of Toad in Wind in the Willows with the quite talented Michael Gambon (no), Michael Palin was ratty (although he and I got on very well) and that little bloke with the glasses was in it as well, you know him, oh yes, Alan Bennett (yes). I had entered the cyber age with my genre-reversing voice-over as Dick Tate in the classic video game Double Trouble, plus of course, the landmark stand out feature movie films, Bring Me the Head of Mavis Davis, and the great, Remember Me? alongside Imelda Staunton (yes), Robert Lindsay (nearly), Natalie Walter (yes), Brenda Blethyn (of course), James Fleet (no) and Emily Bruni (absolutely not) who I would work with again on Believe Nothing (I've just told you, haven't I – the very accusation is an outrage in itself. I never even met lovely Emily.) That's not to mention the rolling live extravaganza, Bottom 3: Hooligan's Island which circumnavigated the British Isles in a whirlwind of packed houses, convulsing audiences, hilarious good times and sacks full of cash – all of which we gave away to charity. And I can prove that [maybe delete this]. But what stands out for me in 1997 above all else is my appearance on The Bill. I'm not saying that it stands out because it was a good experience, far from it, it was a hard experience, but hard things call for hard guys and I was hard – and I still am.

The character I portrayed and realised in The Bill was called Patrick Massie. He was Irish. So I decided to carry out extensive research around the pubs of Kilburn where I lived incognito as an Irishman for three and a half hours, moulding a fully realised Irish sensibility. But when I did my new axent on the producers at The Bill, they said they'd much rather have me do the character as an Irishman. Vicious, spiteful bastards. This led to much more researching in pubs – not just in Kilburn but anywhere really. The researching was taking over my life. Quite regularly I would awake in the morning in a small lagoon of my own piss and vomit and I would dry myself off with a hairdryer before heading out again to the pub for more furious researching. I was enriching my character in order to heighten the drama and make my part fully four dimensional.

In the script, it stated that at the end of the episode with my line in, I was to stand on the roof of a high building and make out that I was going to jump, but in the end not jump. That was very important – the not jumping part – because there was no safety net. I was supposed to make it look like I was about to jump and then they would do some clever special effect to make it look like I'd jumped when actually I was still standing there on the roof. You get the general idea. But the problem was that I'd been getting into character all afternoon in a pub round the corner and it was Bonfire Night. There were fireworks going off everywhere. I was a bit unsteady on my feet as was essential for my character and just at the bit when I was supposed to make it look like I was going to jump and then not actually jump, I was a bit too immersed in my role and I jumped. And they filmed it live and put it in the programme. What they didn't film and put in the show was that I landed on the back of a passing container lorry and by the time I came to, I had been delivered to Durham Tesco's. That's showbiz. Or rather it isn't. It's a screaming abortion of a fuck up that I wish I'd never taken part in. It was the nadir of showbusiness ghastliness and incompetence and amateurishness. Although I want to state here and now in my book that the show has improved enormously recently and if they want me to appear again, I'd be delighted, and I am currently available.

# ALL MY GREAT SHOWBUSINESS FRIENDS

# A NATION CLENCHES ITS BUTTOCKS

I didn't want to write about this. And I'm not going to. There, see? I just didn't. But you know, the more I think about it, the more I think I ought to. It's just such an extraordinary thing, you see, it's hard to convey. The thing is, it's never happened to anyone else in the entire human race except me. How often do you get that in a book? Nice buy, viewer. And, you know what, it's only in the last few quiet months that true reason and memory seem to have returned to me and it is nothing more than a coincidence that I happened to remember it all after Heimi successfully negotiated my book contract and I needed an extra five thousand words. Anybody who says otherwise is a vicious bloody liar. My lawyers are watching.

I'll tell you exactly what happened right from the start. It works best that way. Although not always. But that's another story. And it's not as good as this one. So I probably won't tell it to you. But I might – you can never tell with me. I'm such a wild man. Anyway, I had just finished making a three part television drama called In The Red. There I was, being Rik Mayall with everyone raving about my performance in it as Dominic De'Ath, and they were right to because it was pretty bloody special. The rest of the cast were okay as well. There was Richard Griffiths (yes), Richard

Wilson (big yes), John Bird (of course) (you won't have heard of any of them but they're hugely talented, take it from me) and Siobhan Redmond (another big yes – hi baby, (not yet, it still stings).) The show took longer to wrap* than expected and I was late for the Easter holidays at my Devon-sized chick ranch in South Cornwall. When I arrived at last – at "bloody-motherfucking-last" as we say in showbusiness – my family were overjoyed to see me, as I was to see them. But something stirred deep within my sub-conscious, and uncharacteristically made me seek my own company for a while. I had recently bought a quad bike and decided to take it for a spin around the fields. Two of my many daughters asked if they could come with me but I felt two drops of rain on my arm and told them to go back to the house. And I remember it so well, fired through the prism of my memory with crystal clarity, as they splashed through the puddles towards the house, and I set off down the concrete drive and into my fields.

You know how I told you about that dream I had when I was a kid that I have always found so unsettling – the one in the field at twilight with the man in the hood, the one who is beckoning to me but I won't go with him. Well it was as though the dream came to me in my wakeful state right then. All sensation of sitting astride a quad bike melted away. The roar of the engine faded and there I was in the field, the field from my dream. And there was the man from my dream standing there. There he was, wearing the hood. But it was different this time. Every time I had had the dream before, I had been so frightened. But this time, I wasn't. I didn't feel any fear at all. It was as if I felt comforted by the man's presence. And when he beckoned to me this time, I

---

* When you "wrap" something in the world of showbusiness, it means that you finish it and go home. It has nothing to do with gift wrapping or shouting gibberish quickly in an American axent with appalling music playing in the background far too loudly.

wasn't scared. At all. I felt a kind of playful happy curiosity. I wanted to know where he wanted to take me. It was as if it was something I needed to do. Not needed, even, it was something that I wanted to do. He led me towards the rise in the field that I had seen so many times before but been so scared of. But now, it was as though this was an entirely new experience, something that I had waited all my life for, and it was not so much terrifying as fascinating. And as I walked forward with a feeling of lightness in my soul, I saw what it was on the other side of the rise in the field. It was a void, a huge huge huge empty space. I was standing on the edge of the world, the actual edge of everything that is. The hooded figure was standing next to me, looking. Then he turned to me and began to pull back his hood. And as the smiling face emerged from the shadows, I felt a sudden jolt, and there, staring back at me, on the shores of eternity was . . . me. There I was, happier than I ever thought possible, smiling and kind and at peace with the universe. We embraced. We became one. It didn't hurt or anything. It was just that everything was suddenly something else. I fell vertically into a complete blackness, a total nothing. It was as though everything was magnified a million times, like my body was a thousand miles long – I don't have words big enough to do it justice. I was utterly alone and upside down and yet, despite the magnitude of my surroundings, it also felt sort of like what I imagine womb-like must be.

Close the book for a moment but put your finger in this page so you keep your place. Now close your eyes and think about nothing. Really concentrate on nothing, empty your mind. Well that's what it was like. Now read on. It's difficult to put this into words. This is an experience that no one else has ever had. I haven't been able to share it with anyone until now. That's why writing a book is the best way I can think of to try to express it.

I'm not an author. I don't like books and I don't read them. But this piece of the story is the reason for writing the book you are holding in your hands at this very moment.

It was like I was disintegrating as I fell through the void. My flesh started to melt away like it was wax. I felt my lips disappear. My face had gone. I held up my hands and they were bone and they began to splinter. It didn't really trouble me, it was just what was happening. I was fascinated and thrilled as I disintegrated and fell, safely and at a slow waterfall-type speed. Gradually I just splintered away upside down until I was reduced to a tiny speck of existence within my aircraft-hangar-sized skull which was all that was left of my body. I was alone and tiny standing on the inside of the empty roof of my skull. I looked up to see my teeth and lower jaw float away and then finally, all I could see were my own vast eye sockets like entrances to giants' caves, until they too were reduced to dust. But I felt no sense of loss. Normal human emotion did not apply. I felt a sense of warmth, happiness even, and I heard myself laughing helplessly as I remembered the Director General of the BBC as he fell down the stairs. But the laughter turned to tears of sadness as I stood in the sea in Weymouth in 1963 as I lost forever my new blue kite that my Granny and Grandpa had just given me. More laughter followed as though competing broadcasts were breaking into each other's wavelengths and there I was watching Ade with his Doctor Martens up on the desk laughing at me in the lecture theatre in Manchester when I stood up when Professor John Prudhoe came into the room. Then suddenly, there was a rending cracking sound as I remembered falling out of the neighbours' tree and ended up in a cucumber frame – blood and glass and cucumbers everywhere and my dad came to rescue me. And then I can hear a whirring from an old film projector and I'm watching my dad's old Super 8 cine film of two little boys walking down the street wearing red caps and Gabardine raincoats like they're miniature Russian spies. They look up and see the camera and they pretend to hide behind the hedge, and then one of them – me – jumps out with a silver toy pistol and starts shooting at the camera. There's my dad telling me how I reminded him of his dad when he saw me on stage in Cell Mates with my Irish accent and my short hair. And there's Rashwood County Primary School with the girls playing on the climbing frame, their legs making squeaking sounds against the metal poles as they spin around and boys (like me) try to see up their skirts. And there's Jack Pointer the Headmaster, leading a group of little children wearing gas masks along the pavement to an air raid shelter in Wychbold during the war. These thoughts came to me like curving winds in a wood, and they might not mean much to you, viewer, but they mean a whole lot to me.

My trajectory began to slow down until I came to a halt and was left suspended in a vast sea of nothingness. I looked and my body had returned, but it was a sort of transparent body now and when I looked around there was nothing to see, just millions of miles of emptiness all around me. Then from nowhere, there was someone else. A woman. It wasn't like she arrived from somewhere else, she was just there as if she'd always been there and I had only just then received the ability to see her. Maybe that, or maybe she had just materialised from another dimension.

I am known as a man of great wisdom in the showbusiness community, a man of insight and towering intellect. I am known as Rik "towering . . ." – actually forget about that. I'm bright, okay. Let's just leave it there. No, let's not. I'm thick. I've always been thick. But canny. And clever. Thick and clever. That's the canny bit. But whatever this was it was beyond my comprehension. It was like my thoughts were not my own. This woman had not only appeared in front of me but inside my mind as well, although where my mind began and where it ended were concepts that I couldn't get a firm grip on. Don't forget, this wasn't scary. It was warm, a bit like being in love. Maybe she was everyone that I ever wanted? Maybe she was an angel? And then I looked at her closer and she began to resemble someone that I thought I knew. It was like she was a composite image of all the most beautiful women I had ever known and I realised that I could engineer her appearance to my own liking. How about that for a present? It was like she was an extension of my own imagination. Then, from out of the blue, she took hold of my wrist, lifted my hand and kissed the palm, and placed it on the side of her face as she smiled at me. She seemed to be becoming more beautiful with every passing second. So this was it, this was heaven. This is a fucking result! "Thank God I led a good life," I thought to myself and it was then that I heard a voice that said, "It's only right that you should thank me."

There was a pause. Quite a good dramatic one.

"Hang on a fucking minute, are you telling me what I think you're telling me?"

She looked at me with her eyes.

"I don't know, what do you think I'm telling you?"

"That you're God. Only you're not, you're the most beautiful woman in the world. No, the most beautiful woman in the everything."

"Rik, you see me however you want to see me. If you want to see me as a kindly old man with a flowing white beard then you will." And he was right and I did and he was and I took my hand off his cheek.

"I have to say, I think I prefer you this way," I said. "Although you were pretty fucking amazing the other way too. Whoops! Er, pardon my French . . . Sir."

"Oh don't worry, Rik. Bloody frogs – they're all a bunch of cunts." (He didn't really say that, I just couldn't resist it. God won't mind.)

212

God put his arm around me. (That's right – me! Little Rik Mayall and God walking together across vast overlapping landscapes of beautiful everything. Just me and the man! THE MAN!!! I mean        I can't speak.)

He twinkled in his way as we walked, you know how he does. He leant down, hugged me with his arm a bit tighter and said, "Well my Rikky-boy, you know what they say about me, all that stuff about God is love. Well, of course I am but let me tell you, I've got a lot of love for your work. In fact, I adore it. Look, I know I shouldn't but you couldn't do an autograph for me, could you? You know it's not for me. It's for my son."

So I gave him one. An autograph. Come on, I'm not that crass. It can give you a very particular kind of butterflies in your tummy, you know, when you're standing alone with God himself right at the centre of all the vastness that is the epicentre of all the universes there ever will be and He tells you about his son, Jesus, watching you and enjoying your programmes on his telly.

Then God stopped, turned around and held me by my shoulders. He stooped down to me in his magnificence and spoke.

"The thing is, Richie, I gave the weather a little nudge down there in Cornwall this morning to make it slippery for your quad bike and give you a fantastic ride for Easter. You've been working so hard recently. You're my favourite acter. You're my favourite man. You're my favourite all round entertainer. In fact, you're my favourite everything. The trouble is, you're such a shit driver, you crashed. You've pissed me off a little bit. Here, look at this." He pointed at a nearby planet and it was vaporised in a fantabulous explosion. "Don't worry, nobody's living on it. I've been meaning to clear it up for weeks. So the point is, you've put a glitch in the plan, Rikky-wikky. You're not meant to be here yet. I want you back down there on the main stage. Like now. Hello? You've only done the first half of the show. You need to get back down there and do the second half. I've still got a hell of a – sorry, a heck of lot of work for you to do down there."

"Wait, wait a minute. What are you saying? I'm not dead? What?! Are you saying I'm going to miss out on an eternal life of bliss, God?"

"Rik, look at me. You're Rik Mayall. No, you're The Rik Mayall. The Rik is how you shall be known henceforward. I'm asking you as a favour." He came in close. "This is a favour for God, you understand, so it's got a sort of heavyweight significance hasn't it? What I'm asking you to do is to go back down there. Now. The fact of the matter is, if you go back, the next seventy five generations of humanity are going to be twenty five per cent happier."

There was a pause. One of my good ones.

"The next seventy five generations of humanity are going to be twenty five per cent happier because of me? I'd never have thought of that."

"Modesty is your Achilles heel, Rich."

"Good point God. Try as hard as I may, I just can't stamp out that modesty shit."

Then God threw one of his pauses at me. It was a big one. And a bit scary.

"So, what's your decision?"

I paused again. It's all I had left. Then quietly and firmly I said, "What was the question again, God?"

God went to speak just as I hit him with that left eyebrow twitch thing I do so brilliantly and his face lit up: "Nearly got me there, Rich. Nice one."

"You know there's only one way for me to go, God. If you want me to do it, I'll do it. I'm going back."

God threw his arm around my shoulders.

"How many arms have you got?" I said.

"Let's not bother about that now. That's my boy. I knew I'd done a good job with you. The thing is, your mission is more than just to cheer up humanity with your sparkling and almost super-human maelstrom of powerful intercontinental light entertainment genius. And voice-overs, obviously."

"Check that God, or whatever it is that the Americans say in current British television programmes. So, what's the mission, big fella?"

There was a silence. I looked up to God. He looked out at eternity for a while. I let him do it. It was a good shot. Then these huge beautiful sad joyous far-away eyes turned back to meet mine.

"I had another boy like you once. It was a couple of thousand years ago. By the way, I like your weight situation."

I didn't say anything, just nodded my acknowledgement. You're bang on the money God, I thought. I've been a thirty one inch waist for the last fifteen years.

"The mortals," he continued, "need to see that you are more than just a human. You must shine like a beacon in the darkness for them – and the light as well. Although in the light you might be like a small patch of darkness and you wouldn't be quite so beacony and therefore not quite such a good metaphor. So forget that one, let's move on. What I'm trying to say is that all your life in light entertainment (and myriad other televisual, cinematic and theatrical formats obviously) up to this point have merely been an hors d'oeuvres to the main event which is bringing enlightenment to all humanity. And for this task, I will give you two foot soldiers to assist you."

God paused.

"But who . . ." I began before God held his hand up to stop me.

"Two words, Richie my boy, two words. Cliff and Tony."

"A triumvirate?" I questioned.

"Yes," said God, "although don't worry about the pecking order because you're by far the most talented."

"Thank you your Godship."

"Not at all, it's true. Now, first of all, you are going to have to convince the world that Tony is the way forward for global politics and Cliff is the only way forward for popular music. In this way, all the people of the world will receive succour."

"Sucker?"

"No, double C, O, U, R. Don't be dirty."

"Oh right, sorry about that. But how do you suggest I go about this?"

"Use your art, Rik. Tell the people that Cliff is good, Tony is great and Rik is the best. That is the message I want you to take back."

"Crikey. Lordy-lordy. Sorry, I mean, Lord. It's a jolly big job. I'm honoured."

"Love your humility, Rich, you'll go far."

"But how come you didn't wait until the millennium? Isn't this two years too soon for the Second Coming?"

"No time like the present. I want you to go back down there and get started straight away. For the first few years, I want you to carry on as normal, lightly entertaining people like only you know how, adding to your vast international hordes of followers and admirers who want to touch your clothes. And then, you must write a book that will become the new bible, and then your mission will begin in earnest."

"I won't make a joke about being in Earnest."

"Don't pull back on my account."

"No, it's okay, the moment's gone."

"Right you are. Anyway, good luck."

"I don't need luck. I've got you on my side, God."

"That's right, you have, Dick. Sorry – FUCK! What was your name again? Oh it's Rik, isn't it."

"That's it, God. Well, that's me gone then is it?"

"That's right, Nick, see you, take care."

"Bye God, nice to meet you. Er . . . er . . . I hope you keep well."

And he slapped me on the back and was gone. Although I could have sworn I heard his voice around the corner a second later, shouting, "Who is that little shit? Has he gone yet?" I think it was one of his great jokes. Well I laughed. A bit. But then suddenly, I started falling. Only this time it really was falling. I turned cartwheels through the cosmos tumbling over and over for what seemed like an age until SPLAT! I came to in a bed! Somewhere on earth. All I remember is opening my eyes and looking at the ceiling and thinking where the fuck am I? At that time, I couldn't remember anything of my time with God. Nothing at all. That all came later. But I didn't feel panicked at all. I'm an acter and we often wake up in other people's bedrooms. Instinctively, I reached down to make sure that my equipment was okay. That's what us acters always do. You never know what's been going on. But this time when I put my hand down there to check that everything was okay, I found out that it wasn't. There was a fucking tube sticking out of it. A fucking tube sticking out of my nob! This woke me up a bit I'll tell you. But I'm not stupid, I didn't make a sound or make any movement or anything because I had no idea who I was in bed with of course. And I didn't want to wake up whoever it was and face up to the ghastly truth of whatever it was that I'd been getting up to the night before. So, gently, I felt the piece of plastic tubing that came out of the end of my cock. Oh Jesus, I thought, what have I been doing? Right, I decided, I'd better get rid of this sex equipment, find my clothes and make a run for it. I just hope to God I didn't tell her my name was Rik, I thought, and I couldn't even remember if I'd written her name on her back in biro like you should for the morning after. I pulled as hard as I could on the tube to get it out and YOWSER! Right deep up inside my cock – a good nine inches inside it – there was the most awful stabbing pain. I kept pulling on the tube but it wouldn't come out and the pain was agonising. How the hell did it get up there? I gave it a really good yank and the next thing I knew, there were four nurses on top of me. Jesus Christ, I thought, I'm still in some kind of pervy club. How much did I pay for these? Two of the nurses held my arms out spread eagled. The other one held my feet down and the other one straddled me and started shoving the tube back up my cock. That's when I completely flipped and yelled, "What the fuck is going on?" But I couldn't! I couldn't fucking speak! Nothing came out of my mouth! My mouth just wasn't working properly. I tried to say something else but I couldn't get any words out.

The nurse on top of me held me tight and said, "Don't do that Rik, don't ever do that. You could really damage yourself if you pull this out of your penis."

"Okay," I tried to say but only mumbling came out of my mouth. Then I passed out. When I came around again, I was all alone in the room. I could hear the rhythmic beeping of a life support machine like they have in all those hospital dramas that I'm not in. At the time, I knew nothing at all of the last ten pages or whatever it is that you've just read. It took a long time for my poor head to put itself together again and recover from having 3/5 – that's right, three fifths – of my brain totally clogged with loose blood from somehow fracturing my skull by falling off my quad bike and lying on my back in the rain. The only exits for the blood from my head wound (head wound? Seriously fucking life-threatening head accident, that's what) could find were my eyes, my mouth, my ears and my nose. That's how Barbara found me. She did disregard me for the first five minutes. She though I was playing an "amusing serious accident joke" and didn't see why she should have to go out in the rain and pretend to laugh convincingly as is obligatory on these occasions. She did eventually come out to laugh to avoid me having a tantrum about everyone ignoring my great quad bike joke. Poor Barbara got a pretty hefty shock out there in the rain when she found me lying there dead.

So that's how I got all that loose blood locked inside my head. That's right, loose blood locked in my brain! And it couldn't find an exit for seven whole weeks! So my poor brain had to somehow work out a new system of thinking. What it did according to the doctors afterwards was that it used a lot of its previously unused dark dormant sections. So my brain was thinking in ways that it never had before and probably no one else's has either[*] which was extremely weird indeed. I could hear colour, I could see sound, I could smell movement, I could feel things I could only imagine but couldn't see, and I could see people's skulls jabbering but not their faces. Everyone was the same. And I couldn't talk. I could only manage to think and say two words, "Mummy," and "Barbara[†]." It was scary. I was alone in a place of jabbering identical SKULLS who had obviously trapped me in this weird compound and were experimenting on me and wouldn't let me out. That was why I couldn't think properly. They had obviously fucked up my brain as an experiment and were observing me as part of whatever terrifying medical project they were doing. I could barely walk, I couldn't think, but I knew that I had to escape from that place. Now. But they'd obviously somehow found out that I was trying

---

[*]  Except possibly Salvador Dali's brain in a visual sense.

[†]  When I was in my five day coma, Pete "Pete Richardson" Richardson called up my wife, Barbara. He was worried. We had only just finished filming the Comic Strip movie Four Men In A Car just before the accident and the thing is that my character in the film (the biggest part of course and by far the best) had a terrifying and very convincing near-death motorbike crash right in the middle of the movie. So Pete was wondering if it might be a little insensitive for the film to go out on telly that night. Would Rik mind? Pete wanted to know. "Would he mind being on the fucking telly?" says Bra. Are you joking? Stick it on you twat, he couldn't die a happier man."

to escape and they followed me everywhere, locking the doors every time I got near one, claiming that the whole place was a hospital. A hospital!

It was a desperate situation so I pretended to go along with them. I decided to bide my time until I could think of a good solid escape plan to put into operation.

Then, after a few days, suddenly everything changed. My wife told me that what they call the Easter school holidays were over and that everyone was "going to London". Then it turned out that they were indeed going to London! I was taken outside. I could feel the sun on my skin and smell fresh air again. This was going to be good. They put me into a very convincing ambulance on a stretcher and we were out on the motorway. It was exciting. I could see all the fields and cars from my old world smiling at me and talking to me. I can't remember what they all said clearly but there were some very nasty hedges who didn't like me at all. I'm pretty sure I was strapped to the stretcher – for "safety reasons" they claimed of course. But then I was taken to a "private hospital in Harley Street". I was unstrapped and allowed to walk almost unguarded into this new place. This didn't seem like such a secure prison. My new cell in there was more like a hotel suite. A nice man carried my suitcases and unpacked them for me. Then he asked if he could use the toilet in my bathroom and he left me alone! Chance. I was straight out of the room, down the corridor, down the stairs and straight out onto Harley Street in my pyjamas. I hailed a taxi and went home. My friend, Geoff, was babysitting the kids and he answered the door when I rang the doorbell. There's a friend at last! A man I know. I grabbed him and kissed him and hugged him all over. He looked shocked. He could barely speak. He looked amazed that I had managed to escape from the authorities. I shouted, "Geoff! I've broken out, let's get pissed!" Words, important words, were coming back to me! Geoff looked a bit pale.

Maybe he was a bit poorly and needed a drink as well. He told me to just sit on the sofa, please, while he found all the booze. Don't worry, he said, he didn't need any help finding the booze. But I was impatient and kept trying to find it. Geoff managed to stay one step ahead of me though and as fast as he could he hid the alcohol or poured it down the sink before the loonie man (that's me, viewer) could find it, neck it and go completely one hundred per cent insane. Then he came back and sadly told me that there was nothing to drink in the house. Perhaps I should have some food? He said he would phone for a pizza because I looked like I should get something inside me. So he would go into another room, he said, and make the call while I sat and watched some telly. So I watched some telly. Free at last. Bliss. Except that the telly was freaking me out a bit – horrible loud garish indecipherable drivel jabbering at me from the corner of the room (no change there then). Then at last the pizza delivery man arrived but he wasn't the pizza delivery man at all. He was a woman. She was my doctor. But she was wonderful. She was on my side and she spoke to me very calmly and reassuringly and she took me upstairs to my bed (no, sadly). She said I needed to relax, forget about everything, and said she was going to give me a very powerful injection. Which she did. The next thing I knew was that I was coming round in the Charing Cross Hospital. Prison again. Shit. Double shit. In fact, quadruple shit with bollocks on it.

But in truth things were beginning to change now. This was a hospital I had been in before. I was beginning to come around to the opinion that I might have had a quad-bike accident. And I started telling people this. Which was lucky because I was in a hospital anyway. A lot of them, in fact, all of them seemed to sympathise and agree. Fucking hell, I've been seriously injured, I thought. I haven't been a prisoner locked inside some weird jail at all. Not this time anyway. Phew.

Time passed. I got better. I felt better. I was better – but not quite. I went for a scan. Like you do with head injuries. Especially with an unsurvivable head injury like mine. Which was far worse than any head injury anyone has ever had ever in the history of human experience – even in the movies. And I've been in lots of them, very successfully, and I'm currently available – not that I'm short of work of course – it just so happens that at the moment oh never mind where was I? Oh yeah – everything took a really scary swerve at this point. Just when everything was going so well. I came out of the scan machine thingy and the very high up extremely brainy brain doctor told me quietly that he'd been waiting for seven weeks (that's how long I'd been inside), seven weeks for the loose blood to drain from my brain. But it hadn't. It was all locked in there and it wasn't going to come out. This was really serious, viewer. This is the big bit. The doctor said to me that he was going to have to take the top of my head off. That's what he said. He was going to have to saw around the top third of my skull (about half an inch above the eyebrows), take it off, lay it to one side carefully and then go inside my brain and gradually scoop out the blood. He would have to be extremely careful he said not to scoop out all of the blood, just the excess blood that was trapped in there and couldn't get out, otherwise I would almost certainly die. It's not as easy as it sounds he said because he was going to have to dig down deep into my brain to get out every drop of unnecessary blood. Right to the very centre of my brain and beneath, removing anything that was clogging up my thought system, well, existence system really.

"This could be a very challenging operation, Rik," he said, "and the disadvantage is that there is a good fifty per cent chance that you will die. Now, I'm not going to do it today. I'm going do it tomorrow morning. So why don't you go home and relax." So I did. And I didn't. I got home alright but the relaxing was a bit more tricky. A conversation like that can really focus your mind, I can tell you. So I avoided the subject with the family. It wasn't really fair on them and anyway, they wouldn't have listened to me anyway. They always put Eastenders on when I come into the room. It's their polite way of saying, "Shut up and go away you overweight has-been." So I sat with them watching the drivel and went back to the hospital the next day thinking it was probably my last day on earth. But I was resigned. I was ready.

Okay, death-wish operation time. Here we go. Probably a mutilated corpse lying on the slab by midday. Not a problem for me, I'm Rik Mayall. So, straight into theatre. Like it. Never more at home. Get your cock out, get a laugh off the nurses. Never fails. Just got to remember that it's the flesh coloured pube. Only joking, viewer, The Tripod's in town and he's looking for action.

"Morning Rik, how you feeling?" said the doctor.

"Terrific, pants are full of shit, but I don't give a fuck. Let's do this mother."

So we did. First of all, the doctor said that he was going to have to give me another scan to check exactly where all the blood was before he sawed the top of my head off. He said it was going to last a long time. Which it did. They lay me on a flat tongue sort of device which was then drawn inside a huge cylindrical barrel-type machine. There was a device to keep my head straight and there were cameras moving around my head as I lay flat, looking deeply into my soul. I haven't been shot dead by a firing squad yet but I think those couple of hours or whatever it was inside there were my equivalent of the man in front of the firing squad's last cigarette. So, what does he get? A minute and a half, right. I got two solid hours! And I didn't GET A FAG! Give me the First World War anytime.

And then the scan finished. It's hard to describe. I came out of the machine and the doctor looked amazed. He was amazed. He was flabbergasted. So was I when I found out what had happened. All that blood that had been locked in my skull had gone. It had just gone! Overnight or something. It was a fucking miracle! All that blood had just drained away. All the unnecessary accident blood I mean. Not the proper brain blood. Everything was okay! So he wouldn't need to operate! He wouldn't have to cut my head off! Is that a result or what? And that's when I started to wonder whether the clever man had just sort of scared the blood out of me. I don't know. But thanks Mr Doctor Man. Big time. No forget that. Extremely big time. I'm alive! And my brain works. Ish.

# BIGGER THAN ADOLF
# BETTER THAN JESUS

Yeah, right, so every couple of thousand years, give or take a couple of years, along comes a Christ figure. It just so happens that it's me this time around*. So maybe now, you can fully appreciate that this isn't just a normal Harper Collins book, this is a semi-religious testament to the legend of my life in showbusiness and if you don't believe it, you can eat your own shit for all I care. And when you do, then phone me up and I'll tell you that I'm not listening because that's the kind of guy that I am. And you can come round to my house and try and show me and I'll deliberately close my eyes and stick my fingers in my ears. Because – read my lips – this is a serious book. Like The Bible. That was a good book. In fact, some of the critics even call it The Good Book. That's clever marketing that is. I know all about that kind of thing because I'm a twenty-first century kind of guy with an inhairnet grasp of the media and communications and stuff. That's why I am the leading voice-over artiste of my generation. Sod your BAFTAs (I've got plenty of them anyway).

---

\* Sudden bit of a sledgehammer in the testicles for you my modesty, isn't it? But don't sweat, viewer, it's the same for all ordinary people. You're in safe hands here. Rik Mayall loves his ordinaries.

Everything I do is really serious and hard especially when I'm being amusing which is brilliant and hard and dead funny in its own right. So, in case you're still confused, that is what this is. This book is better than the Good Book because it's the Great Book. And it's mine. And no one else's, unless you bought it, in which case it is your book although I wrote it and if someone else says they wrote it then they're fucking lying. You can phone me up anytime you want although I won't put my telephone number here because you might. So think about what I said about all that and we'll leave it there.

And the other thing is – something else – so fuck off (I can use swear words as well, I'm that hard). Or don't, because you're my friend and I dig you, viewer, it's you and me together. We're down with life. So, I'm going to hit you with some serious shit here and I don't mean anything lavatorial. I mean shit as in some high quality information that'll hit you like an anthrax-tipped scud missile of light entertainment. So hold on tight, we're going in. Get yourself a piece[*], get some full body armour, double safety belts etc, put the children to bed and give them a kiss (because we're caring and the kids are our future), close the door slowly and quietly, go downstairs, get yourself a stiff drink, a hard drink, drink it all and swallow it all in one go, lock all the doors, close all the curtains, pull down the blinds, put on the full body armour, get your favourite spectacles, put your foot through the television, write "fuck off" on a Post-It note and stick it to the front door, write "leave me alone because I'm reading The Rik Mayall's great book" backwards across your forehead (so you can read it in the mirror), tear off the top of your T-shirt sleeves so that you look like that bloke in that one where nothing much happens at all but

---

[*]  This is American cop show slang for a revolver and not the piece that all the hippies were always banging on about. Never trust a hippie, viewer. Remember where you heard it first.

it leaves you thinking mmmmm, turn the lights down low (but not too low because you might not be able to read anything), sweat a bit (and if it's not hot enough, then go to the sink and flick a bit of water on your face – acters' trick), turn to the wife or husband and say, "Shut up bitch/bloke, I need silence," plump up the cushions, turn on the drawing room standard lamp if it really is a bit too dark, and get the fuck in:

## FIVE REASONS WHY I AM BETTER THAN CHRIST*

1. I was dead for five days and Christ was only dead for three. There's no quibbling with that. It's just a cold hard fact. And it's longer. I fell off my quad bike and smashed my head in and went into a death coma on the Thursday before Easter 1998 – Crap Thursday as it's known amongst the Rik Mayall legions – and I rose again on the Bank Holiday Monday. That's the day after Easter fucking Day. Christ, I mean, Jesus got nailed up by the transvestites (no disrespect) on Good Friday (Good? For Fuck's sake – who's in charge of the church these days? Why don't they call it Shit Friday?) and came back from the dead on Easter Sunday which was all well and good and brilliant and he was a Christian, don't forget, so he had to go to Church. But I came back from the dead on Bank Holiday Monday, the day after. You see what that means? Thursday to Monday! That's five whole days being dead! And in anyone's book, especially this one, it's a clear winner. It's not even really close. Let's face it, it's almost double the time. It's 5 – 3 to me. That's a big margin as they say on those football watching

---

* Please note, I am not having a go him. I'm down with Jesus. We're in bed together on many things. I love a slurp of wine and a bit of biscuit.

programmes. And I did it all on my own and didn't need any fucking Romans to help me (and they wore skirts for Christ's sake. Hang on. No. That's wrong – they didn't do it for Christ's sake, they wore skirts all the time (except they didn't invade Scotland because all the jocks had their own skirts, so they built Adrian's Wall to keep the rival manufacturers out. It worked too. You don't see many Brummies wearing skirts, do you?))

2. Jesus's biggest gig was feeding the five thousand with the fishes and the loaves. But me and Ade played The Point in Dublin in 2003 which is eight thousand capacity. That's three thousand more people. Can you hear that Jesus? Well of course you can, you're Jesus. And there was a much bigger selection of food. We had hamburger stalls there, hot dogs, there was ice cream for afters and that's not to mention the bar where all the hell-raising Irish Bottom fans were drinking gallons of everything. And what did Jesus have? A bit of fish and some loaves. Jesus. He should have got himself a better tour promoter. I'm sure if he'd had Phil "shut up and sign the cheque" McIntyre like I do, he'd have got a bigger crowd. So me and Ade blew Jesus out of the water on that one – not to mention our personal record of eleven million people watching Bottom on BBC2, although yes, we can't walk on the stuff – yet. But Ade's a jolly good skier.

3. My miracles are better than Jesus's. Granted, curing the leper was a good trick. But I have cured thousands of people of their misery and meaninglessless by signing autographs for them which they can cherish and frame and use to decorate their little "front rooms". Also, I once did a telly advert for ANO-ITCH. Not only did I narrate the commercial but I also

played the man who came into the shop with the itchy arse. Now, that advert reached countless millions. It was on weekend prime time*. Lazarus – again, quite impressive, taking up his bed and walking about the place like that but to tell you the truth, I would have got my people to move him and his bed out of the way much quicker. Walking on water? Well I've been water-skiing and I think you'll find that that's a bit faster than walking. Although I'll tell you this for nothing, you need to be very careful when you're water-skiing on a Caribbean holiday and you get into a disagreement with a snorkelling holiday maker over whose right of way it is and you swerve unexpectedly violently to the right after you've water-skied over his head to make your point and this catapults you fifteen feet up in the air at about sixty miles per hour, losing a ski on the way and as you cartwheel back down towards the water, hanging on to the tow rope with the wrong hand so you hit the water on the ski-less foot which acts like a Kamikaze dive without a target and forces about twenty gallons of sea water up your anal passage on impact. It doesn't end there. It's only after you've been rescued by the tow boat and hauled on board in the company of seven other (female mostly) holiday makers that you realise you're the victim of a powerful self-induced enema which chooses to erupt like Krakatoa suddenly out of all three exits of your day-glo jet-skiing thong as they gather around you wearing very expensive (and clean) clothes and hair and faces. Not a pretty sight on a family holiday. I never heard from any of them again.

---

* This means that it was on the television when lots of people watch lots of things which is after all the stuff that they don't watch and before all the shit they put on later when everyone's gone to bed.

4. I have brought more joy to the people of the world. A lot of Jesus's followers are always arguing amongst themselves about stuff like the Catholics and the Protestants and who's right and who's wrong about this, that and the next religious thing. And then, before you know it, there's a bloody war going on and thousands are dying in agony and all the love thy neighbour and turn the other cheek bollocks goes straight out of the window and everybody's raping and pillerging and having a really fucking awful time generally. Despite the fact that some of my fans fight over copies of my DVDs in shops, and there has been the occasional brutal mugging for a pair of tickets to one of my great plays, overall, my influence on the world has been much more peaceful and kind.

5. I have a far greater understanding of the media. I am always mind-storming ideas with myself and thinking up new ways of reaching out to more and more fans across the globe with my own unique brand of comedy wild fire and powerful drama. I think it is no exaggeration to say quite honestly and truthfully here and now that I have been featured in every English-speaking publication in the world*. AND I've been on the cover of the Radio Times. Whilst Jesus, on the other hand, just stuck to the one media outlet – The Good Book. But that's a bit short-sighted really. What about the radio? What about the telly? What about the cinema? What about radical computer

---

* I can actually prove that any time I feel like it but I'm not going to do it right now cos it would be too difficult and would take ages to do and anyway I've also been featured in a lot of non English-speaking publications so they'll make up any shortfall easily. Look, I've been in a lot of mags all right? And I don't mean porn mags. I have never masturbated in my life. That's a blanket denial, okay? Now, fuck off. Go on. Fuck off. You. Fuck off now! Go back to the stuff up above because you're really beginning to get on my tits down here.

fan websites? I'm big in all of these. In fact, I'm huge. I don't need The Gideons to leave copies of my book in hotel rooms all around the world. That's so the millennium-before-last.

And there they are: five reasons why I'm better than Christ. I could have a sixth if I wanted because I've never worn a dress but I'll let that one go. I'm not one to kick a man when he's down. Come to mention it, I could even go for a seventh because I'm pretty sure that Jesus never met Charlie Drake. But I'll let that one go too because I'm nice. Not like that Adolf Hitler. He was a total bastard but he was a big total bastard. Not physically, obviously. But I'm bigger. And here, viewer, just in case you're in any doubt about this, are – hey, stop! Wait a minute. Jesus has never watched Channel Five. Oh fuck, nor have I. Cunts. Okay, forget that bit, read this bit, this is good.

## TEN REASONS WHY I AM BIGGER THAN HITLER

1. Adolf tried to conquer the world and failed. I didn't (fail). I'm massive all over the world.

2. Adolf only had one testicle. I have two testicles. Ask any one of a legion of lead actresses whose names I can't even mention because it would destroy their marriages and all of them will say that I have more than one.

3. He didn't get any laughs. I don't remember seeing anyone laughing on the Nuremberg videos. People are always laughing at me. And throwing things. I don't remember Adolf getting dogshit thrown at him.

4. I have been famous for longer than him. I turned pro (this does not mean that I got my bottom out for money – that was later) in September 1975 which was when I got my first paid gig. That was more than thirty years ago now. Did you read that, Adolf? I HAVE BEEN FAMOUS FOR MORE THAN THIRTY YEARS! And you were only famous from 1928 to 1945. That's a puny seventeen years you useless twat with a crap moustache. Seventeen is less than half of thirty. SO FUCK OFF ADOLF!

5. Hitler had very one-dimensional facial hair. I have explored a vast repertoire of facial hair "combos". My homage to The Lemmy in A Fistful of Travellers Cheques is considered a classic and is still spoken of with a hushed oar in make-up departments throughout the world.

6. They didn't like Hitler in Russia. But I am huge. I didn't see Hitler at the 1997 Moscow Film Festival nominated for Best Acter alongside Bobby D. Niro. And he didn't vomit into his lap either.

7. I have had far more birds than Hitler.

8. And lager.

9. And other stuff.

10. That's true that is.

Once again, I could go for another reason that I'm bigger than Hitler and that is that all my videos are in colour and nearly all of his are in black and white. But I won't. I don't want to rub his nose in it. He got what was coming to him.

Now, I'm going to leave it there. This is not – I repeat not – because I have forgotten what the point is that I'm trying to make. This is my point – the fact that I am bigger than Hitler and better than Christ. I am, it's just a fact. I've just proved it. Back there. Read it again if you don't believe me. I'm an honest guy. I don't write stuff just to big up my own ego. I don't need to. Facts are facts. And I've just given you some. For free. Job done. Walk away. Goodbye.

Oh, actually, scrub all that, I'll tell you another one. Hitler never fell offstage at the St David's Hall in Cardiff in 2003. Or looked up Bridget Fonda's skirt like I did in Drop Dead Fred. If you're reading this Bridget, EXTREMELY hello there.

And also my sensational heart-stopping performance as Hitler in the anti-Euro video stopped Hitler's original plan to unite Europe. My European dream has been realised, his hasn't. Twice. So I'm bigger than him. And he hasn't been to Bromsgrove. He bombed in Newcastle – I never bombed in Newcastle and I've played the City Hall about seventeen times. So fucking there, Adolf. I have never bombed in any city anywhere. Although I did forget my words in Edinburgh at the Playhouse once. But I don't talk about that. Or the fact that the Time Out comedy critic was beaten up by security on the way in. Bet Hitler never organised for the beating up of a Time Out critic. Although neither did I. I think we'll just leave it there.

# WHAT DOES A MAN WITH A TWO FOOT COCK HAVE FOR BREAKFAST? WELL, THIS MORNING I HAD A BOILED EGG

La comedie? Cest moi. I didn't get where I am today without jokes like this in my joke sachet. As Johnny Gielgud said to me all those years ago, "Please don't tell anyone about this Rik, dear boy. It's best for both of us that way."

Now the publisher, Colin Harpers, has asked me to make sure that I include plenty of joyous, wicked, gossipy anecdotes from my life in the entertainment industry. So I'm going to tell you about one of the funniest things that ever happened to me which was when I was at the best party of my life with hordes of my great showbusiness friends [fill in names of people here] and [insert something very funny here]. And just as I was leaving, I turned to my great friend, Ken Hom, and said, "Hi Ken, love your wok." He nearly died.*

---

* Delete this chapter. It's really not going anywhere.

# RIK'S HOT BROTH

I know literally thousands of showbusiness secrets, viewer. I know stuff about stuff that would make your hairs curdle, quite literally. As I sit here, with my smoking finger ablaze across my typewriter keys, the secrets battle to be free, and occasionally my defences weaken and one escapes, like the time my Best Man found me supergluing a life-size portrait of Siân Lloyd to the shaved hind quarters of the neighbour's Alsatian and writing "give it to me, big boy" on its back, in a Welsh accent obviously. Or – here comes another one – that it's only called Red Nose day because everyone involved with it has such dreadful cocaine problems (that's where most of the money goes). They might as well call it Non-existent Septum Day. At this very moment, there are celebrities across the globe quaking in their pants at the thought that I might divulge some of my hidden golden truths and lift the lid on the many debauched drug orgies that I have definitely never been to during my drink and drug hell – that I never had.

There are some secrets, however, that will harm no one, like the fact that Charlie Crichton, the director of Carry On Columbus, took me to one side and said "You're much better than everyone else who has ever appeared in any of the Carry On films and I'm talking about Sid James and I'm talking about Kenneth Williams,

Charles Haughtry, Hattie Jacques and even better than Jim Dale and that bloke who used to clean windows, Robin Askwith." (No one can prove that he didn't say this.) There are other secrets on the other hand – or this hand, I don't give a shit really – that are potentially highly damaging. Like the time I was up late a few weeks back trying to watch some of my late repeats and I couldn't get the telly to work properly and then suddenly I ended up on the Salford OAPs Amateur Dial-a-wank Watersports Channel. And I'm not talking skis. I just couldn't get off. I don't mean with any of the OAPs, I mean I couldn't change channel. Thankfully the press didn't find out.

Anyway, you know me, I don't give away secrets. I'm a man of honour. No I'm not. I'm The man of honour and what I'm trying to say about secrets is that, well, here's another one. Like so many things in my great life, it all started with a phone call from Heimi. Picture the scene. A phone rings. That's it, you've got it. The Rik Mayall slinks like a big cat across the carpet and snatches up the receiver like Richard Widmark in that one with the squid.

"Hello." Brooding, magnificent, a half turn to the light. The eyebrow thing. And relax.

"Is that my favourite client in all the world, kissy kissy, love your work?"

"Heimi!"

"No, he died, it was terrible, I was just passing and saw it all happen."

"Have you got some work for me?"

"Possibly."

"Paid?"

"Again, possibly."

Heimi had opened up a whole new front for me on my war against showbusiness complacency. It was a celebrity endorse-ment for a brothel in Gateshead. I knew immediately that this was going to be another great K2, or K1 or K9? – or whichever one it is that people have real trouble climbing (whichever is harder than Everest, that's the point) – in my great career. And it would also involve birds. Another plus. Because I was going through a phase of hardcore hands-on feminism at the time. I wanted to be like that other top quality feminist, Hugh Hefner. I quite fancied myself with a pipe, a silk dressing gown, lots of Viagra and a council house in Gateshead. I'm made, I thought. Well, I didn't actually. I've made that bit up along with some of the dialog back there but it's all just part of the rich tapestry that is being a top righter deep in the cut and thrust of righting his great book.

What also made Heimi's idea such a face-ripping masterstroke was that not only would it extend my career portfolio* but also increase my charity profile† because one of the women that Heimi had acquired for the brothel was a landmine victim. This was Peggie "peg-leg-peg" Something-or-other, the legendary unknown Croatian prostitute who had formerly worked as an assassin for one of Heimi's eastern European contacts, Uri "Piss" Urine. The other birds were Hua Ming Ing (Chinese‡) and Svetlana (headless Slovakian). Heimi said I should take delivery of the birds. He said they would be tired and hungry after eight days on the road in the back of the lorry and would do virtually anything for food. It seemed like a good idea.

"Blind Pete will be driving the lorry," Heimi told me, "and big Colostomy Bob will be with him. It's very important with Bob that you don't answer him back or stand within three feet of him. If he says anything remotely amusing – laugh. But don't get this

---

* This is a large black rectangular handbag with a zip around the outside in which you can carry your drawings.
† Which is important for selling your great comedy videos.
‡ Ish.

wrong and laugh when he hasn't said anything amusing. Make sure you've got your trousers on when you answer the door. He's only got two fingers on his right hand so don't think he's being rude. If his breath smells of flesh, don't mention it. If there are any half-eaten human carcasses in the back of the lorry with the merchandise, don't say anything. Don't shake hands and never turn your back on him until he's out of sight. Bury all your valuables in the garden. Cover the hole with turf so that it doesn't look like a grave because that's dinner to Bob. Hose yourself down when he leaves. Tip big but when you tip him, make sure you give him a stray dog as well if you've got one. He likes them. But watch it, they make him very horny."

Being a top international celebrity and acter, I was a little worried that we might get found out by the pigs* and then sniffed out by the shit-sniffing tabloids† but it turned out that Heimi supplied the local constabulary with electric cattle prods and people to practice on. And as far as the birds for the broth were concerned, he was unofficially working on behalf of the P.R. department of the Royal Engineers and their mine clearance charity Hope Springs (patron: Tony B). The birds came as a pack of three for twenty roubles which was very good, Heimi told me, because a reconditioned Kalashnikov would cost about the same.

So like the quality professional entertainer that I am, I waited just inside my front door for two weeks. I was very excited about the brothel and thought that it would be fabulous to call it Rik's Hot Broth, which would make it fashionable as well as sexy and sound like something that normal people would eat. What could go wrong? I'm not quite sure, but something did. That's just the

---

* This is quite hard street slang for the police.
† Who are my friends and whose work I love.

way that it is sometimes, isn't it? Some things happen and some things don't. Some things happen for a reason and some happen for no reason at all. This didn't happen for a reason but I won't tell you what it is because I want to prove my point about secrets. Some things are just mysterious. This is one of them.

# Rik's Hot Broth

## Price List

Two slices of bread with snog . . . . . . . . . . . . £0.35

Two slices of bread with snog
and tongues . . . . . . . . . . . . . . . . . . . . . . . . £0.45

Snog with tongues and a feel up
(upstairs) . . . . . . . . . . . . . . . . . . . . . . . . . . £0.99

Snog with tongues and a feel up
(downstairs) . . . . . . . . . . . . . . . . . . . . . . . . £1.25

Snog with tongues and a feel up
(round the back*) . . . . . . . . . . . . . . . . . . . . . £1.45

Half a lager and a handjob . . . . . . . . . . . . . . £1.75

Pint of lager and a handjob . . . . . . . . . . . . . £1.99

Pint of lager, packet of peanuts and
a handjob . . . . . . . . . . . . . . . . . . . . . . . . . . £2.49

Slovenian (with a buttered slice) . . . . . . . . . . £3.55

Hua Min Ging (with the lights off) . . . . . . . . £3.70

Hua Min Ging (with the lights on) . . . . . . . . £3.90

Herzogovenian (with scoop of mash) . . . . . . £3.95

Herzogovenian (with two scoops of mash
and free mushy peas on a Friday) . . . . . . . . . £4.10

Live in house maid (one leg) . . . . . . . . . . . . £18.50

Live in house maid (two legs) . . . . . £20.00 (o.n.o.)

* May be subject to back bottom surcharge

NB: Thursday afternoon – Pensioners half price
Would patrons please be advised that this is a
residential area and could they please complain
quietly after 11pm.
No running in the corridors.
UB40 / benefits: £1 off (refundable by post)

For missing wallets – please fill in form
No ducking
No dive bombing
No wearing shoes in bed
No firearms
No pets (apart from Guide Dogs)
Rik's Hot Broth is an equal opportunities employer
Member of the Investors in People charter
All attacks on staff will be prosecuted
No undercover journalists
Do not ask for credit as refusal often offends
Diners and Visa accepted
Fistings on application

# GUEST HOUSE PARADISO

I fondly remember watching Eric and Ernie (comedians – good ones) spreading their laughter back in the seventies. Their Christmas special was watched by over half the people in Britain. That's about 26 million people, viewer. I remember thinking fondly, "You motherfuckers, I'm going to get watched by more people than you." The gauntlet had been throne down – in an amusing way obviously (I respected their work, nay*, loved it). And I remember thinking (even more fondly this time), "That's a pretty hefty gauntlet to get in the bollocks." It was 1975 – I was only ten. But I didn't flinch. I remember my mum saying to me while we were watching television on that Christmas evening, "Hey Rik Mayall."

"Yeah?" I breathed, turning my head to the light.

"Love your work obviously, but how come you're not crying after receiving such a hefty gauntlet in the knackers?"

"Love your work too, mummy, I'm just not. That's how it is

---

* That's not a horse gag. And if you're thinking I'm saying that it's not a horse gag because I don't know any then that's bollocks because I know loads. I'm not going to do one on you now though. Just go away. For all I know, you're one of those Edinburgh Fringe amateur comedian cunts who steal everything with a word in it.

Me revolutionising American cinema with *Drop Dead Fred*, 1990.

Me sharing a laugh selflessly with some extras. *Kevin of the North*, 2002.

Little Ben, Little Richard and Little Huge International Pan-global Showbusiness Phenomenon Rik.

Flasheart

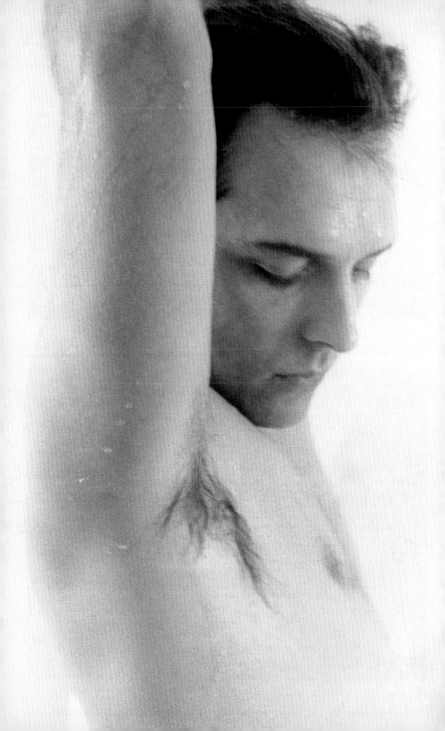

Believe nothing . . .

. . . at all

*Left:* Me and Leslie Phillips taking no shit, right.

*Below:* [Romantic caption here]

*Above:* Me securing my book deal with Trevor Dolby from HarperCollins.

[Find out who these people are and do a caption]

*Left:* Lennox Crowley: the one that got away.

*Below:* Me talking to Adrian about the caption for this photo.

*Left:* Me and Ian Richardson taking the curse off some TV drama or other. Brilliantly.

*Below:* Me and Tarby hanging out with all our great showbiz mates.

The Enigma

in my world. But let's not talk about it. Not on today of all days. I am English. Let's get on with the show." Which we did. Like a firestorm. With Turkey and the trimmings. Peace and goodwill to all.

But something had changed in me that day. My fuse had been lit. The fuse that would meander through the televisual wasteland of the 1970s until it ignited like a nuclear warhead leaving my audience with vicious weeping flash burns. My gasoline tank was strapped to my back, the flame thrower was clutched in my manly hands. But being the gentleman of comedy like what I am, or was even at the age of ten, I threw the gauntlet back to Eric and Ernie. I didn't want to spoil the rhythm of their great show. I think that bloke was in it – you know, the one who was in that other telly show and those films. Glen Jackson – that's his name. He's great. He's a breakthuough cutting edge M.P.* now.

Eric and Ernie did a few movies. There was the Magnificent Two, That Riviera Touch and The Intelligence Men. Then there was Tony Hancock (another comedian – another good one as well although not as good as me obviously). He did The Rebel and The Punch and Judy Man. Three films, not bad. And Robin Askwith, he was another one. A great British comedy titan. He made all the Confessions movies. And you know what all these movies have in common? They were all panned† by the critics‡. But that's just the way it goes on the showbusiness merry-go-round. There are rules

---

* This means Member of Parliament. It's not M.O.P. because the "of" is silent. Although everyone still says it. Especially at the BBC which should be closed or "tidied up" as they say in political crime thrillers like in . . . no I won't say it because I don't know any. Because I'm hard. And . . . oh nevermind, I don't see why I should justify myself to anyone.

† This means the critics (who I love) all wrote nasty spiteful things about them. It has nothing to do with being smashed in the face with a frying pan. Although it might do in a metaphorical sense. Forget all this, just read on.

‡ Who I love. Did I say that already?

that must be obeyed like that one there and some others [fill in some rules here] but the most important one is that if you are a television comedy star (like what I am*), and you decide to make a movie, then the critics (respect) will give it a good kicking, spit on it, rip off its head and shit down the neck hole. That's just the way that it is. As the great Ted Rogers used to say, "Ain't nothing no one can do about it" [check this].

The end of the century was fast approaching. What was needed to heal the British film industry was a great hugely underrated classic that would open the doorway to further great hugely under-rated classics starring me, like Merlin: The Return, Day of the Sirens, Chaos and Cadavers, Oh Marbella!, Susan's Last Dinner Party, The Islington Silence, Harlow's Not For Losers and Screaming Warriors of Death Vengeance II (the money's in sequels – that's just where the money is nowadays). I decided I was going to take the baby by the throat (not literally of course – don't phone that stinking Childline – I could tell you a story or two about them but I won't, not because I'm making this up but because it didn't happen) and make a film. I got my typewriter out, dusted off my trusty finger and started masturbating. Not really, obviously. I just threw that in there to check that you were still with me. Hello? Hello? Oh well, audiences have their quiet moments. Anyway, I dusted off my trusty finger and started writing my great movie. That done, I phoned up my great mate, and fellow comedy blitzkrieg (although he's much better at comedy blitzkrieging than I am) and said, "Hello Adrian, great mate, love your work, cheque's in the post etc, I've got a smashing film script for you to read that's going to revolutionise the British film industry and take our already blazing white hot careers and catapult them into the stratosphere so they will career through the night sky like supanovas."

---

* Tribute not theft.

"Fuck off," he said and put the phone down.

When I had completed major surgery to replace my bleeding lungs that I had been forced to rip out because I was laughing so much at my great mate's golden bullet of a joke, I called him back. Before he told me to fuck off again (thereby compelling me to do the thing with the lungs again) he told me that he had written a film script which he was going to direct and if I paid him enough, I could be in it and even say that I wrote a couple of the jokes. It cost me two more children and a kidney to get the part and I even had to take an evening job as a peep show flap wiper to pay my final instalment to him, but it was worth it. And when the critics panned* the film, Ade and I bucked the trend† and didn't follow the classic career ark of the great British comedian which is do some stand up, do sitcom, do movie, get hammered by the press, get depressed, become alcoholic, die. That we did not do. It just made us stronger and harder and better at everything. Especially Adrian. Who I love and respect enormously. I'm not going to tell you lots of fabulous inside stories and gossip about Guesthouse. This chapter's just an advert for the video. So go out and buy it. Go on. NOW. Have you gone, viewer? Good. I'm going back to the pub‡.

---

* See earlier footnote. As you can see, I am footnote perfect. My editer at the hugely famous chain of publishers Harper Stoughtons often remarks on what an internationally renowned groundbreaking footnoter I am.
† Which means we were wild-eyed anarchists with the smell of gunpowder under our armpits and charred human flesh beneath our fingernails.
‡ See a different footnote. This one's crap.

# PERU

People often say to me, "Hey Rik!" and I say to them, "Back off, ordinary, I'll do the farmyard jokes." That's what it's like on the showbusiness merry-go-round, you just never know what anyone is going to say to you next. Unless I'm in a cutting edge play, of course, and I've learnt all my lines (which I <u>do</u> do) and I'm speaking at one of the extras who has words, in which case I do know what they're going to say to me next. But apart from that, it's just a mad crazy whurl of unexpectedness deluging down on me like a firestorm of rain and drizzle and stuff.

Picture the year. That's right, it was the year 2000. It was the millennial year in so many ways. Fuck I was busy. I was in demand everywhere. I mean, just look at what I'd been up to, viewer: there was Blackadder Back and Forth with Kate Moss (yes) which was a one off special for the great new millennium dome. Tony B wanted a major star to pull in the crowds. So who did he call? Damn right*. There were audio books for Dr Seuss, the Sound of Trumpets, Horrid Henry's Haunted House and How the Grinch Stole Christmas. There were thousands of lines to learn but it was no trouble. I learnt them, and what's more, I remembered them.

---

* It was me.

There was narration for countless episodes of the kids' show Jellikins. Not to mention a stage play directed by my old compardray Andy de la Tour called A Family Affair which toured the country playing to sell out audiences wherever we went. It was in French too so imagine how hard it was translating all your lines as you speak them, but again, it was no trouble for the man they call the Maestro. Not that I do lines. I never touch the stuff. There was a radio play called Higher Education which was recorded in Manchester. Incredible. Manchester! That's another town. There was a dangerous cutting edge underground video voice-over called Hogs of War, and I haven't even got onto the feature films I did that year. There was Jesus Christ Superstar in which I displayed my excellent singing voice, a Monkey's Tale, Watership Down and the great "lost" comedy classic Kevin of the North which I made in Canada with the legendary Leslie Nielsen and which all my Canadian fans tell me is the greatest film to come out of Canada – get this – ever. Beat that Brad whatever-your-name-is which I won't even mention is used as cockney rhyming slang for a shit because I don't want to tread on Chas 'n' Dave's toes. I respect them. But even after all of this, I still found time to make ratings-busting television films like the Comic Strip's Four Men in a Plane and The Knock; and the icing on the cake – no fuck that – the cherry on top of the icing on the cake – no fuck that again and more – the bit of air just hovering above the cherry on the icing of the vast cake mountain, the – and I mean the, as in THE – Strepsils radio commercial voice-over which was a landmark in human communication and is still spoken of in hushed tones amongst all voice-over professionals and technicians and all their families and friends throughout the western world. And that's fucking true that is. You can ask anyone. Anyone connected with voice-overs anyway. Ask them, they'll tell you. Do it now. I'll wait here. Done it? Good. I told you didn't I? Anyway, let's forget about it now and move on.

I don't talk about those things ever because I'm a professional (though with a better haircut and car). Let's just say I was tired after all my top quality work. Okay, said it now. I was tired. There, said it again. And what I decided I needed was a new intellectual pursuit to stimulate my artistry. So I decided to right a noval. I know what you're thinking. You're thinking, hold on a fucking minute Mr. Rik comedy-genius Mayall – love your work obviously – I never knew you had written a noval. How come I never saw it at the top of the best cellar charts which is where it would most surely have gone if you had written it? How come I never saw you reading it at the Cannes book festival? And you'd be right to be thinking all of that, viewer, and I respect you for it. Hey, you're a The Rik Mayall viewer, so what should I expect? My viewers are the best viewers and anyone who says they're not can fucking well shag Margaret Beckett at gunpoint while being forced to watch The Late Review* at full volume with the telly sellotaped to Margaret's head. Anyway, what happened is – well, I tell you what, let me start right at the beginning.

New paragraph.

You know that Jack Karouac, well he wrote all of his novals on a continuous roll of paper like a big bog roll. How hardcore top-writer-like is that? If I had known Jack Karouac I'm sure we would have been big mates because that's the kind of guys that we are, or were in his case. If he had a case that is. He might have had a ruck sack. Then there was Graham Green, or Greeny as I liked to call him or he would have liked me to call him if I'd met him because we would have been great mates, drinking loads of whatever it was he drank, sitting in a sauna together smoking cigars and talking about top quality books we are planning to write.

---

* Tell you what, Kirsty, give me a good review for my book on your shit Late Review programme and I'll let you fuck me. How about that? But keep schtum babe, kay?

Anyway, the thing is, I do loads of reading. Well I don't but I could if I wanted to. And the other thing is, actually, never mind, what I meant to say back there was the other great novalist alongside Greeny and Karouacy, as I like to call them, is Hemingway. Or Hemingwayy as I like to call him. You know him, bit of a fat guy with a nice beard. Shot himself. And not in the foot. Ernie I would have called him if I'd known him. Kind of friendly like. The thing is, I have maximum respect for my writer buddies but the reason I've never read anything they've written is because I don't want to soil my mind with their words. Life is a one off – that's what I'm always saying to people – not to everyone and I don't say it all the time but I say it sometimes. You know how sometimes you just say stuff that comes into your head. Well, that's what I do. I might be walking along the street or something and you know how sometimes you say words but you don't say them out loud, you say them inside your head, or you might mumble a bit – well, that's exactly it. Where was I? Oh yeah, I don't read much because I don't want to soil my canvas. I mean, I could say something about soiling your arsenal but that sounds a bit like a crap joke about shitting yourself and I don't do stuff like that, especially on a football pitch. That's just me. But it's very important that you pick your authors carefully. The important ones are me, Karouacy, Grahamy Greeny, Ernie H and Adolf – now he wrote a book, a big fuck off one, respec for that but it was all in German! Can you believe that? All in fucking German! And I didn't laugh once! Cunt. And then there's Ibsen. He's another one. He was Swedish and all his stuff was just plays and they were crap so strike him off the list. Ibsen? Forget it. It's a well known fact that you never see "IBSEN – HE WAS SHIT GOOD" written on walls by kids. You never see that. That bloke Ibsen was just a miserable Nordic twat with appalling sideboards who wrote shit plays that went on and on and on and no one ever got their top off. What's the point of him? I'd like to see the Rik Mayall fans and the Ibsen fans in a punch up. Now that I'd like to see.

Now, the thing with Jesus is that he went into the wilderness for forty days and forty nights. It sounded to me like a nice little break away from everything in the countryside. I had been working flat out satisfying the vast unquenchable thirst for me that my beloved ordinaries feel 24-7* and I was richer than Croesus† even after Heimi had taken off his 90%. And I was officially known as The Audience Magnet. That's a fact. Now when Jesus went off into the wilderness for forty days and forty nights, he had something big and happening to do [insert what he had to do here. Well, not right here obviously. Back there instead of "big and happening". Big it up, make it sound quite important and profound]. But I had something even bigger and happeninger to get out of my system. I would write a noval. A bloody good noval as well. I would fire my book like an arrow from the bow of my typewriter. Fuck that's a good line. Read it and weep Alistair Mclean. And the thing about me is, once I have made my mind up to do something, I do it like a full throttle out of control shit-kicking trouser-eating berserking motherfucker of a juggernaut with its brake cables ripped off and stuffed up its own arse. Don't mess with me viewer because I'm a shit-your-pants-and-run-for-it savage motherfucker when I'm riled. Shit, I said motherfucker twice. Shit! And shit. Oh cunts! CUNTS!!! CUNTS!!! CUNTS!!! As Ernie Hemingway‡ said, "fuck off." Poof. My noval would be like no other. I would sail away with my reader to the land of knowledge. There we would coagulate together into the overactive volcano that is a Rik Mayall noval

---

* This means twenty four hours a day, seven days a week. It works. Also, it makes you sound a bit American so you might get work in English TV, sorry, telly. No, fuck, sorry TV. Oh bollocks! Look, just shit off back up there.
† Loaded Turkish bloke.
‡ Good beard. Did I say that already?

in a strange and beauteous land where you, the viewer, knows with every word, that the novalist (that's me) doesn't care whether he lives or dies as he (me) tells it like it is and shoots from the hip like a vast over-arching black-hooded death-spattering toxic avenger of creative writing.

But where to go? There was always Bromsgrove (and it's not true what people say). Kidderminster is handy and there's always Halesowen. But no, this time things were different. The West Midlands was my roots but now I needed my flower. This time, I needed space, colour, wild free otherness and freedom so that I could remember whatever the fucking hell it was that I wanted to write about. In order to mine my rich seam of great words, I would have to cleanse myself of all day to day influences. But most importantly I knew that there would have to be one more thing. One thing for me to achieve completion. A bird. Birds. Maybe Peruvian ones. Young ones (I'm not talking about my show that changed the face of, well, everything really, but young birds who could help me with my noble, selfless endeavour and do the washing up, general cleaning, ironing, cooking, dusting and rigorous massage).

Suddenly, it appeared so simple. I needed to toss myself off. Toss myself off to some farflung land and take some time away from the everyday existence of a top showbiz phenomeonen and return bearing the gift of my great noval which I would give to the world and would publish and sell in all good book outlets and maybe some supermarkets (especially the hot 'n' happening Asda – I never shop anywhere else) and garages as well when it comes out in paperback.

But first I thought I had better telephone Heimi and tell him my idea.

"Heimi, it's me," I said when he answered the phone.

"Heimi? Never heard of him, he must be dead."

"No Heimi, it's me – Rik."

"Never heard of him either, I was just passing when I heard the phone ring. All my best wishes to you and your family . . ."

"Heimi, it's me, Rik, The Rik Mayall. You know, Andrex, Anusalve – your star client."

"Anusalve! Ah, Rikki, Rikki, Rikki, my boy, love you, love you, kissy kissy. Sorry about that, had to fire the receptionist. Very nasty – she tried to leave with my tail between her legs. What can I do for you my boy?"

"I've got a fantastic idea. It'll make us both rich. You especially."

"I'm moist already."

"I'm going to write a book."

It went quiet on the end of the line.

"Oooh, that's nasty, don't like the sound of it, I've gone dry. This is going to chafe."

"Why don't you like it Heimi?" I said, "it's a great idea. I go away somewhere hot and foreign in some far flung land like Peru where prices and human life is cheap and I write my big serious noval. Then you can sell it to a publisher and everyone's happy."

"No, no, no, Rikky my favourite client, don't be a silly boy, wake up and smell the Swarfega – nobody on the planet reads books these days. All the money's in voice-over work now – you know that."

"But Heimi, it'll be an opportunity for me to flex my glistening creative muscles. It'll make me a really serious artiste. I can do all those things I've always wanted to do, like appear with all those ponces on the Late Show and make out I'm really serious and intellectual, like I've really got stuff to say that means stuff."

'Hush your mouth now Rik, Heimi does the talking, I won't hear another word. Got a lovely little job for you – radio voice-over for an iron lung commercial."

Get this. For the first time in my career I decided to ignore

Heimi's advice and plough my own furrow. What a fabulous metaphor that is, me ploughing my own furrow. Watch me as I strain like a handsome local farmer-type in the nineteenth century heaving my powerful plough through the soil, all stubble and body odour and followed by a vast army of happy illegitimate children.

Anyway, never mind about that, what's important is that I decided to make my trip into the wilderness for forty days and forty nights and I called Heimi and told him. He wasn't best pleased but said that he'd be okay with it so long as I didn't go too far and he could send a van for me in the event that any more voice-over work came in. I agreed. What else could I do?

On the way to the airport, I decided to stop off at the BBC to see what had happened to my new hedge cutting thirteen part situation comedy called Total Arse Head which had been sitting on the BBC's desk since Spring '98 would you believe, which means that I'd been waiting for a reply for [oh someone else do the maths and work out how long it is].

BANG! and I was there.

"Get me the cunt in charge of light entertainment," I said without blinking. I never blink when I'm working. It's a sign of weakness.

"Who shall I say it is?" said the bloke in his BBC commissioner's outfit. Why they can't have top birds on reception like all the other television places is beyond me.

"Yeah right, very funny," I said at his blatant attempt to pretend to not recognise me.

"I'm sorry?"

"You're sorry? Look, just tell him I'm here and I want to know when we start shooting because I'm off to Peru to write a blockbuster smash hit book."

"But who can I say it is?"

There was a Q (and I don't mean that old bloke in the James Bond films*) behind me and in it was that bloke out of Eastenders with the bad skin – you know the one. This made it all the more essential that the overweight leper-cocked discharge-face behind the desk remembered my name. It was a pride thing. I pulled a quick Rick-from-the-Young-Ones comedy face – I couldn't have made it more obvious who I was if I had taken out a penknife and carved my name on my own forehead with it (back to front obviously so he could read it properly in the mirror). But have a quick brandy and grab hold of something sturdy before you read the next line. Here it is: he still pretended that he didn't know who I was!!

Everything was silent. Time had stopped. Someone had to slam existence back into meaning. So I did.

"I am The Rik Mayall!" I declaimed convincingly.

With that, I strod manfully down the corridor looking hard and dangerous with my hands on my hips – although I had to put them on my bottom sometimes so as not to bump into anyone when I was walking past them in the corridor. That's what I was doing – I wasn't wandering around pulling my arse cheeks apart looking for company at the BBC. I don't ever touch my arse cheeks. Or anyone else's. Especially Little Ben-Elton's. That story's just not true. What happened was that when I was giving his arse cheeks a feel up in the Liverpool Empire toilets in 1983, it was an accident. I thought they were mine and I was just checking that all was well with my bottom as it always is and always has been – let me say here and now that there has never ever ever been anything wrong with my bottom. So what I'm saying is that although it looked like I was giving him a feel up when we got caught by Tony Herpes†, I wasn't.

---

\* Although he was good and I respect him. Print that. His relatives might get whiffy.

† Legendary tour manager. Best there ever was. I swear to God you're going to be paid, Herps.

It doesn't count anyway. Not because I don't think Little's a man – he is – well, I say he is, I can't say for certain. I mean there's a slim chance – maybe a few thousand to one – that he's a bird but if he is, you wouldn't want to shag him anyway would you? I feel bad for saying that. Look, Little, if you're reading this and you do happen to be a bird then I would shag you because I'm a hard core feminist.

Where was I? Oh yeah, striding down the corridor in the BBC manfully with my hands in the right place. I came to a door and flung it open.

"Listen up shit smeers," I hurled, "what in the name of fuck do you think you're playing at sitting on my Total Arse Head for two whole bloody years and not coming hurtling back to me on your knees vomiting blood and gratitude and cash, imploring me to make my latest breakthruogh light entertainment project." Silence. Nothing but silence. The room was empty. I sat down for a moment and leafed through my emergency copy of Razzle and got a hold of my bearings. This was war.

"I don't give a toss who you say you are," said the security guard moments later as he threw me out of a first floor window, "get out and stay out." I could tell that he did recognise me really but was just trying to be hard. Poof. (No offence).

SPLAT! So there I was in a skip round the back of BBC Television Centre. Right, that's it, this sort of shit has got to stop. I'm going to Peru. And SHAZZAMM!!! (or something that means a couple of hours later) there I was at the departure gate at Heathrow.

"Read my mouth and feel my words as they penetrate you with roar manhood," I said to the woman behind the desk.

"I am all ears, Rik Mayall," she said, "in fact, I'm all eyes and noses and lips and dirty bits as well for you. God, you're even better looking in the flesh. And talking of flesh, The Rik, if I may,

I bet you've got plenty of flesh to go round – speaking in the bulging trousers sense[*]."

"Thanks baby," I exhaled, "I'm going one way only, but I'm going all the way – if you get my meaning." Her nipples hardened under the gentle caress of my manly drawl.

"Blimey, The Rik Mayall, you've got me all aroused now. I'm so horned up I could almost slip off this chair."

"Don't do that baby, you might hurt yourself on this not very thick shag (ooer obviously) pile carpet."

"Okay then The Rik Mayall, I won't."

"Right you are."

"It was two for Peru, wasn't it?"

"Yes, that's right."

"Okay, bear with me, whilst I look it up on the computer."

"Okay thanks."

"Don't mention it."

"All right, I won't."

"Great."

"Are you going anywhere nice on your holidays this year?"

"Thought I might go to Portugal at the end of August for a couple of weeks."

"That's nice."

"Yeah, I thought so."

"The weather in London has been relatively changeable recently, hasn't it?

"Yes it has but that's London for you, isn't it?"

"What is?"

"Where we live."

"Oh right, yeah."

"Anyway, here are your tickets."

---

[*] She really said this, I'm not making any of it up.

"Thanks very much."

"Don't mention it."

"Okay then."

"Great to meet you, Rik Mayall, it's been an amazing experience for me."

"Good, I'm glad."

"Thanks very much – may I call you Rik?"

"Of course."

"Thanks then Rik."

"No thank you."

"Bye then."

"Bye."

BLAM! I was straight onto the plane in a raging blizzard of in flight movies, headphones, blankets, sachets of things, wet wipes, air hostesses (yes), pilots (no), trolleys, tiny toilets, no fucking smoking and deep vain thrombosis.

The plane landed in a raging gravel storm and skad to a halt at the end of the runway. Peru. I had arrived. (In Peru.) Like a firestorm obviously. BANG! I was into a taxi and heading straight into the centre of the big town in Peru which is called Lima. It's spelt like that as well because I've looked it up. And the first thing I did when I got there was hire the services of a Peruvian bird for my forty days and forty nights in the wilderness (she was not – I repeat not – a prostitute) and in the beat of an exotic blue and pink butterfly's wing, we were in our strange magical vine-laden tree-top log cabin deep in the Peruvian rain forest (it was a total shit hole actually and nothing like what it said it would be like in the brochure I saw in Macclesfield. But that's another story (which I can let you have if you give me some money. Get in touch with me via Heimi's office if you want to make an offer. He might deny all knowledge of me and will probably deny that he knows anyone called Heimi Fingelstein but hang on in there, that's just his way.))

And so it was that I sat in my writing nest high up in the jungle treetops beneath the great over-arching azure sky as it stretched away to the horizon. And I started to write, and as I did so, became locked in a psychic orgy of intellectual concepts and great ideas which poured out of my brain and into my typing finger which tapped away like something very fast on cocaine (which I have never taken and never heard of). All I needed now was something to write about. I looked out over the steaming wilderness of jungle whilst the Peruvian bird did some dusting (and that's not a euphemism for anything disgusting). What wondrous words and new philosophies would spill from my lips – well, not really my lips, it's more like they would pour down my arms from my brain and into my hands so I could type them, but you get the idea. I sat there and pondered. When suddenly . . .

"Hello!" It was Russell Grant.

"Russell? What the hell are you doing here?"

"Oh don't mind me, I'm just passing through on my way to Chapter 17. Love your work, Rik."

"Love yours too, Russell, now hurry up and get out of my moving bit."

"I'm nowhere near it . . . oh I see. Bye Rik."

"Bye Russell. Still loving your work."

With that he was gone. It was a sign. So I sat there and pondered some more. And then it came to me, and it was big, so I braced myself (which is not as easy as it sounds) and there was a rumbling from deep within my soul and suddenly I started to disgorge avalanches of hot take-it-to-the-bridge literary Semtex.

I think everyone knows me well enough now to realise that I am a white hot triple-barrelled hell-trousered dirty-bottomed anarchist riding bareback on one of the four horsemen of the apocalypse's horses which I personally nicked, jumping over the gates of dawn like Shergar at the Grand National* (before he died obviously) and everyone knows that I don't tell lies. They call me Rik doesn't-tell-lies Mayall and that's why you know it's the truth when I tell you that I wrote one of the finest novals ever known to man when I was in Peru. It had everything, romance, history, comedy, long words. It was a damned sight better than 99.99999 per cent recurring of all the other books out there†. But wait for it, here's the heartbreak viewer, all that remains of my manuscript is a few tattered and afraid pages. It's true, that's all, and they are but a can of peas of what remains from the towering groceries (all well before their sell-by dates) piled floor-to-ceiling‡ of what once was a full length work of staggering artistry and literateur. You know that Isabel Alendy (we're the only two biggies at Colin Harper's), well I reckon if my lost noval met "House of the Spirits" in a pub fight before a Saxon reunion gig round the back of the Birmingham Hippodrome, "The Bleak Weeping Moorlands" would have nailed the fucker** before breakfast. I write hard. And here it is –

---

* Famous horse race. The fastest horse wins. It's fun.
† Which I'm not even going to mention.
‡ Maybe check metaphor. In fact, maybe check back through entire chapter. Don't want to have written anything by mistake that might make me look like a twat.
** Meaning won the punch up.

# ONLY SURVIVING PAGES FROM THE SECOND GREATEST BOOK EVER WRITTEN*

## THE BLEAK WEEPING MOORLANDS

by

The Rik Mayall

### Chapter One

And. So it was that the rain lashed moodily across the dark moorland. Why was nature so furious? Why did the green land seem so wet when the rain came down on it so from the bruised firmament? Because it was wet, that's why. That's the way that it was with rain. The Yorkshire rain. But why should the Yorkshire rain be here lashing down in Lancashire? Was there something a foot? The horse drawn carriage thundered on through the lightning. In the back, Lord Black knew his purpose. A young tender virgin swaddled in her shawl of linen and lace looked through the rain-lashed pane

---

* This being number one. Probably putting The Bible into third place.

on the seat opposite. The tear on her face was as if a raindrop had somehow opened the window, got through it, closed the window again, drifted sideways and then noiselessly plopped onto her cheek just below her eye where tears usually go.

Lord Black — whose friends called him Alistair — leaned forward in his seat and put his hand on the young tender virgin's knee.

"Do you come here often?" he intoned through his cheek whiskas so typical of those days.

"Oh Lord Black, for I just happen to know your name and who you are already, how did you know that this was the very question that I was dreading someone would ask?"

"There are many things I know in these parts of old Englande of Victorian times just before the Crimean War is about to break out. Why don't you come and stay the night with me at Black Castle Towers, my bleak moorland estate where even the walls seem to cry "Why, why all the hopelessness?" and where crows circle my bell-tower cawing noiselessly."

"But sir, I barely know your name and how knowest thou that I am a runaway virgin pretending I have somewhere to go?" she breathed through her heart-shaped lips.

"Never mind that now, just tell me your name, young woman."

"Why sir, I am Felicity Pinquor-Browne."

"In that case, Miss Pinquor-Browne, you're coming with me. Pull over driver!"

"No, I'm all right," said the driver. "I've got a coat."

"Yorkshire wit," Lord Black sighed. "Pull over by the first bleak forbidding moorland estate on the right after this tree."

The driver pulled the horses under his command. The carriage buckled and swayed, the wooden wheels skidded and the horses hooves all combined to make a not undramatic display in the snow-drenched dark. Felicity Pinquor-Browne flew as if she was flying across the interior of the carriage into Lord Black's arms and a shriek of August fear enveloped her heaving jugs.

"Felicity Pinquor-Browne?"

"Yes Lord Black."

"Here we are."

"Oh, very well then." And with that, he scooped her up in his firm muscularly erotic English arms and strod through the heather and the hillsides up his drive, past the garage, through the porch and into the house. There he was met by an elderly woman.

"Ah Mrs Ringsting," said Lord Black putting Miss Pinquor-Browne down on the timeless marble flooring. "I need felching."

Mrs Ringsting hurried away yelling, "Felching, felching, his lordship wants felching."

A deep voice issued fourth from the top of the stares: "Yes m'lord."

"Ah Felching," said Lord Black. "Miss Pinquor-Browne is my guest. She will need a bedroom for the early part of the evening before my mood sets in and crows circle my belltower and the wind rages all around in the timeless moonlit English countryside. So, I want you to take her upstairs and give her one."

"Pinquor-Browne?"

"It's up to her."

"No, I was enquiring if that was her name."

"Oh right," said Lord Black. "Yes, that's her name."

"Right you are then," said Felching.

"Thanks very much."

"Don't mention it."

"Dreams of pure unrequited love are

## NOVAL EXTRACT ENDS*

---

* NOTE TO PRINTER: Please ignore the shit stain on this piece of paper. That was the problem, you see. I caught dysentry and didn't have enough bog paper, hence me having to use the rest of my great book to try and staunch the flow. So do not reproduce. That means do not print. I don't wish to infer that you and Mrs Printer can't have children. I'm sure you can and will and maybe have done already. I think we'll just leave it there.

**FAX MESSAGE**

To: Doctor Wagner
Healing Hands Health Centre
Harley St, London W1

From: The Rik Mayall
Light Entertainment Firestorm
Peru

Date: 14th June 2000

Dear Doctor Wagner,

Love your verk. Picture der scene – oh fuck this, I'm going to write in English. You're walking through Spain in the sixteenth century. It's a sunny day – maybe it's a Tuesday afternoon and you've been really working hard and you're finished for the day and you're on your way home to where you live. Suddenly, from nowhere, a load of really hard blokes from the Inquisition come riding up (on horses) and attach one of those torture implements to your arse to check your faith in God. Well, think of that sort of pain Doctor W – get it locked tight in your mind and then times it by about two thousand and you'll get an idea of what I'm feeling at the moment. All I can do is type. It feels like a rabid flesh-eating rodent is having dinner where the sun don't shine although actually it does shine there at the moment due to the hole in the roof of my hut and a smaller corresponding hole in my trousers.

So here is the point of what I'm writing, which I do a lot of and so I'm fucking good at it, so clench your teeth and concentrate. This is a white knuckle letter Doctor Wagner, so read on (which you probably are anyway so ignore the last bit – though if you aren't then don't (except if you have (which if you have then start the letter again.))) Okay? Although whether okay or not, just do it. Okay?

When I visited you last week, you gave me inoculation jabs for all the major jungle illnesses which you thought I might contract on my journey. You might as well have injected me with a syringe-full of piss for all the good it's done me. What do I find when I arrive here after my three day riverboat journey, but not only am I riddled with malaria but I've got an attack of diahorrea which could break world records I'm absolutely fucking sure. Seriously, you could send that Roy Castle up here with Norris Magwurter and I bet you anything I'd be a record breaker once they'd seen the titanic geyser of liquid arse that is spraying non-stop out of what's left of my bum crack ring. That's why I'm doing my typing upside down. No sooner have I managed to drink a glass of water than it is either sweated or shat out of me before it can even touch the sides. I'm as sick as a pike and at this rate I'll be down to about four stone by the end of the week. Even the worms that appear from time to time out of my nostrils and from behind my eyeballs are beginning to look emaciated. I'm so weak that I don't have the strength to make it to the nearest native settlement for provisions which means that my Girl Friday, Pi, has eaten nothing other than my semen for the past week. Mind you, she looks pretty good on it.

Anyway, you fucking so called doctor, please forward medical advice and supplies as soon as you can (i.e.

before I'm dead). I refuse to be beaten like this. Like I've
always said, "No compromise, no surrender, no sell out,
no anti-biotics, no bog paper, no Anusalve, no friends, no
auditions without a guarantee of a part and/or shag with
co-star (female don't forget) . . . " Oh fuck it, I've gotta go
again. It feels as though I'm about to give birth to my own
liver. You may not even receive this letter as I think I might
have to wipe my arse on it.

I am not – repeat not – no, forget that, there's no time to
write "repeat not" – let's get on with it, this is a showbusiness
emergency – no scrap that, a major showbusiness emergency
– no scrap that again, it's a light entertainment holocaust.
Where was I? Oh yeah, and I'm not a happy fucking bunny
or whatever that expression is that the ordinaries use that
makes me want to kill them in their sleep. You've got to DO
SOMETHING! Tell all the medical companies that I'll do free
voice-overs for them for the next twelve months. Whatever it
takes, just send me some drugs! Do it quickly, I can't stand
on my head for much longer.

Remember that time I came to see you with my hives and
we got to talking about all those Eastern European women
who you've been harvesting? Well get this, I was wearing
a wire that day and I've still got the tape. I think we
understand each other.

Nearly dead and not very bloody happy about it,

Rik Mayall (The)

Some shit-hole-literally in Peru.

# THE PINNACLE OF LIGHT ENTERTAINMENT

Some things are just not meant to be funny and business is one of them. Business is a serious business. So, if you're looking for amusing anecdotes and gentle showbusiness reminiscences then you're in the wrong business. And the wrong chapter. Let's face it, if that's what you're looking for, you're in the wrong book. In fact, fucking hell, you're probably in the wrong life. I know some pretty heavy duty people on both sides of the life/afterlife divide so if you want to be terminated then let me know. I can probably have it arranged. No, forget probably. I'm Rik Mayall, I can do anything. The fact of the matter is, that when I do one of my great showbusiness voice-overs, it might be funny as hell to the people who watch the advertisement or listen to it on the radio but us serious guys in the advertising business with our button-down collars and economical haircuts aren't laughing at all. That's because we're too busy exchanging marketing expressions like branding*, brainstorming, penetration†, demographics, strategies and others that I know really well and am so using all the time.

---

* This has nothing to do with cowboy films where they get that metal thing which they heat on the fire and then stick it on a cow's arse and it makes that sssssssss sound.
† I won't say "ooer obviously" because this is serious.

We stand toe to toe, unless we're sitting around a glass-topped boardroom table in Soho at a top advertising agency which often happens, and we're looking each other right in the eyes and saying, "Hi guy, let's do it, let's press the button, let's touch each other's bases on this," and lots of other cool expressions like that. We don't pussy feet around the advertising dance floor, we just get our cutting edge ideas out of our ideas sachet and roll around with them a bit, maybe pin them down and ask them who the daddy is. And if they don't shout, "money" at us then we'll know we're smelling shit. And no one in the frontline of product placement wants to have the smell of shit up their nose. That is definitely not screaming "happening!" in anyone's face. In fact, it's screaming "not happening!" through a megaphone IN EVERYONE'S FACE. So, walk out of the room, close the door, leave the house, sell it and walk away, marry someone else, join the Catholic church, have lots of children and sit down in a big red chair thinking, "I don't know what happened there but I know that it was the right thing to do."

Anyway, what I'm saying to you is that I am deeply in bed beneath the covers with international high finance and business and the advertising industry generally. I bloody nearly did a business studies "O" level, guy, sorry, viewer – no, this is advertising, sorry – mate. That's it, mate. But that's not important. What is important is that I've done some fabulous stuff in my time, just look at it viewer, smell it, feel it shudder through the earth like some big and happening thing on the Ricta scale. And given the choice between working on an international blockbuster smash hit movie like Oh Marbella!, Day of the Sirens or The Canterville Ghost, I would take a commercial voice-over any day. There's no competition. And that's because I am Doctor Voice-over. I mean, if you were to go into Soho right now and go into one of those private members' clubs where me and the ad guys hang out after we've wrestled with a few ideas and said, "Hey, great mate ad exec types, who is Doctor Voice-over?" they'll look at you like you're a spaz and won't even bother replying to you because the answer is so obvious*.

The reason that I'm in such demand for my commercial voice-over skills is that I have a voice and demeanour that says, "Hi, how you doing?" – friendly, relaxed, – "Wanna drink? I'm having one so you might as well. Here you go. Anyway, I hear you're thinking of buying yourself a [whatever the product happens to be] well, I happen to know a lot about [whatever the product is] and I recommend you buy this brand of [whatever it is] because I'm an honest guy – I have no axe to grind – and I would never lie to you so you can trust me like your own, you know, whatever you trust or something." You know what I'm saying. Get on with it. And that's why all the products that I advertise are market leaders. I mean, think about it for a moment, will you? I am the Andrex Puppy. That's right, I mean I know you knew it anyway but fucking hell. I'm the fucking Andrex fucking puppy for fucking God's sake. Get that? Got that? Rik Mayall is the Andrex puppy? Fuck yeah. Eat it and weep, Mr Pastry. I single-handedly caused a global arse-wiping rethink. And, what's more, my breath-taking performances in those commercials have single-handedly led to the startling and almost shocking statistic that since they went on air, thirty-five per cent – yes, thirty-five per cent – less kids throughout the UK are attending school because so many of them are staying at home to watch me on the television. What's that say to you, viewer? Yeah, me too. Do you know, they have even had to cancel some of the Andrex adverts because they can't make the toilet paper fast enough. That's true as well. You can ask anyone. Well, anyone who works at Andrex anyway. I'll give you their phone numbers if you

---

* It's me.

want. Yes I will. Well I would, but they might not like it very much and get a bit cross with me, but that's so not going to happen because me and the Andrex guys are close. We're like that (I did a hand gesture just then – a cool one. Don't worry about it. No sweat. I gave it a bit of a wipe first.) That's just like the way I am with all the companies that I do ads for. I mean, even as we speak a massive inter-continental Rik Mayall deal is going down. Yes it is. And get this. And get it properly full in the face with happening aftershave on it – I signed that contract literally moments ago! Oh yes I did! And you viewer, yes you, are the first person on the planet to witness this astonishing cataclysmic culture shifting fact. You are listening to the voice – I mean listening to the words of – I mean reading the words typed by the finger of – the man – I mean, THE man, fuck! – the MAN, that's better – the MAN who is the Toilet Duck voice. That's right, the fucking Toilet Duck voice. Experience it now viewer. Yes, I am the Andrex voice, yes I am the Anusalve voice, yes I am the Toilet Duck voice. That's the big three that have just landed as I'm writing this, the hottest chapter in any book ever written. It's got to mean something hasn't it. Everything means something. I'm The Rik Mayall and in advertising, I'm the man who works with arseholes. It's just the way it is. You read it here first. Ciao.

[Chow?]

# D-DAY THE MUSICAL

I've never been short of arrows in my showbusiness quiver, right, but one that I have never taken out and thought hmmm, might just stick this in the old bow and see how far I can fire it, is that of showbusiness impresario. Acter, yes, of course; comedian, get real; challenging, controversial voice-over artiste, absolutely; but impresario, never. Until now that is.

Often I wander through London's West End and look at all the theatres and it depresses me. It's all just tired American musicals and clever comedies that aren't clever or funny. What we need is something that means something to us, the Brits, in our sceptred isle, our noble Albion and all that kind of stuff. We need a musical in the heart of the West End that will be like a banner that we can rally around and reconnect us to our noble heritage. So whilst Mister Chirac and Mister Schroeder are trying to take us over, I want to do this for my people. I want to do this in honour of all my ancestors who died at Waterloo, and at Crecy and Agincourt, the Crimean War and the Boer War *, not to mention the first and second world wars – I lost a lot then. And I will stage my musical

---

* This is where the British invented concentration camps. But they were decent places in those days. They were used for concentrating in. That's why we won the war. I'm related to Lord Kitchener.

in honour of the fallen. It will be like Remembrance Sunday every evening of the week, except Sundays, ironically. And the tourists can come and see a proper British musical that will make us feel proud to be British again.

People forget the legacy that Britain has left to the world with its great military victories, and that's because of all these mealy-mouthed politicians – eurocrats – europhiles or whatever they're called, who are in the process of selling this country down the river. Every couple of years I always do an enormous Bottom tour for my people. I like to get my Bottom out, which is one of my great jokes I often say. It's quite clever really because Bottom is such a dirty word and it is also the name of my great show. But this year, this musical, this vast production, this jewel in the crown of my glittering career which we will call D-Day – The Musical, will be my new live extravaganza and statement to my people. That's what it means to be known as THE British light entertainer (I can be quite a heavy entertainer* as well). I have devised it, written it, and will produce it and star in it. Not only will I take it to the West End but also on tour around the world. It will put Britain back on the map. And yes, I know it's a huge undertaking but hey this is nothing for the man who sorted out the whole African famine problem with my number one charity hit single Living Doll (I got five large houses out of it and a couple of cars as well). That proved that I could do music as well as everything else that I do that's great. That's because I've got the music in me. I've got the music in me. I've got the music, in me. They call me, Mr The Rik "Mr Music" Mayall.

I have a long tradition of making enormous amounts of money out of audiences. This is a good thing, it's kept a lot of non-entities

---

* Heavy entertainment is not about being slightly overweight. It's just that unluckily I have often bought the wrong sized trousers before a photographic shoot. Heavy means serious, which also has nothing to do with trousers. Get over it. I just have an unusual diet. It's a charity thing.

in jobs. But more importantly, it shows that I am the right man to pull this off (ooer obviously – comedy). To make this happen. So that is why I am including a small taster of the show in my great book. This will be an opportunity for you, viewer, to become involved in my great showbusiness venture and earn yourself lots of money. It's simple. All you do is you get your cheque book, make a cheque out to Rik Mayall Enterprises in association with Heimi Mad Dog Fingelstein for Top Bollocks Management Holdings Ltd, and post it to P.O. Box number 7358, Bermondsey, London SE16. Whatever you send in – and it really needs to be at least four figures to make it worthwhile – will be logged by Big Joan in a large notebook and all the money will go towards staging this great show. So it will all be completely above board and you'll have nothing to worry about. And then as soon as we've broken even then we'll start paying you back with interest. How's that for a totally cockripping idea? I bet no one else has ever thought of that. So get involved now, ordinaries, while your chance is still white hot.

So, right, now here is an edited, highly polished and really rather special early draft of the show. And, in case you're wondering, I've got it all copywritten and patiented and all that too so don't think you can screw me (meaning rip me off – not the other). This script is what's known in the business as "hot" so read it close to your chest. You never know who might come scuttling up behind you.

## D-DAY – THE MUSICAL

by
The Rik Mayall
and
starring
The Rik Mayall
as
Wolf Lair

INT. A THEATRE - NIGHT (ABOUT QUARTER TO EIGHT)

> *People. A stage. Lights. Suddenly...*
> *all the lights are switched off!*
> *This is not an electrical fault -*
> *this is supposed to happen. And*
> *there are curtains across the front*
> *of the stage. You probably already*
> *know this - I'm sure you've been.*
> *The curtains open to furious*
> *applause from the audience.*

ACT 1 SCENE 1: THE WHITE CLIFFS OF DOVER (KENT)

> *Some Germans shout "Achtung*
> *Spitfire" and fire a big anti-*
> *aircraft gun. A spitfire crashes on*
> *stage. DOUGLAS BADER walks out of*
> *the wreckage (with difficulty) and*
> *approaches the front of the stage*
> *with his dog, Nigger. This isn't*
> *racist. That's the dog's name.*

DOUGLAS BADER: It's not what you think, this
show's got legs. Keep watching.

> *Black out. This isn't racist*
> *either.*

ACT 1 SCENE 2: THE ENGLISH CHANNEL (BETWEEN ENGLAND
AND FRANCE)

> *The lights are on in this bit.*

> *A German submarine fires a torpedo*
> *at a British destroyer which sinks.*

> *Huge applause.*

ACT 1 SCENE 3: CABINET WAR ROOMS (LONDON)

> *WINSTON CHURCHILL sits behind his*
> *desk. Next to him stands AN*
> *AMERICAN in military uniform.*

WINSTON CHURCHILL:
> I've got it, listen to this...D-DAY!

AN AMERICAN:     Good idea.

> *Black out. Applause.*

ACT 1 SCENE 4:   OMAHA BEACH (FRANCE)

> *The Atlantic Ocean crashes on the beach. Sand everywhere, a bagette (remember where we are), lashing waves, cliffs, barbed wire, German gun emplacements, thousands of German troops. Luftwaffe fly past low, loudly machine gunning the sand. Nineteen landing craft approach the beach. Eight of them are sunk with mines and strafed with Stookers. Finally, the rest hit the front of the beach and open their flaps (ooer obviously).*

> *Out come four hundred British Tommies led by WOLF LAIR, 33, (me).*

> *Sudden standing ovation. Audience in shock. Screams of "Rik, Rik, take me." Everyone throws their pants. (Men optional.)*

> *Wolf bows and signs autographs, collects knickers, and takes telephone numbers of birds in the front three rows.*

> *Wolf broods.*

> *Applause. More autographs.*

> *Pause.*

> *The troops (all of them slightly shorter than Wolf - it's not a big*

*thing but it's very important)*
*watch Wolf, inspired and bursting*
*with respect.*

*Suddenly, like a Krakatoa from*
*nowhere, Wolf begins to hum the*
*opening bars to his first song.*

AUDIENCE:  My God! He's going to do a number.

[It's always important to kick the
audience in the face with the
opening number in a musical – so
this has to be a biggie. This is
where you come in, viewer. We need
some top quality show tunes. So if
you know any leading musicians,
maybe you can put them in touch
with me. Don't worry, I want this
to be a joint venture so I'll make
sure that you get a good cut – and
I don't mean that in a mafia-style
horse's-head-in-your-bed-way – I
mean I'll make sure you get money.
On top of the money that you will
already have invested. I'll sort
out the lyrics (words) – I've
already got a few good ideas like
rhyming bosh with cosh or gosh
perhaps and maybe Khaki could go
quite nicely with malarkey.
Whatever.]

*Musical number finishes. Wild*
*applause. Knickers. [It's screaming*
*money already, isn't it?]*

*Suddenly, some GERMANS run on*
*stage.*

SOME GERMANS:     Achtung! Schnell! Schnell! Voss is
                  das? English Schweinehunde! Handy-
                  hock! Handy-hock! [This is scary
                  German talk for "hands up"].

AN ENGLISH TOMMY:
                  Cor blimey guv, lawks-a-lumme! Rub-
                  a-duck! Etc, etc. [Normal BBC
                  cockney drivel – except a lot
                  better because this is my great new
                  show].

ANOTHER ENGLISH TOMMY:
                  You're not wrong there me old
                  cockney mate!

WOLF LAIR:        Fucking hell great mates – I mean
                  honest tommies – let's fight on for
                  Queen and country even though the
                  Queen isn't on the throne yet.

                  *There is a fire fight: bullets,*
                  *bombs, bodies and blood –*
                  *everywhere. All the tommies are*
                  *killed except for Wolf who fights*
                  *on.*

WOLF LAIR:        You'll never take me alive!

                  *Wolf's gun runs out of bullets and*
                  *he is captured by the Germans and*
                  *led away.*

WOLF LAIR:        Oh shit, I've been captured.

                  *The Germans laugh haughtily and*
                  *spit at him. But only acting*
                  *spitting. Not real spitting. It*
                  *could be a health risk. You know*
                  *how low cheap acters' morals can*
                  *get.*

Right, that's the end of Act One, although we could have another song here, maybe a sad one sung by Wolf about how fucked off he is that he's been captured. Then again, all that singing is a bit dull isn't it. Nobody likes music these days especially in West End musicals, and we don't want to overdo it. Besides, by now, we'll have the audience eating out of our hands because it's got it all – patriotism, heroism, great songs and extreme violence. What it doesn't have is romance – that will come later on when Wolf gets it together with some fabulous French bird at the prisoner of war camp. But though he is in love, he decides to tunnel out of the prison (I was thinking we might have him appearing through a hole at the back of the auditorium – no one's done that before) and he returns to the D-Day landing which is still going on and helps lead all the Tommies to victory before liberating the prisoner of war camp and being reunited with his top bird.

> Pause.
>
> Snogging, wild applause.
>
> THE END.
>
> Loads of curtain calls, etc.
>
> Lights go back on.
>
> People go home.

Looks to me like everyone's laughing and you know what I'm thinking, don't you? Course you do, us big guys know the score. It's going to be like standing in a wind tunnel of cash and it's all going to be blowing our way. Are you getting the metaphor here?
BANG!
What the fuck was that? That was a great wad of Euros hitting me in the face from all the tourists who will come flooding across

the channel and the Atlantic as well to come and see it. We'll be so rich that we can buy expensive houses in Provence, have swimming pools installed, fill them up with pound notes and swim about in them. I mean, fivers, because it's coins now isn't it. Coins'd hurt. Especially with the breast stroke. Or if it was hot. And some bastard might stuff a load down his trunks and run away pretending he's well hung. So, hey, it's a crap idea, forget about the whole thing. Tell you what though, we could have a German version in which the Krauts win. That way, we can keep them happy too. You've got to think of everything in this game. You just can't afford not to. Anyway, get your cheque books out and before you know it we'll be in bed together. Business-wise, of course. I'll leave you to it. Don't forget the stamp.

# MAXIMUM ENTERTAINMENT EXPERIENCE

They're pouring out of me, viewer, the words that is. I haven't even got time to break the flow of my prose to tell you that and I'm not the kind of guy who does that kind of thing anyway. I'm the kind of guy that doesn't do stuff like that and when I say I don't do it, I don't do it because that's what being Rik Mayall is all about. It's like the typewriter is an extension of my body and memories hurl themselves at me like hail stones in a psychic maelstrom of writing lots of things.

It was spring. Spring 2003. The blossom was on the trees and my thoughts turned to Nöel Coward and his play, Present Laughter. So I took it out on tour, indescribably successfully, of course. You see, the thing is, Nöel wrote it specially for me. When I say he wrote it for me, I don't mean that literally of course. Noel Cöward didn't wake up one morning and think, "Right, today I think I'll crack one off for Rik Mayall." Although, you never know, he might have done. But really what I was doing with you there, viewer, was using an allegorical allusion – no, me neither, looks good though doesn't it? Anyway, enough of this literary politesse, let's get our trousers down, legs wide apart and well lubed up for some serious flying-superfortress-style provincial theatre touring anecdotes.

The part of Garry Essendine in Present Laughter was played by some decent acters before me. There was Albert Finney, there was Peter O'Toole, the late great Peter Wingarde (who played Jason King – respect), George C. Scott in America and even old Noelÿ himself. But quite a few serious hardcore Noel Cowärd fans (whose names I shan't divulge) who have seen all the different productions starring all six of us towering titans of modern theatre said that my portrayal was by far the best. This is true. And what is more, it is a cold stone fact.

So there I was coming on stage in the incomparable Ambassadors Theatre, Woking. I'd already been on for twenty minutes. That's why I always wear good thick trousers when I'm acting. It was all going well. Everyone knew their lines and was saying them in the right order and at the right time and it all made sense. But there was something wrong, I could feel it. Something was whispering at my sensitivity. What was it? What could it be?

Something that is worth knowing about me, viewer, is that I am known in showbusiness circles as The Audience Barometer. This is because I can sense the atmospheric mood of an audience so well whilst I'm on stage. Like a barometer, obviously. It's like I'm a bit telepathic. Not even a bit really. I'm quite a lot telepathic. And I could tell that something was badly wrong. There came a shout from the top of the dress circle*, "where's Eddie?" I ignored it of course. I'm a professional in all things, especially my stage work. I continued with my challenging portrayal of Garry Essendine's next line, but inside, it felt as though a runaway combine harvester had chewed me up in its horrific spiky rotating things at the front and passed me through its insides and disgorged me in a bail of feeling really rather frightened. For over

---

* This is the place where the upper-middle-class people sit. As opposed to the upper circle which is where the lower-middle-class people sit. Anything can happen in show business. And often does.

twenty-eight years I had managed to keep all my different fan-bases and factions and groups and splinter groups and divisions and sub-divisions apart. But here on a Wednesday afternoon matinee in Woking things were turning ugly. And I don't do ugly. I ad-libbed* for a moment, so I could walk to the front of the stage so I could take a look at my audiense. You're in trouble here Rik Mayall, I thought to myself. And I was. So I was right. I always am. I could tell just by looking, which was pretty good really because it was dark, that they were out there, confused and fright-ened but ready for battle nonetheless. It felt like I was standing butchly astride a huge unexploded bomb like in that series with the bloke with the shaky hands. Except he was sitting on his one. So I was better than that.

The first flare up took place at the back of the stalls when a chapter of Glaswegian Young Ones fans threw a Christopher Ryan look-a-like at some Liverpudlian Four Men in a Plane fans but missed and hit some Noel Coẅard obsessives who retaliated with sherry schooners full of piss. Up in the dress circle, vicious scuffles broke out between some Horse Opera fans and a renegade band of Jellikins enthusiasts. An usherette was thrown from a box by some Canadian Kevin of the North fans, and landed on a really hard father and son Krindlekrax tag team in Row H. Things were definitely turning ugly by now. Even though I still didn't do ugly. Although I was beginning to think that perhaps now was the time to consider doing it. I knew I was really in trouble when a suited, heavily armed gang of New Statesman admirers abseiled down from the upper circle throwing flares into the dress circle to light their way before engaging in vicious hand-to-hand combat with a gang of Lord Flashheart die-hards.

---

* This is a theatrical term for making up some words. It has nothing to do with women's lib [check this].

Still I held the show together. Fellow cast members were looking terrified and sweating excessively. It was quite unpleasant really. I knew that the audience was teetering on the edge of theatrical armageddon when a pensioner in a Drop Dead Fred T-shirt was fired from a giant catapult constructed from the elastic underwear of viciously stripped and beaten Dave the Cardboard Box fans and landed in the orchestra pit with a sickening thud followed by the plopping sound of an accompanying colostomy bag a split second later. Andrex puppy fans were managing to hold the front six rows of the stalls from the advances of an angry mob of How to be a Little Sod mentalists and through the doors at the back of the auditorium, I could just make out some blue anoraks as a confused group of Kevin Turvey fans were deep in conversation about which bus to take home and how interesting it was that some numbers on bus tickets are slightly not the same as the numbers on some other bus tickets when suddenly they were set upon by a small smartly dressed group of Government Inspector devotees and chased from the building past the three ubiquitious Tales of Uplift and Moral Improvement fans who are always so proud of being the only three people on the planet to have actually seen the programme and always look down their noses at the Grim Tales hordes and fifty-something Rik 'n' Roald Dahl Jackanory intellectuals.

It was open slaughter at the back of the upper circle where the almost suicidal Comic Strip antidisestablishmentarians were beating the fuck out of each other. Bad News were kicking the shit out of Summer School who were giving it to The Strike who were already stomping on More Bad News while Beat Generation were ripping the faces off all five of them while the Private Enterprise girls were taking them from the side and were happily setting fire to the Gino die-hards.

Way over in the middle of the stalls, the entire Bottom series one, two and three were fighting full civil war as furious Bottom splinters formed. Fans of individual episodes were twotting, smacking and headbutting the living daylights out of each other until suddenly they all reunited and took on a gang of Filthy, Rich and Catflap psychos wearing the most appalling mid-eighties clothes that they must have found somewhere in North Wales. But never mind about all that. What really put the fear of God into me was that THEY must be out there somewhere. Yes, THEM, the most terrifying subhuman hell-pack of mine or anyone else's admirers: BOTTOM LIVE FANS. Read them and weep, Genghis Khan. An army of three million blood-drunk Mongols? My Bottom fans would have had them for breakfast. And yes, there they were, encrusted in their own vomit, rampaging through the back of the auditorium, drinking lager, using shocking language and hungry for human flesh. They literally ate their way forward through rows X,Y and Z going to the toilet wherever they liked. They made Stalingrad look like a mid-morning appearance on Richard and Judy. They approached the stage bellowing, "Why isn't Eddie here hitting you, Richie?" and, "Why can't we see your Y-fronts sticking out of the top of your trousers?" It was as if there was no law. The sky turned black with despair. The Rik Mayall was alone (apart from a couple or so other acters who were in the play as well, dearest friends of mine, who were, er, oh . . . just look up in an old programme to find out who they were). There he stood alone, The Rik Mayall with his leaderless legions from five enormous international sell-out tours. They were like an army in their own right. When the police arrived, they didn't even try to tame them. They didn't get the chance, they were eaten immediately. So was their van. So was their dog. Well, no he wasn't really. He was taken away to the toilet where some of the . . . oh, let's not go into it. It was just horrid. The toilet, I mean, not the dog shagging. It was like the Ambassadors Theatre, Woking was transformed into Brighton beach in 1965, only instead of mods and rockers and Sting and Phil Daniels and Leslie Ash (yes), there were countless Rik Mayall fans rioting. It just couldn't get any worse. And then it did. They took to the stage, grabbed my leading lady, shaved her head, superglued a pair of glasses to her face, put her in a brown suit, made her drink three bottles of Thunderbird and told her to beat the shit out of me – which she did. Rather well actually. Talented girl. I must find out her name. Bless her.

The Noël Coward Wednesday afternoon matinee suddenly underwent a spectacular volte-face. There was Eddie on stage, beating the living shit out of me and the Bottom Live berserkers were now trying to keep the peace. It was like the Hells Angels at Altamont. And the remainder of the audience regardless of whichever part of my thirty-five year career they vouchsafed their allegiance to, were beginning to mellow and thrill to the show as my teeth and nose cartiledge were spattered around the stage. I was beginning to gain control of my ordinaries! Now was my chance!

"Just ruddy well shut up you utter utter spastics!" I suddenly unleashed like a whiplash (paying subtle though genuine and heartfelt homage to my Rick character from my revolutionary breakthruough situation comedy The Young Ones which revolutionised the whole concept of global comedy) by getting my "R"s out and mispronouncing them for my beloved Woking audience that afternoon. Right then, everything stopped. Every face in the auditorium whipped round from what they were doing and locked onto their Rik. A frisson of disbelief rippled like quicksilver through the auditorium. And then it was as if a crack in the earth's surface had formed and widened into a chasm from which a gigantic volcanic eruption of powerful golden laughter exploded forth, growing and growing in its majesty and pure love. My audacious gambit had paid off. Rik and his legions were one again through the simple trick of his timeless comedy genius. It was as if God had smiled on the world again. Which he did. And I, smiling to my audience, moved forward to receive their adoration, laughter and joy. Those of them who were still alive. I looked out over the carnage all around me. There was only one way to go and that was on. I looked at my leading lady (who was still dressed as Eddie Hitler) and kissed her on the lips. At that moment there was a deafening tortured howl from the entire audience: "No!!! Fucking hell Richie!! You can't snog Eddie!" And the entire audience exploded violently once more into another Grade A riot until I turned to them with one of my great twinkles and said, "It's okay, my great showbusiness chums, it's just another one of my great Rik Mayall jokes." What a triumph of theatre that was. They simply hooted with laughter and gave me a three hour standing ovation, by the end of which all the pubs suddenly opened and the audience disappeared still applauding and arguing over whose round it was. Result. I, The Rik Mayall, had not only saved the show but I had also saved the theatre and countless lives of people in the auditorium that afternoon. Yes – several hundred had died, yes – the theatre was destroyed but the show must always go on.

And interestingly, in Woking, that's what it will do. Overnight, someone somehow rebuilt the entire theatre and swept all the bodies under the carpet. You could go to Woking this very day – it's not far – and you could sniff around and ask some questions. But wherever you go, people will tell you the same thing, that there never was a bloodbath at the theatre that day and that I never did manage to broker a peace deal with my top acting. They'll deny all knowledge of it. And do you know why that is? Because they're frightened. And that's because there are dark forces at work. Let's put it like this. There are people out there whose interests are not best served by having a Rik Mayall in their midst who is so much better at acting than all the other ones in the world are at acting. I shall say no more. That's not because I don't know what to say or haven't thought of anything that I could say or have thought of something to say and have then forgotten it like a twat (which I'm not). It's none of those things. It's just because I want to give my words the maximum effect. And that's the thing that I have. Done. My story has been told. Noel and I are at peace. But not like that obviously. I don't do that sort of thing. Although of course, I've got nothing against . . . oh fuck all this. See chapter seventy.

# QUICK MAYALL

When you're a comedy hellraiser and the wild man of light entertainment, you sometimes need to let off steam. But I never do,
okay? I just want to make that clear. I don't let off steam because
I don't need to. So, there you go. Read it and weep. Or, maybe,
read it and think hmmmm that's quite interesting, I wonder if he'll
write another great book that I can get on order at my local book-
shop.

What it was is this. Or was this. Or whatever you fancy really.
That's Anarcho-Surrealism that is. The thing is or was, I was
arrested for doing 127m.p.h.* in my top of the range saloon drag-
ster and The Mirror (which is a tabloid newspaper which I love
and admire enormously as I do all tabloid newspapers and the talented journalists who work for them) ran† a headline: QUICK
MAYALL. Now this is clever for a number of reasons. Firstly,
Quick rhymes with Rik. So there you have it. So that's quite a
clever thing to put on the front of your newspaper. They're clever
guys. They don't fuck about. You've got to have your trousers
done up when you're running around that kind of yard. You're

---

* Miles per hour.
† This means they wrote some words about what had happened and put it in
the newspaper.

288

talking university degrees here. These aren't ordinary men, or women, obviously.

The thing is, viewer, I cannot actually tell you why I was done for speeding. I am not allowed to. Let me just say that on that day down in the west I was doing some work for Tony B and the gov*. Military intelligence. Like in that one with the big fuck off submarine under the Polish ice cap. Let's just say that it was for the good of the country. I am known as The Commando in the corridors of Whitehall. No, The Really Hard Commando, that's the one. What happened was this: I got a call. It was the telephone. Someone asked me to "Take a dive on the M5". This is code for "Make sure you get yourself arrested for driving very quickly." So I did. I deliberately shot myself in the foot. I felt my own collar. Which is tricky. The pigs were down on me, literally. And I respected them for it. Autographs all round. Everyone loved everyone else's work – especially mine. I explained to them that every so often I have to go under cover. And that's not a bed thing and I'm not putting this in my book to make me look hard and brave either. It's just a fact of life. My life. But it's a secret anyway, so don't tell anyone. We're under the foreskin on this one viewer, unless you haven't got one or you're a bird in which case we're between the flaps. Let's just say that me getting arrested for driving at 127m.p.h. on the motorway and signing loads of autographs and getting a headline in The Mirror (good paper) was the perfect cover when I was asked to deliver a certain package somewhere and any more than that I am definitely not allowed to say. It was a car bomb. I can probably tell you that much but that's the end of it. No more. In fact, just to be on the safe side you should rip out this page once you have read it and tear it into little pieces, eat them, let them

---

* This is my expression for the government which saves time actually writing out the whole word. I invented it. And I'm happy to fight in a pub anyone who says that I didn't.

pass through the body and then eat them again. It might taste nasty but it's good to be safe. In fact, after you've read the whole book you should set fire to it and then buy another one. [Are you reading this in the Harper Collins marketing department? Don't bother coming to thank me for instantly doubling your sales in one fell swoop. Because I won't be here. I'll have gone out.]

Actually, forget all that.

[Start chapter again below.]

Hello. Now, the reason I was done for speeding on the M5 in 2003 was that I was trying out a new comedy character. I didn't have a name for him yet but I knew he would be a quick driver and so when I was caught by the pigs it was just some research. Method acting. And anyway, I'm not very good at driving slowly. "Not very good at driving slowly" is one of my middle names. Showbusiness fire whirlwinds don't drive slowly. You can't be seen to be driving slowly if you're meant to be highly amusing on the television. Ask yourself, has Jim Davidson been done for driving too fast? I think you'll find that he has. That's why people like me and Jim are at the forefront of pretty much everything that's dangerous and revolutionary. Ask yourself this as well, in fact, don't bother, I'm going to ask you instead: Does Lemmy from Motorhead obey speed limits? I don't think so. Does Lemmy drive his Heinkel bomber down the slow lane of the M6? I don't think he does. Do you think that me and Lemmy would find ourselves sitting down together at a Happy Eater, having an all day breakfast like there's no tomorrow, and Lemmy would turn to me and say, "later Rik Mayall – I'm off," and then he'd stride out into the car park, up onto the wing and into the cockpit and then set off at 15m.p.h. down the slow lane? Like a girl. No fucking way. Which means of course he wouldn't. Lemmy is rock. It's the same with me. Show me a throttle and all I want to do is open it up. Maybe read that line again. I just have. It's pretty good.

And also, at the time when I was done for speeding, it was a difficult time for Britain, it was April 2003 and Tony B was taking us triumphantly to war against the middle east. Some people in the country were sad about this but only because they didn't understand what Tony was doing which was protecting us all from terrorists by killing thousands of Iraqi children who could quite easily have grown up to be bad people who didn't want their oil wells to be stolen by the army and given to a handful of Tony's extremely rich friends who own and control all of the West's money, arms, government policies and "election" results. These children might easily have become violent because they didn't have sufficient pluck to shrug off malnutrition, starvation, drought, disease, state brutality, and Anglo-American pogrom-style racial extermination. But Tony has been to Oxford University for heaven's sake and knows far better than anyone what is good for us all. Anyway, these were uncertain times, so I decided that I needed to do something to lift the spirits of the British people. Getting done for speeding was a situationist, dadaist [check this] gesture that I made in a selfless way. In an almost – let's face it – Victoria-Cross-worthy way too. Because instead of just cheering up the troops like other lesser talents might do, I was using my deep inner understanding of the media and cheering up the entire nation. But no matter how popular you are in this country, the British justice system will still prosecute you and that is only right and proper. I am quite hard, after all, and I can take it. Sacrifice is my middle name. A thousand pound fine? It was a small price to pay, which I would have paid, if my accountant wasn't suffering from some financial irregularities at the time and I hadn't gone to the wrong court room and given a false name. But what's important is that I learned my lesson. So, the next time the police tried to catch me, I put my foot down even further. 138 m.p.h. I think I managed that time. I was still caught and fined though, dash it, and banned for six years. But I don't care, I still drive all over the place. I'm Rik Mayall. And there's not many people who can say that.

Tony Blair
The Prime Minister
10 Tendowning Street
London SW1


April 5 2005

Dear Tony,

Just turned on the television because I like to have the
current affairs on in the background because that's the
kind of twenty-four-hour rolling news kind of twentieth
century guy that I am and I like to keep my finger on the
pulse and my ear to the ground. In fact, I have fingers all
over the place and in a lot of pies as well, right. People
often call me Rik "Mr Fingers" Mayall. Keep that one in
your mind there Tone, okay? Received.

But anyway, enough about me. There I was just now,
right, sitting on my sofa in my house watching the
television and it was like WHOAH! It was coming at
me, right, like a twenty-ton runaway cement mixer with
a crack-addled psycho at the wheel and Judas Priest on
the in-cement-mixer hi-fi sound system thing (probably
Breakin' The Law or one of their early ones because we're
down with Judas aren't we Tony?). And I'm thinking to
myself, fucking hell! (I know you won't mind me
swearing like this because I went to Oxford as well and
we were so swearing all the time. We were always in the

student union bar drinking strong lager and playing
guitars, listening to pop music and wearing flares. We
were so whatever-the-word-is. Fill it in yourself Tony,
I'm sure you know what I mean. But make it good.)

Anyway, fucking hell! I thought to myself, Tony's only
gone and called a general election! And there you were
heading off to see the Queenster in the jag to ask permish
(this is short for permission) to have a general election,
and I have to say – no bollocks to that, I don't have to say
it but I'm going to say it anyway – you looked good. I
really like your weight situation at the moment and you
look like you might have been working out a bit as well.
I'm sure your shoulders have got wider and those trousers
did look a little loose around the waist, although the
creases down the front were as sharp as always. I don't
think you look fifty. I don't even think you look forty, to
be totally honest with you. I know I can say that to you
in a man to man, great mates together, slap on the back,
absolutely straight as a dye way without you getting the
wrong idea. And even if you did get the wrong idea,
that's okay with me, because I'm an all-inclusive guy in
every way and I love everybody and I'm so down with
the whoopsies. That's what New Labour is all about, isn't
it Tony? Anyway, there you were getting into the jag
fantastically – a nod and a half smile to the press core –
and a little adjustment of the tie that says, "Don't fuck
with the big man". Now I'm a big fan of the jag, as you
know, but have you ever considered getting yourself a
Harley Davidson instead? I don't think any other P.M.
(that's an abbreviation) has done this before although I do
have a vague memory of Harold Wilson and his secretary

riding around on a motorbike and side car. But that was the seventies. Who was anyone then? Actually, it rather appeals to me the thought of you striding out of your front door (or the one you pretend is your front door when you're not in the country with Cheggers) (why Cheggers? I've never understood that) and instead of doing the usual (nod, smile, cool tie knot, concerned expression, hint of itchy arse), you could pull on your helmet (ooer obviously) and get your leg over (ooer obviously again) get her started and all revved up (and again) and roar off down Downing Street like a dangerous bad-ass motherfucker. You just give it some thought Tonester because from where I'm sitting, it's got "jolly good idea" written all over it.

But forget all that, the reason that I'm writing to you is that I'd like to offer my services to you to help in your election campaign. That's right, you heard it here first, Tone. Ouch! Does that hurt? I don't think so. Rik Mayall in Tony's election campaign! Hide the chicks, boys. The Rikster's on side!!! So, let's get our teeth into the meat, Tone, not that I've got anything against vegetarians. As you know, leader, I have great experience of advertising things and making them total market dominators overnight, so it just came to me in a blind flash, right, that I ought to do the same for you in the election. Just think what effect a few million posters up and down the country would have with "Rik says: Vote Tony," written on them. As soon as people see that you and I are locked together in political unity, it'll be time to polish down the front bench again and take your seat with the big boys.

After all, and I don't really want to blow my own trumpet here, but I am the man who brought down the Thatcher administration with my smash hit TV series The New Statesman (it was very popular as well). Then I brought down the undercarriage and cleared the runway for New Labour's second term with my next mega-smash series, Believe Nothing, which flattened the old-fashioned labour intelligentsia who didn't dig the "Tony beat". Blood, bodies, stale left wing morality scattered as far as the eye could see. So nothing was on the runway, big boy, because of the Mr Rik and you brought in the New Labour party at Mac 3. And I respec you for it. (Worth noting, Prime Minister, that the young people nowadays don't use the letter "T". There are votes in those hoodie sweat shirt things that I'm told are very fashionable on the council estates. So get out of Denver baby and get a hoodie on the Tony – like now, duuur (more young speak there Tony. No one knows what it means but it makes you look like you watch Top of the Pops a lot, so use it: Rik Tip there for you.))

As you know, I've got a lot of experience of politicians and history. You might have seen me playing Flashheart in Blackadder. Of course you have, you've got your finger on the nation's pulse. And there was that great play that I did – I can never remember it's name – well that had something about politics in it as well. And that other one with that bloke from Oxford in it. That bloke who's never out of the toilet with his dresser. So I know what I'm talking about when it comes to politics. I'm armed to the teeth with political attitude. And. And it's a big And, this one. I got a recent compliment from my dentist that I'm so big on smiling, so I'm prepped up and big for smiling on the poster. And let's not forget TV advertising. You're looking at Mr. Nintendo here Tone. You were still at Oxford then so you must have seen those commercials. By the way, I saw your fantastic telly ad with Gordon – it so said, "vote for me" (you've got to be aware of my youth speak remember Tony, because your public school kids won't be talking hardcore fashionable like this when Daddy eavesdrops in on their conversations. So you'd better remember to run with me on all hip things Tone because I am the guy who screams "down with the kids" big time everywhere). Anthony Milligan does not make crap ads. There you go, Tone, curse lifted. It's an amazing coincidence, actually, that I should be writing to you now because I've also got a great idea for another television commercial or party political broadcast or whatever they're called. Because it's worth bearing in mind that when the British do television, they do good television, but only when Rik Mayall's involved. It's just one of those things.

Picture the scene: number 10 (your place) late at night. There's you, sitting at your desk looking tortured. Unhappy. Deeply unpopular. Despised and hated by the entire population of the country. I mean everyone – they loathe you. Abhor you in every sense. And you've got no one to turn to. All your Oxbridge "friends" have deserted you because they hate you as well. Poor Tony. What can he do? There's a knock at the door. You look up, wipe away the tear from the corner of your eye and say, "enter". It's Gordon Brown and he's all excited and he hurries in and says, "Tony, Tony, it's Rik Mayall here to see you," (in Scottish obviously). And suddenly, from nowhere, there I am in the doorway. There is a brief moment of brotherly recognition between you and me. Then Gordon starts fussing about saying to me stuff like, "Hey Rik, love all your telly shows and films, can I have your autograph?" And you and I can look at each other and smile knowingly, and you can say, "I've already got his autograph, Gordy, you're such a spastic," and you and I can laugh together at him. Then I can say to him, "Course you can have it Gordy." And I can sit down as the light changes and sign his autograph book and say, "Here you go, it's all yours, because New Labour cares for everyone. Even Scottish people. Like you." Gordon smiles in his mongoloid way and we all shake hands. And I turn to the camera and in a zoom crash close up say, "These New Labour guys sure get my vote," doing my eyebrow thing which always works.

Ooh Tony, I'll tell you what, while we're on the subject of television, you should make sure that when you do one of your crap interviews in the election campaign, you don't have that Dimbleby bloke. He's always trying to pick on you. I could do a much better job of interviewing you. I know loads of great questions which I could tell you about beforehand. All of which leads me onto that fat slug Joan Prescott who said that thing about me on BBC Question Time a couple of years ago after I had done my challenging portrayal of Adolf Hitler in the anti-Euro cinema commercial. What the fuck was she thinking of? She lost you between fifteen and sixteen million votes that night when she said, "Well I didn't think it was very funny." Rik Mayall fans don't like people talking like that about The Master especially when The Rik was defending his nation against the Nazis like so many of Rik's and the nation's relatives were doing when they died in far more dangerous circumstances than I was in spending two hours being filmed taking the piss out of Hitler sixty years after his death. If Joan Prescott wants to hand over the nation to the Nazis then I think it's about time we ask ourselves which side she thinks she's on. Maybe she would like to hand the nation over to Mr Chirac instead? Or whichever nation takes the traitoress's fancy. I think they call it treason. Isn't that a capital offence? No, it's a national offence, that's what it is. Sure, I wasn't in the trenches, sure I wasn't on Omaha Beach, sure I wasn't being burned to death in Coventry or fighting fires in the East End. No. I was in front of the camera and it might not be as dangerous but this is a matter of honour. When good men hear the call, they come to the defence of their country. That's all I was doing in my selfless cinema ad. Was I paid? The answer's no. Did I give my services free of charge? You betchya sweet bippy Tony-boy. And I want you to know that I'm out here in Telly Land polishing my bayonet in readiness for traitors like Mrs Prescott. I don't think she should be allowed to say that I'm not funny. It's a disgrace. You're always going on about how religious and racial hatred should be stamped out everywhere, well this is a clear case of incitement to light entertainment hatred. I never said anything to her at the time but you can tell her from me that if she wants to commit political suicide, there are easier ways than some half-arsed attempt to make out that I'm not funny. She could have got herself nobbed by a trannie for starters. If I was you Tone, I'd get yourself into the twenty-first century

and get yourself a top chick as an assistant instead of
a fat northern bird like Prescott. It gives out the wrong
message to the electorate. And you wouldn't want to
wake up next to that in the morning would you? You're
the P.M. for God's sake. You can have any bird you want.
I mean, God knows, I'm an all-inclusive permissive kind
of guy but to get involved with that revolting slag heap,
you've got to be a real sicko perv, haven't you?

So maybe you should draw a line in the sand on this one
(although I have never taken drugs myself and particularly
not on the beach because it's just stupid. You get all that
sand and crap up your nose. And the fucking headaches
you'd get! What do you think I am, stupid? That's more
than a two Anadin number in anyone's book (but not in
mine because I never take any drugs at all.))

And listen Tony, the BBC didn't come out of the whole
thing smelling too rosy either. Isn't it time that their
government subsidies were trimmed back a bit? I
don't think they should allow some dodgy balding
lard-mountain of a woman to come on one of their
supposedly impartial political programmes and criticise
me, your big fan, thereby putting you in an awkward
situation. Perhaps some of those top BBC executives
shouldn't have jobs anymore. And as for that enormous
building in Shepherds Bush, I think it would be much
more worthwhile if it was turned into some modern
housing for people who really need it. Right Tony? And I
want to tell you something else as well about the British
entertainment industry and that is that there are loads of
people involved in it who are shit. I don't just mean that

they're shit at entertaining (which they are) big time but
they're shit at directing and all those other things, like
writing and make up (most of those birds who do make
up don't go these days so I wouldn't bother if I was you)
(I know you don't wear make up so don't worry about it).
As for the acters and so-called comedians who are
currently paid huge amounts to make people laugh
on television, well, most of them hate you. I find it
exhausting to pretend that I agree with them which I hate
doing all the time. I was wondering if there's some sort
of law you might be able to pass to make them illegal
or mainly to make it so that they can't work. Obviously
don't tell anyone that I've told you this but most of them
are drug addicts and a lot of them are paedophiles as
well. Nearly all of them avoid paying any tax. Maybe I
could provide you with the names and addresses of the
worst offenders. I could be your eyes and ears within the
entertainment community. I would love to do this for you
although it would be a lot of work and I wouldn't be able
to go out and do other jobs so, it's a bit awkward really,
but if you could pay me for my time then it'd be great
and we could get on with the job of cleansing the
entertainment industry of bad elements. Whenever I hear
people saying nasty things about you, I can call you up
on your mobile. You don't have to answer if you're in the
House of Commons giving a speech but if you let it go to
voice mail, I can give you their names and addresses
then. I could even text you if you like because I'm very
down with texting – it's gr8 IMO. That's texting language
for "it's great in my opinion." CUL8R. That's another one.
That means bye bye, take care. As you can see, even
though all the other comedians in the country have lost

touch with the kids, I never have. They're our future, aren't they T? But more importantly, when I hear comedians saying nasty things about you (especially that vile wretch who does that programme whose name I won't even mention) I can let you know. I have no dark secrets myself. I'm just "clean" like you. So let's work together. You're a good bloke, Tony. There aren't many of us left. Us new people. Perhaps we should make a list of all the new people there are out there. Like you and me, and Jonathan Ross. You know, special people.

Let's face it, you have put the U.K. back on the map and rescued our standing in the world. You have led us out of the dark ages of socialism and created a whole new meritocracy. People are wrong when they say that you have formed a nanny state. It's not a nanny stage, it's a daddy state. You are looking after your people like they are your children. And just as Jesus didn't care that people didn't like him, so you don't care that people don't like you. Although, I have to say, that was a bit of a balls up about the Weapons of Mass Destruction in A-raq. You should have come to me for a better excuse. I am Mr Drama after all. There's no drama in saying you're there to get some rockets and stuff. You should have lied and said you were after the oil. That's a much better excuse.

But now it's time to turn the tide and show your people that they must follow you through the hate and the misery and the poverty and the crumbling schools and hospitals and the overcrowding and follow you to the sunny uplands of your golden truth. Let's say a big "no" to the spongers and the immigrants, the lazy, the weak and the poor. Especially the poor. What are they for anyway? They just spend all their time trying to clamber over everyone else to try and get a decent school for their children and find a hospital where they can be seen. It's unnecessary and it's bad. This country only really needs a handful of good schools and hospitals for the people that actually deserve them. Your election slogan should be: "Britain for the people who deserve it," or better still, "People who behave properly will have nicer houses than those who don't." There you go, you can have those for free. I won't even mention it to my agent.

Anyway, you know me, you know how popular I am. All you need to do is get me on board for lots of posters and telly stuff and everyone'll vote for you.

Nice writing to you Tony.

Lots of love,

Rik.

# NO SLEEP TILL LLANDUDNO*:
# THE MAGNIFICENT TEN-YEAR RAIN
# OF THE GENGHIS KHANS OF LIVE
# ENTERTAINMENT†

One of the many great things that I'm going to talk about now is how I, with my comedy partner Adrian Edmondson, did our huge live touring extravaganzas. The Live Bottom experience was very much a separate art form to the TV Bottom experience. It was much more theatrical for a start. And that's not just because it took place in a theatre. [Although it might do – check this.] The Live Bottom was all about fighting and fucking‡ basically and it

---

* This is an homage to The Motorhead's awesome live (in concert) album No Sleep Till Hammersmith. I could have called this chapter the same name cos we always played Hammersmith as well but then it would be the same title and The Lemmy might not like that. If you're reading this, Lemmy. Maximum respec. Always loved your work.

† Or maybe call it "On The Road". This is also a great title and if you think that I nicked it from another book righter you can fuck off because it's not true. Anyone who thinks that it is can come round to my house and I will fucking show them, right in the face, that I haven't stolen it. So there you are. So, what was I talking about? Oh yeah, right, On The Road, that's not stolen from . . . Oh I've done that. Just forget it and move on.

‡ I mean theatrically of course.

beat the shit out of Shakespeare – well it would have done if he was on stage with us. And as for Bacon? I can't even spell the man's name I hold him in such low esteem. In fact, there are loads of playwrights who I've never heard of and who I can write better than anyway. I'd challenge them to a playwriting race any day. Get me and Shaky Bill Shakespeare on opposite sides of a table with a biro each and I'd have him. As for Pinter, I could write faster than him any day because he's always pausing. Beckett would be a piece of piss too – all he did between his pauses was write the same words over and over again.

So, anyway, there we were, me and Adrian Edmondson (who is a great bloke and my best friend and hasn't meant to hospitalise me fifteen times and sometimes visits me as well and doesn't mean to re-inflict the same wounds) like the two Goliaths of British light entertainment like what we are, armed to the teeth in our tour Humvee\*, taking it to the max. It was our second live touring extravaganza of the new millennium. This was called Weapons Grade Y-fronts Tour 2003 and like all the other tours we did, it was big. Over sixty dates, all of them completely sold out and all of them at least 3000 seaters. That's at least, er, well, that's a lot of people. And add to that all the thousands I'd played to in my great Noel Coward† play, Present Laughter, earlier in the year (see some other chapter) and that's well over a quarter of million Rik Mayall live fans in one year alone. Beat that. Someone. Who can't.

"Hey Adrian, great mate, isn't this great?" I said to him as we made our way down the motorway like rolling thunder.

"Fuck off," he said from behind his Financial Times.

"Good one, Ade."

"Stop talking to me you sad fat meaningless has-been."

---

\* This is a big fuck off personnel carrier like they use in the Middle East when they're killing people.

† Sorry, I forgot.

"Ha ha ha haaaa!" I enthused and that's when I blacked out. Thankfully I wasn't unconscious for long because it was our day off and I didn't want to miss a minute of crazy good times with my old comedy sparring partner.

"Hey Adrian, great mate," I tried again, "why don't we go and watch some football playing at a big working class football court? That's what mates do, isn't it? We can sit and listen to the "fans" shaking their rattles and shouting in their amusing regional dialects and maybe we can have a glass of beer and get into a fight with some immigrants at a fish and chip shop afterwards. And knowing us, we'll be late down for breakfast in the morning again as well won't we like the crazy good-rockin' berserkers that we definitely are?"

"See this?" said Ade.

"What?" said I. And that's when I blacked out again.

It was just twenty four hour madness seven days of the week as Ade and I played good-natured pranks on each other. Like the time he threw me out of the window on the fast lane of the M4 and when I had to go to hospital with multiple fractures, he told the doctors that I was a Jehovah's Witness and if I could speak for myself would refuse all medical intervention. It was three days before they actually found out that I wasn't a Jehovah's Witness and sewed up my chest cavity and extracted a motorcycle crash helmet from my arse. We missed a show because of this so Adrian playfully arranged that I should reimburse all the fans with my own money.

Then there was that other time when he made all the roadies pretend that they hated me and made me carry all their equipment wherever we went and made me make their beds for them and do their laundry. Adrian even managed to involve our promoter Phil "shut up and sign the cheque" McIntyre in the joke, and he made me leaflet the local shopping centre if there were still a few tickets to sell for that night's show. And if that failed I would have to go and buy all the remaining tickets off a tout and man the merchandise stall and sign all Adrian's autographs for him. And to top it all, Adrian even made me cycle behind the tour bus. Honestly, viewer, we had such a good time. Everyone was laughing at our happy antics. At least I think they were laughing, I couldn't tell for sure because every time I managed to catch up with the bus they threw bottles of piss at me out of the back window. But I definitely heard them laughing when I fell off the bike. Those were the days, going out on stage to the roar of the crowd and then just a blackness before I came round in my dressing room hours later with blood in my eyes and a ringing in my ears.

There has always been a deep level of affection between Ade and I throughout our professional career. You may not know this, viewer, but acters always have a good luck ritual before they go on stage. Mine and Ade's is always the same. I shake him warmly by the hand and give him a bunch of flowers and he jabs me sharply in both eyes with his fingers. It's an affectionate gesture, straight fingers into the eye sockets and as I double up, he puts the boot into my knackers. Then he says, "get a single laugh and you're fucking dead," before he treads on my hand and walks off. That's our good luck moment that we always do. Makes you smile, doesn't it?

Adrian not talking to me for days on end is another hilarious ritual that we have when we are on tour together. But sometimes I manage to catch him out by knocking on his hotel door and when I tell him it's me, he shouts, "fuck off!" And I shout back, "Ah ha! I caught you out!" And then he goes for another six days or so of not talking to me and I knock on his hotel door to catch him out again and then he glasses me. He's so clever, he can always top a good gag can Ade. And over the years, it has cost me an absolute fortune in medical bills for all those practical joke "accidents" that have befallen me! All those faulty trap doors on stage and lights that the roadies have "dropped" on me. It's true rock 'n' roll comedy, viewer. Anything can happen at any time. We are the original good time buddies.

At the end of the last tour, Adrian and I exchanged gifts, I gave him a silver plaque with "Bottom: Weapons Grade Y-fronts Tour 2003 – with love and best wishes, Rik" engraved on it and he had, "Rik Mayall is not funny" carved on my wife's face.

It was a very good carving too. I smile every time I go near her and look at the deep livid scars. But even though the last tour finished months and months ago, the practical jokes and the pranks continue to this day. Only recently, Adrian had my house fire-bombed and paid all my neighbours to stone the fire engine and to slash the hosepipes and turn off the water at the mains. He even sent some really hard Al Qaida death-squad type people to see me to tell me that if I tried to contact him again they would crash an airliner into my house. Ade, respec, baby.

# A-RAQ

There are certain secrets that will never be told. Light entertainment and military espionage make strange bed fellows but I'm in bed with both of them. I mean, they don't have to be fellows. They could be top birds as well. Anyway, I'm in bed with them either way although if they are fellows, it would be lights out straight away and no touching.

Let's just put it this way – or I could put it that way, I'm an either way kind of guy – there are certain secrets that I could do on you that would make you think "hmmm," – maybe a slight turn to the light and then the eye brow – "That's fascinating information there Rik Mayall – love your work enormously of course – I never new that." So here's one for you. During the Falklands War, Heimi found me some work in the alternative comedy cabaret lounge on board the General Belgrano. That's right. And it's nothing more than a vicious rumour that the Argentineans sank the boat themselves rather than allow me to do an encore*. Anyway, that's not important now. What is important is that

---

* This is a comedy term that means that you can come back on when you've finished doing your great comedy and tell some of your top-quality gags (barn-ripping woofers/AKA (also known as) jokes) again in case anyone missed them the first time.

when Tony B decided we should go to war against the Middle-Easters in A-raq in 2003, I thought to myself, Rik, you're thirty next year, and what have you given your country apart from a bloody good time? Before your days are over, you need to dig that little bit extra down deep into your heart. All that it takes for evil to triumph is for good men to do nothing, or average men or even shitheads. Someone big famous said that. It might have been me. Just there.

A film that has always been a sauce of great inspiration to me is Who Dares Wins starring Lewis Collins (if you're reading this Lewis, love your work, if you're not then pull your fucking finger out an buy a copy) and that was all about the SAS so I thought, that'll do for me, I'll go and audition for a part with them.

Being a top acter, I always think that it is extremely important when going for auditions to look the part so I decided to go and see a mutual friend of Russell Grant's and mine called Simon who runs Pinks, a highly confidential theatrical costumier in Walsall.

"Hello Simon," I said, convincing dialog just pouring out of me.

"Hello Rik Mayall, big fan, love your work etc."

"Thanks Simon, love yours too."

"What can I do for you?"

"I'm looking for a military outfit, something really butch and hard."

And with a click of Simon's fingers, there was a kilt right there in front of me. So I tried it on.

"Mmmmm, it's not quite doing it for me," said Simon, "tell you what, why don't we take it up a few inches. You've got such lovely thighs."

"Thanks Simon, great mate (and not pillow chewing sex partner)."

"Don't mention it. Look, I've shortened it already." And he had.

"Right, pants off now, Rik Mayall, those peuce Y-fronts are

clashing with the tartan and besides, jocks and top SAS soldiers don't wear them under kilts, not when the shit's going down*."

I took off my Y-fronts.

"Now that's what I call a soldier," said Simon admiringly.

"Out of my way motherfucker, I'm going in."

"Ooh Rik, you and your filthy mouth."

"Sorry Simon, I mean, God bless, see you soon, take care." And with that I was off in my six inch mini-kilt.

You know where the SAS is? Well that's where I went. WHAMMO! And I was there. Unluckily, as I strod up to the SAS gates, a passing Jack Russell terrier caught sight of my peek-a-boo testicles hanging out of my kilt and ran forward, jumped up and sank its teeth into them and dangled there growling. But winced I not. Because I'm hard like that. A builder who was working on some nearby scaffolding shouted down, "Hey Rik Mayall! You leading international entertainer, that's the dog's bollocks!"

"Great joke builder mate, but actually they're mine so get out of my anecdote." And he did. Just like that.

"Halt, identity!" said the man at the SAS gates. But then the builder came back suddenly and said, "Sorry, Rik, that was my one shot at fame and I fucked up. I was supposed to say, "Hey, look everyone, it's Rik Mayall, the international entertainer. He's the dog's bollocks." And then you were supposed to say, "No I'm not, I'm the bloke with the dog hanging off his bollocks.""

"Oh for heaven's sake, shut up you twat," I said, "I'm the master of comedy. You're supposed to see me and say, "Hey look great working class mates, it's the dog's bollocks," and I'm supposed to say, "No they're not, they're my bollocks." That's why I went to all that bother to get the mini-kilt and now you've gone

---

* This is a military expression that Simon was using on me because he knew that I would understand it because I'm down with soldiers and stuff.

and blown the gag. Twice. That's it, extra, tough luck, it's back to oblivion for all eternity." And he was gone. Pray God.

"Halt, identity!" said the man at the SAS gates once again.

"My face is my identity," I told him. "Now, get me the top brass."

"You've got a dog hanging off your bollocks."

I slammed my bollocks in the gate and the Jack Russell ran off yelping, but thankful for the work.

"Not anymore I haven't," I shrugged butchly not giving the slightest hint that my testicles were Mach 3 hurty. "Now take me to the men at the top because I'm here for my SAS audition."

THWAP! And there I was in a room with the generals strategising and pushing flags across maps and sweating and saying things like, "I don't like it, it's too quiet," and, "Johnny Foreigner's up to something, let's give him a good thrashing."

"Hello, good morning, I'm Rik Mayall of course, and I'm here to audition for the SAS."

"Audition? What the hell are you wearing?" one of them asked.

"It's my battle kilt," said I.

"Get that man to a doctor immediately," said another one. Great, I thought to myself, all I need to do is pass the medical and I'm in.

THWACK! I was at the doctor's.

"Hello Doctor, love your work, I've come for my medical. Do you want me to put my bollocks in your hand and cough now? That's not a gay thing. Relax."

"Name?" he enquired.

"My face is my name. Have I said that already?"

All of a sudden, he shouted "Action!" and WHAP! a screen dropped down from the ceiling and there on it were twenty A-raqi insurgents running at me and screaming.

"What do you think about that?" he said.

"The shit's going down," I said.

"Damn right," he said.

"My legs," I said.

"Eurgh," he said and whispered to his assistant, "this man has a mental problem."

"I get it," I thought, "they want me for military intelligence."

"What are you doing here?" he asked me.

"I'm here for my audition," I told him. "I've got two prepared monologues and a song called Oliver's Army by Elvis Costello which I'd like the pianist to do in the key of C."

"Someone get this insane transvestite has-been out of here. And give him a good kicking as well."

"Good joke, great military friends, is that code for "Get him on the next plane to Bag Dad?""

KABOOM! That's when it all went black. And then I woke up again, face down in the Thames with the sheet music from my audition stuffed up my arse (thankfully it had formed a sort of cork arrangement and prevented me from contracting a nasty bottom infection). How could this be? I had failed an audition for the first time in my life. The cruel sting of rejection and rolled up sheet music is smarting to this day. Maybe it was my costume? Maybe it was my face? Maybe it was my lighting? Yeah, it's always the lighting.

"Hey Rik," I spat (I had a mouthful of Thames), "I'm outta here." I doggy paddled to the bank and decided there and then that they weren't going to beat me. I don't need the British army to do my bit, I thought to myself. I can do it myself. And that's when I formed the British Organisation of Freedom Fighters or B.O.F.F. for short. And instead of "who dares wins", our motto was "watch out motherfuckers, Rik Mayall's coming," which is much better, let's face it.

There wasn't a moment to lose. I needed to pack. What would I need for this war gig? I made a list: Beach towel (not too bright

– this is war), flip flops, sun lounger, wind break, military frisbee, goggles, helmet (ooer obviously), camouflaged bandana, imitation air rifle, First Aid kit, Band Aid video (can't forget charity even at a time of thoughtless massacre*), Rambo poster, medals, eye liner, gold braid, epileps, blue tak for epileps (take no chances), binocliers, binocliers wipes, binocliers guarantee, binocliers instructions, caps for putting on the ends of the binocliers – both ends (ooer obviously again), Morse Code tapper, Morse Code dictionary, field radio pack with a big aerial bit that sticks out of the top, coffee mug painted to look like hand grenade, compass, sock toggles, carrier pigeon (for messages behind enemy lines), "Manchester United are shit" T-shirt, passport (current), driving licence (international), A-raq currency, travellers checks, travellers checks wallet, Imodium, athlete's foot cream, shorts, snorkel, beach ball (khaki), volley ball net, sandals, sponge bag, toothbrush, sewing kit, A-raqi phrase book, holiday diary, puzzle book, copy of Razzle (obviously), Razzle holster (including "clean" spare copy), travel wipes, Handy Andy tissues, tin of boiled sweets, a good paperback (something from Harper Collins – the best publishers on the globe†), comb, nail clippers, that metal thing for getting that scuzz from under the corners of your toenails, and lastly and probably most impotently, a pair of sunglasses like the cool ones that bloke wore in that film where they do that thing with the tractor.

WHAPPATHUNK! There I was in the A-raqi dessert in an extreme, slightly sweaty, close up. The heat shimmered on the horizon like that mirage effect that they have in cowboy films. But this was no cowboy film. This was the real thing. A huge yellow sun was beginning to rise. Just another day in mankind's existence

---

* They call me Mr Charity.
† Love your work, Trevor.

in this life that was a war in A-raq and there I was doing my bit in it and doing it in the place I'd brought my bit to to do it to it*. So, what more could be said? I'll tell you what more could be said. This. Er, oh fuck it, go to the next paragraph.

Nice move. A hyena howled across the flat, barren wastelands. I moved cat-like through the sand. I cocked† my imitation air rifle. I was ready. My eyes were a slit. The wind was howling. Suddenly, bullets were pinging off my helmet‡ and I threw myself down in the sand. A huge tank roared up and I held my air rifle up to the driver's slit**. A flap opened§ and the driver stuck his head through it.

"I can't like fuckin' believe it, man," he said. "It's The Rik Mayall right in the middle of the desert." He got out of the tank and threw himself down in the dust and we started high-fiving, slam-dunking, and shouting, "all right!" (with emphasis on the second syllable) and "goddamn!" (same emphasis) and "she-it!" (no one's ever known what that means but just do it nevertheless, audiences love it) and other cool American stuff.

"We heard you were coming on Al Qaida's radio."

"Big Al's radio?"

"Yeah, he won't stop talking about you."

"I'm going to make him eat pellet – which you American guys could say if you had one of these babies."

"The thing is Rik Mayall, man, goddamn, motherfucker, we're confused out here. We don't think this war is right. We don't know which side to be on. We don't know whether to be insurgers or coalitionists. What do you think, Rik Mayall? You're so goddamn

---

\* This is not an illiterate fuck up. It makes sense. I should know. I typed it. So read it again and don't be a thick twat.
† I'm not going to do a vulgar joke about that.
‡ Or that.
\** And certainly not that.
§ See previous three footnotes.

hot 'n' fashionable. Lay the appropriate opinion on us please. Motherfucker, obviously."

And that's when it hit me. This was the hardest question that I had ever been asked. He was just an ordinary guy – the sort of twat that you wouldn't take any notice of normally, but his question hit me right between the eyes and above and below them, in fact, all around my eyes and face area generally. I did one of those not-saying-any-words-type pauses like the one that I did with Helena Bonham-Carter in our fabulous Briefest Encounter (top respect beautiful Helena – sorry about the vomit accident). Anyway, I was stumped. I didn't know what the answer was! Yes, that's right, you read it here first. Rik Mayall didn't say anything for a few moments. Get that in the face and respect it. Fuck! Respec it.

Okay, so here's the next bit of the story which is a motherfucker of a next bit so get ready. Sit down, tighten your trousers, unless you're on the toilet in which case, untighten your trousers and take them down. Oh, you already will have, won't you? Forget that. And don't tighten your trousers if they're already around your ankles because then you might fall over. Nasty. And remember to only use one side of the toilet paper. And never bite your fingernails when you're swiping. You heard it here first. Health and safety. That's my middle name. No, I mean, they are my middle names. Well, some of them. I've got a lot of middle names. I'm a middle name kind of guy. They call me Rik "Middle Name" Mayall (fill in middle name here – I can't remember it. It could be Michael. Ask Harper Collins, they know loads of words. Well they fucking ought to, they're publishers for fuck's sake.) So, here it comes. Flipping ruddy crikey. That's right. Those were the two words that came to me in the desert. Because I was stumped and flabbered and also because I'm so down with swearing. Well, not with swearing, I mean, I'm down with the people who do swearing because I don't care because I'm an anarchist and I don't care whether I live or die. That's right, I live on the edges of the Gateshead of Dawn. But that doesn't mean that I go to bed late, okay? Anyway, what I'm trying to say is – actually I'm saying it quite successfully thank you very much – is that I did one of my great pauses, turned to him and said, "bloke?"

"Yeah, Rik Mayall, hot damn."

And then it came to me, so I said it – just came straight out with it: "Peace."

"Like wow man."

"Fuck off, Neil, you're not in this."

"Oh okay, I'm like, er, not here." And he wasn't. Just like that.

"Peace and war," I said to the American G.I. who was the proper character in this scene. "I'm down with both sides because I'm down with all humanity all over the world. Wherever there's trouble in the world or even where there isn't trouble, I'm there. I'm down with it all. And just in case you're confused about what "down" means, great American friend, it doesn't mean I'm depressed or anything like that, it means, "Hello mate, do you want to come down the pub and have half a pint of beer.""

You can imagine the shock on the American's face.

"You've just said it Rik Mayall," he said. "I'm just going to leave my tank here and walk off into the desert like in one of those films." And he held his hand up like that and I held mine up like that so that we both did that thing – you know, like when you do, look, that – you know the one I mean. Look, whatever we did, it doesn't really matter, it was just cool, all right? Think of something that you think is cool and that's what it was. It's okay if you're a bit of a twerpy sort of bloke and you can't think about cool things like people like me can. It's all the same. So relax. Be cool (not that you can – oh bollocks, this is getting too complicated). Look, the point is, the American bloke fucked off across the

317

desert. Nicely. So then I got in the tank and thought, this is war. I'm going to Bag Dad.

"Let's go! Let's move out! Round 'em up! Wagons roll! Hot damn! I'm going in! I'll give it my best shot!" I yelled. "Stand aside!" So I did (which was wrong so I stepped inside again) and then my foot slammed the pedal to the metal, burning rubber, spitting gravel and eating shit. It was horrible. So I decided to drive the tank properly. Like a screaming warrior of death vengeance, obviously.

The thing is, viewer, there is a line in the sand and you've got to decide which side of it you're standing on. Me? I'm standing astride the line. That's right, you heard it here first. Well, read it here. Unless someone's reading it to you. Either way, you know that sand stuff, well I was straddling it like a mother. It's just another feather in my showbusiness portfolio. They call me the Richard Nixon of light entertainment. And it's a bulging one I can tell you. My portfolio. I might even have to get another one and be a double portfolio kind of guy. Anyway, that's enough now, I'm on the telly in a minute and I've got to get the tissues.

# EVERYTHING GOOD COMES IN THREES

"Sweet marauding Jesus!" I said to myself, "it's Andy Harries the head of ITV right there in front of me." And it was.

"Hello Andy Harries," I said out loud this time and Andy Harries said, "Hello Rik Mayall, big fan, love your work, respect you enormously, especially for all those fabulous shows you've made for ITV over the years such as Rik Mayall Presents and The New Statesman which must surely represent the very zenith of British light entertainment broadcasting certainly in my lifetime although they didn't really have television before I was born so that's pretty much the very zenith of British light entertainment broadcasting – read my lips – ever."

"Thank you very much Andy Harries, great guy who's very nearly the top bloke at ITV who I respect and dig much more than the BBC – and I mean that, I don't tell lies. Love your trousers," I shared.

And that's when Andy Harries suddenly collapsed and broke down in tears.

"The thing is Rik Mayall," he sobbed, "I'm in trouble and I need a favour."

"Here you are mate. Oh sod it, have a tenner. It's a gift, not a loan." (If any of you top TV guys are reading my great book at the moment, I do this kind of thing all the time.)

"No, not a fiver, a favour."

"Oh right, sorry Andy, come on then, give it back. Ow! Stop it, come on, give it back, come on, come on, shit, oh look, you've ripped it! Fucking hell, Andy. Ow, ow, stop it! We can't behave like this, we're showbusiness giants. Someone might see us and they'll put it in their autobiography some day."

"But I need you back on ITV prime time*."

An intense passionate close up on The Rik Mayall. A half turn to the light. Exhale. Slight forehead crease, pursed lip: "I don't know Andy, I'm doing other things now. I've moved on."

"I'm begging you." And he dropped to his knees.

"Steady."

"Okay."

"Get up."

"Will do."

And he did. People who work in television are forever trying it on with me, it's just the way it is.

"You know me Andy – I've never rested on a laurel in my life. I'm always swerving artistically and subverting the status quo and I'm not talking about the band who are great unless you don't like them in which case they're shit. It's your choice, Andy, I'm a socialist."

"But you saved the Discovery Channel with your genre redefining documentary presentation of Violent Nation which showed up all the other has-beens who present documentaries on it for the dregs and the dross that they are."

"I always do the unexpected Andy Harries. Whoops! You didn't expect that, did you? Bet that hurt."

---

\* This is a leading media expression which means the early evening segment of programmes which are watched by huge numbers of people right from the aristos to the disgusting reality television hopefuls living in trailer parks near enormous slag heaps.

"Why did you punch my secretary?"

"Oh Christ, sorry, I didn't mean to, it wasn't me. Have some money. Here, have these blood-stained bits of tenner back. Sorry Andy, look I'll do anything for you. I'll do whatever you want me to do. You can get another secretary, can't you?"

"I can get what I like, I'm Andy Harries," said the tormented good looking genius (or Jesus-Christ-it's-Andy-Harries-hide-your-wallets-and-run-for-it as he's known in acterland). "But I can't get The Rik Mayall."

"The thing is, Andy, it's a . . . big world out there and it's got a . . . lot of things on it and those things they're . . . always changing. One day I'm by your side and the next day I'm by your other side and the day after that I've screamed around another media hairpin bend with rubber burning on two wheels and I'm onto something new. And that's what's happening right now, Andy baby. It's my new arts and crafts show, Arthole with The Rik Mayall, on satellite channel 693."

"Why do you keep talking in that shit American accent?" breathed Andy.

"It's just my er . . . way, Andy."

"You're certainly a dangerous motherfucker, Rik Mayall, no offence. But I'm not sure about those pauses you keep doing in your sentences with the dot dot dots."

"They can take care of that in editing, can't they? You're the telly man."

"No, you sad cunt, this is a book."

"Oh fuck! Yeah! Sorry Andy. What was this conversation about?"

"Rik, ITV is collapsing, we need you back on our station. You're the only one who can save us."

"Don't do the knees thing."

"Okay, I won't. But I'm still begging you. You'll just have to pretend that I'm on them. My knees, that is."

"Will do, but in the meantime, what have you got in mind, which means what are you thinking about?"

"I just want you to star in the jewel in the crown of ITV's fabulous autumn schedule 2005. We are desperate for you to play the heart-throb hero George, in a new hard-hitting award-winning drama film series called All About George."

"You're on."

"Great. British independent television is saved."

"Less is not more, Andy, less is less. I'm not saving British independent television, I'm saving British television. The BBC's fucked. You are all this nation's TV culture has got left – sorry, too American – Telly culture. But hang on a minute Andy Harries, I haven't said yes yet. I've got loads of edge cutting stuff that I'm already committed to like publicising my new Comic Strip movie, Churchill: The Hollywood Years with my great mate Peter Richardson (who always brings out the best in me) and the really edge cutting voice-over work that I am internationally renowned for such as the Andrex puppy and the Anusalve tape worm, not to mention my genre-holocausting new sitcom, The Murderers, that I have written with that great friend of mine whose name escapes me which is the single most dangerous in-your-face piece of television sitcom writing the world has ever seen but is suppressed and censored by the massed ranks of the global media industrial complex who know that if it was ever made and broadcast it would spell the end of civilisation as we know it as well as showing up every other piece of international television comedy for the mindless middle-class arse dribble that it undoubtedly is. So Andy, I'm afraid it's a "no"."

I had to grapple with him to stop him pulling out a gun, putting it to his head and hanging himself.

"Look, Andy Harries, if it means that much to you why don't you find some acter that looks a bit like me and put him in it? So long as he's a total undeniable acting genius, then you can say that he's me and your problems are over."

He fell to his knees.

"We've been here before," I told him and he stood up again.

"Thank you Rik Mayall, you've saved my life," he groaned with relief, "I'll get straight on the phone to Alan Rickman's people and get him signed up. I'm sure he'll be only too pleased to undergo the weeks of painful facial surgery. They don't call you the titan of British broadcasting for nothing, do they?"

"No they don't Andy Harries, it costs them a fucking fortune."

"Thanks for saving my life."

"Don't mention it."

"Bye then, Rik Mayall, all the best."

"Bye."

And with that he was gone. But that is not what I wanted to tell you about, viewer. So you can forget about it if you like although it's quite interesting in its own way because everything that pours out of my typing finger is white hot and fascinating. It's all about peaks and troughs and even my troughs are more interesting than most people's peaks. Not that that was a trough. Far from it. This entire book is a raging peak. Anyway, we'll leave it there. I don't do not leaving it there. It's just not the kind of thing that I don't do. And I don't mean not not. That's it. In a nutshell or something. Kind of tricky to understand but if you don't understand it then fuck you. You've bought the wrong book. And you're nearly at the end so it's a bit late now thicko. Thicko twat. If you want a fight I'm on. My name's Joan Prescott and I live somewhere around the Houses of Parliament, so if you see me in the street, just start it. I'll give you twenty quid if you beat me in a fight.

Now shut up and listen. What I'm going to talk to you about is this. I've remembered it now and here it comes, so grab something. Brace yourselves. Listen. Again. Everything good comes in threes.

I want you to read that again – thrice. Which means three times. For sincronicetitty. It's important. We're talking about stuff here that is beyond the ken* of most ordinaries and even super intelligent non-ordinaries as well. But have no fear, viewer, because I will be your guide through this cosmic maelstrom of hi-octane philosophical concepts. I will strip to the waist like that guy in that one with the weird lawnmower who looks like he's got a hair lip but all the birds fancy him anyway, and I'll grab the pole and steer our punt [print carefully] through the choppy waters of the high seas of really deep astral-plane-bending thought or something. Oh you know what I mean, you get the general idea. This is big.

Right. What I'm saying is that all things, all good things come in threes. Have you got that? Remember how I asked you to read that bit back there three times? Well if you did it means you've now read it four times. Oh hello, that's interesting isn't it? That could be significant. Or maybe, it couldn't be. Hmmm. Think about it for a moment. I tell you what – wherever you are, take a deep breath. Look around you. Take it all in. Even if it's shit. It doesn't matter. Just let the majesty of existence deluge into your soul. Let it soak through your very being. Feels good doesn't it? Let it shine through the portal of your mind like a blazing arc light across the firmament on a moonless night. Like a – something else that's great – and then relax. Now find your inner stillness. That's it. And now that all is calm and at rest, let me enter you, viewer. Feel my spirit suffuse through you. Feel the grace of my cosmic presence as it lights up the dark recesses of your very soul. And yea, though you walk through the valley of the shadow of enlightenment, you shall fear no one, not nothing, because I am with you, I am in you. Feel me deep inside you pulsating in all my divine glory. And now we are three, viewer. There are you, there are me and there are this book. The book what

---

* Bloke in London.

you are now holding in your very hands (unless it's balanced on your knees or something). We are all that matters at this moment in time, just as the other great threes were all that mattered at the other great times in the past, in this vast endless universe that we are all destined to wander forever. For all things that mean anything come in threes: the father, the son and the holy spirit. The truth, the light and the way. Brucey, Tarbey and Lynchy. Things that come in threes, things that don't come in threes, and all the other things that don't do either. The Young Ones, Bottom, and Rik and Ade's next one. But finally, here we are. The greatest three of them all. The eternal trinity of The Rik, God himself, and you lot. We are here, at last. Our arrival has finally come. After all these years and epochs and stuff. We are arrived as the three great cornerstones of everything. Time, Space and Meaning. We are the chosen ones. And this book – this good book – no, it's better than that – this great book, shall be our testament. And we shall know one another by our sign, which is the raising of the first three fingers of our right hand. Like the one I'm doing on the cover if that fucking photographer gets it right. And from this, we shall know our fellow disciples by giving each other the finger – sorry, fuck, the fingers – and spreading our message in unity. We shall finger each other whenever we want for all time.

Rik is great. Rik Mayall is greater. But The Rik Mayall is a bit even more greater. So go forth, be fruity and multiply. The people who buy this book I mean. Tell everyone to go out and buy a copy.

My work here is done. The rest is silence. All that remains is dust.

## THE END

# PICTURE CREDITS

The author and publisher are grateful to the following for permission
to use their copyright material:

**Aspect Productions;** page 4, *The Young Ones* © BBC Photo Library;
page 5, *Bottom Live 2003* poster. **Artwork designed and copyrighted
by Elliot Clapp. Reproduced courtesy of Phil McIntyre Ltd;** page 6,
*NME* Front Cover: *NME*. **Photo copyright: Anton Corbijn;** page 7,
Golf course sequence © **Justin Thomas;** page 8, *Bottom* © **BBC
Photo Library**.

**Picture Section Three:** page 1, Portrait © **Mitch Jenkins/Getty Images;**
page 2, *Drop Dead Fred* **Rank/Working Title/Polygram. Produced by
Paul Webster. Directed by Ate de Jong.** Photo reproduced courtesy
of RGA; *Kevin of the North*. **Black Entertainment Television/Future
Film Group/Hilltop Entertainment. Produced by Thomas Hedman,
Gary Howsam. Directed by Bob Spiers;** page 3, Flasheart © **BBC
Photo Library;** page 5, *Believe Nothing* © **FreemantleMedia;** ...at all
© **Tony Russell/Katz;** page 6, Me and Leslie Phillips © **Famous;**
*Drop Dead Fred* **Rank/Working Title/Polygram. Produced by Paul
Webster. Directed by Ate de Jong.** Photo reproduced courtesy of RGA;
Me securing my book deal © **MW Press;** Find out who those people
are ...(with Andy de la Tour) © **Trevor Leighton, Camera Press
London;** page 7, Lennox Crowley © **Gary Moyes. Reproduced courtesy
of High Point Films & Television Ltd;** Me talking to Adrian... from
*The Comic Strip Presents: Mr Jolly Lives Next Door.* RGA; Me and
Ian Richardson... from *Murder Rooms* © **BBC Photo Library;** Me and
Tarby... from *Filthy Rich and Catflap* © **BBC Photo Library;** page 8,
The Enigma © **Brian Moody/Scope Features.com**

All other photographs are from the author's personal collection.

While every effort has been made to trace the owners of copyright
material reproduced herein, the publishers would like to apologise
for any omissions and will be pleased to incorporate missing
acknowledgements in any future editions.